DK EYEWITNESS TOP 10 TRAVEL GUIDES

BOSTON

PATRICIA HARRIS
DAVID LYON
JONATHAN SCHULTZ

DK PUBLISHING, INC.

Left **Boston Harbor** Center **Massachusetts State House** Right **House of Blues**

LONDON, NEW YORK, MUNICH,
MELBOURNE, AND DELHI

Produced by Departure Lounge, London
Reproduced by Colourscan, Singapore
Printed and bound in Italy by Graphicom

First American Edition, 2003
04 05 06 10 9 8 7 6 5 4 3 2

Published in the United States by
DK Publishing, Inc.,
375 Hudson Street, New York,
New York 10014

ISSN 1479-344X
ISBN 0-7894-9193-1

Within each Top 10 list in this book, no hierarchy of quality or popularity is implied. All 10 are, in the editor's opinion, of roughly equal merit.

Floors are referred to throughout in accordance with American usage; ie the "second floor" is above ground level.

See our complete product line at
www.dk.com

Contents

Boston's Top 10

The information in this DK Eyewitness Top 10 Travel Guide is checked regularly.

Every effort has been made to ensure that this book is as up-to-date as possible at the time of going to press. Some details, however, such as telephone numbers, opening hours, prices, gallery hanging arrangements and travel information are liable to change. The publishers cannot accept responsibility for any consequences arising from the use of this book, nor for any material on third party websites, and cannot guarantee that any website address in this book will be a suitable source of travel information. We value the views and suggestions of our readers very highly. Please write to:
Publisher, DK Eyewitness Travel Guides,
Dorling Kindersley, 80 Strand, London WC2R 0RL, Great Britain.

Left **Barking Crab** Center **Store, Newbury Street** Right **Singers, Berklee Performance Center**

Left **Claude Monet's *La Japonaise*, Museum of Fine Arts** Right **Memorial Hall**

Key to abbreviations
Adm *admission charge payable* **Free** *no admission charge* **DA** *disabled access*

BOSTON'S TOP 10

Top 10 Boston Highlights

"The Hub," "Beantown," "Baaahstin" – call it what you will, New England's largest city exists to be explored. Its colonial-era architecture, vibrant seafaring heritage, and irrepressible Yankee character make it one of the country's most distinctive locales. Yet for all its big-city amenities – world-class restaurants, museums, and shops – Boston remains surprisingly compact and eminently walkable.

1 The Freedom Trail

Boston's best walking tour is free, self-guided, chock-full of history, and open year round. Just follow the painted red stripe threading its way past historic buildings such as the Massachusetts State House *(Hall of Flags above; see pp8–11)*.

2 Faneuil Hall Marketplace

What was once a dilapidated, post-revolutionary mercantile area now sets the standard for urban-renewal projects worldwide. It boasts an indoor food court in Quincy Market *(left)*, shops, and street performers *(see pp12–13)*.

3 Boston Common & Public Garden

Swan boats drift beneath weeping willows, children splash in fountains, and a bronzed General George Washington *(right)* oversees the proceedings from his lofty steed *(see pp14–15)*.

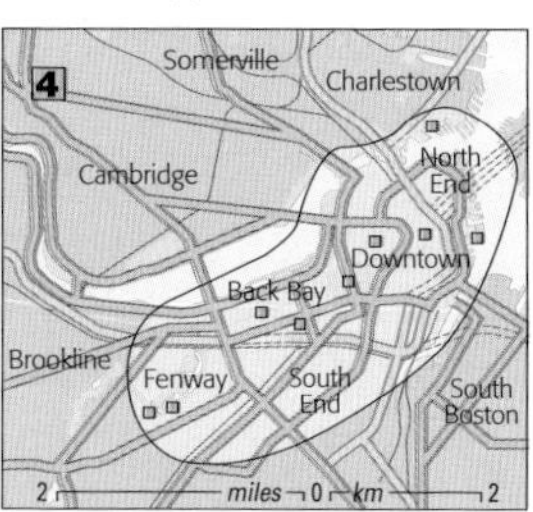

4 Harvard University

Boston may have its legendary blue blood, but neighboring Cambridge claims the Harvard Crimson. Pumping vigorously since 1636, the undisputed heart of American academia has cultivated some of the world's greatest thinkers *(see pp16–19)*.

5 Around Newbury Street

Where fashionistas share the sidewalk with punk rockers. Nowhere is the city's myriad fashions *(left)*, faces, and fortunes on more vibrant display *(see pp20–21)*.

6 Museum of Fine Arts

The MFA, Boston's undisputed queen of the visual arts scene, boasts some of the most extensive collections of Japanese, ancient Egyptian, and Impressionist works of art in the world. Van Gogh's *Houses at Auvers* (1890; *left*) is just one of many treasures in the European Art collection *(see pp22–5)*.

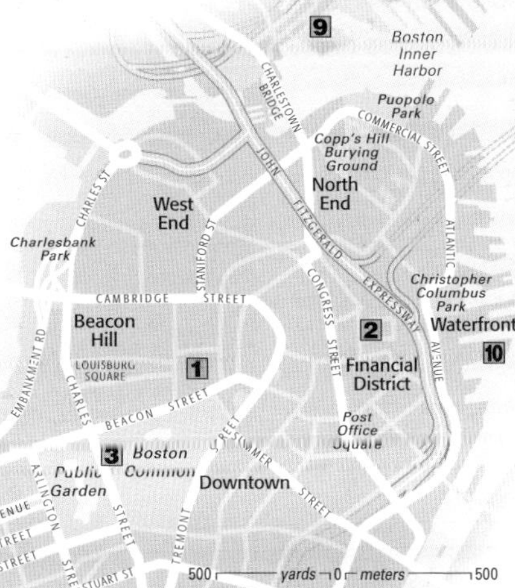

7 Trinity Church

This Neo-Romanesque church is regarded as the finest execution of architect H. H. Richardson's distinctive style. Equally impressive is La Farge's stunning *Christ in Majesty* window *(above; see pp26–7)*.

8 Isabella Stewart Gardner Museum

The works of Rembrandt, Botticelli, and Sargent appear all the more masterful in Isabella Stewart Gardner's Venetian-style palazzo. The courtyard's *(left)* myriad treasures include an ancient Roman marble sarchophagus dating to AD 222 *(see pp28–9)*.

9 Charlestown Navy Yard

Boston's deep harbor made it ideal for one of the US Navy's first shipyards. USS *Constitution (below)*, the most famous of the yard's progeny, is still docked here *(see pp30–31)*.

10 New England Aquarium

Get personal with three species of penguins, harbor seals, and many other creatures of the deep. The vast 200,000 gallon (900,000 liter) Giant Ocean Tank *(right)* is the aquarium's centerpiece, where an upward-spiraling walkway guides you around the ecosytem *(see pp32–3)*.

TOP 10 The Freedom Trail

Snaking through 3 miles (4.8 km) of city streets, the Freedom Trail creates a living link to Boston's key revolutionary and colonial-era sites. Stroll from highlight to highlight and you'll see history adopt a vibrancy, palpability, and relevance unparalleled among US cities. Some of Boston's most unique shops, restaurants, and attractions are also located along the trail.

Freedom Trail plaque

Give your sweet tooth a workout at Mike's Pastry ***(see p94).***

Maps of the trail are available at the Boston Common Visitors' Center.

Most of the trail is indicated in red paint with a few sections in red brick.

- *Start point: Boston Common. "T" station: Park St (red/green lines)*
- *Finish point: Charlestown. "T" station: Community College (red line)*
- *Map: P4 (start)*
- *www.thefreedomtrail.org*
- *Copp's Hill Burying Ground: Snow Hill St; 617 635 4505; open 9am–5pm daily; free*
- *Park Street Church: 1 Park St; 617 523 3383*

Top 10 Features

1. Massachusetts State House
2. Park Street Church
3. Old Granary Burying Ground
4. King's Chapel
5. Old South Meeting House
6. Old State House
7. Faneuil Hall & Quincy Market
8. Paul Revere House
9. Old North Church
10. Copp's Hill Burying Ground

1 Massachusetts State House

Arguably Charles Bulfinch's *pièce de résistance*, the "new" State House (completed in 1798; *above*) is one of the city's most distinctive buildings *(see pp11 & 75).*

2 Park Street Church

Founded by a small group of Christians disenchanted with their Unitarian-leaning congregation, Park Street Church *(above)* was constructed in 1809.

3 Old Granary Burying Ground

A veritable who's-who of revolutionary history fertilizes this plot *(above)* next to Park Street Church. One of its most venerable residents is revolutionary Samuel Adams *(see p38).*

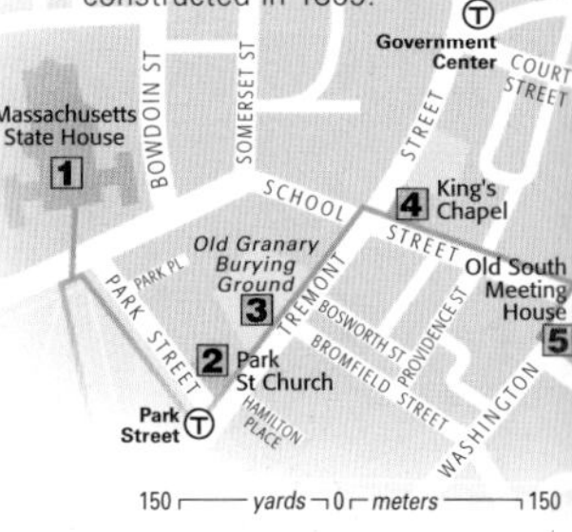

Key

- Freedom Trail
- "T" Station
- Tourist Information

4 King's Chapel

The current granite building was erected in 1749, although the chapel was originally founded in 1686 by King James II as an outpost of the Anglican Church. Don't miss the atmospheric burying ground next door, which shelters colonial Governor John Winthrop *(see p98).*

For more information on these areas see chapters on Beacon Hill and Downtown & the Financial District **See pp74–9 & pp96–103**

5 Old South Meeting House

What Berkeley's University of California was to the 1960s, Boston's Old South Meeting House was to the colonial era: a crucible for free-speech debates and taxation protests *(see p98)*.

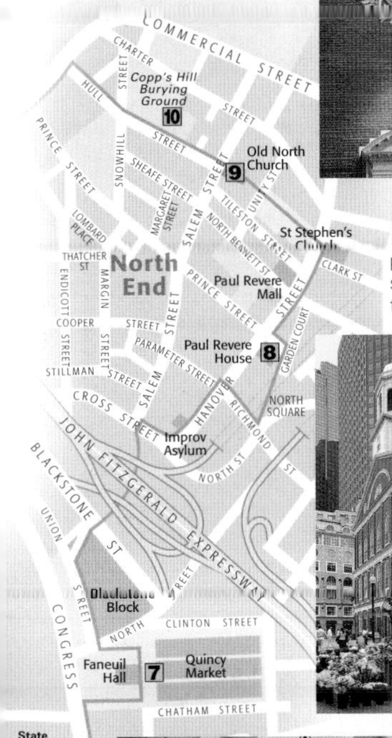

6 Old State House

Built in 1713, this exquisite example of colonial architecture *(above)* served as the HQ of the colonial legislature and the royal governor *(see p97)*.

7 Faneuil Hall & Quincy Market

Known as the "Cradle of Liberty", Faneuil Hall *(left)* has hosted many revolutionary meetings in its time. Neighboring Quincy Market, built in the early 1800s, once housed Boston's wholesale food distribution *(see p12–13)*.

8 Paul Revere House

Nestled in North Square, the Paul Revere House is Boston's oldest private residence. Its principal owner was well regarded locally as a metalsmith prior to his fateful ride *(see p91)*.

9 Old North Church

This church *(above)* occupies a pivotal place in revolutionary history. Prior to his midnight ride, Revere *(see p38)* ordered sexton Robert Newman to hang lanterns in the belfry, to indicate that the British were approaching via the Charles River rather than by land *(see p91)*.

10 Copp's Hill Burying Ground

With headstones dating from the 17th century *(left)*, Copp's Hill is a must for history buffs. It was named after William Copp, a farmer who sold the land to the church *(see p91)*.

An Hour of Freedom

For visitors tight on time, consider this condensed trail. Head up Tremont Street from Park Street "T" station, stopping in the Old Granary Burying Ground. At the corner of Tremont and School streets – site of King's Chapel – turn right onto School and continue to Washington Street and the Old South Meeting House. Turn left on Washington to the Old State House then finish up at Faneuil Hall nearby on Congress Street.

Note: *From Copp's Hill Burying Ground, the Freedom Trail continues across Charlestown Bridge to Charlestown Navy Yard* **See pp30–31**

Left **Bunker Hill** Center **Statue of Paul Revere** Right **Reenactment of the Boston Tea Party**

TOP 10 Moments in Revolutionary History

1 Resistance to the Stamp Act (1765)

The king imposed a stamp duty on all published materials in the colonies, including newspapers. Furious Bostonians boycotted English goods in response.

2 Boston Massacre (1770)

Angry colonists picked a fight with British troops in front of the Old State House, resulting in the deaths of five unarmed Bostonians.

3 Samuel Adams' Tea Tax Speech (1773)

Adams' incendiary speech during a forum at the Old South Meeting House inspired the Boston Tea Party, the most subversive action undertaken yet in the debate over colonial secession.

4 Boston Tea Party (1773)

Led by Samuel Adams, the Sons of Liberty protested against the king's tax policy on tea by boarding three British East India Company ships and dumping their cargo into Boston Harbor, a watershed moment of colonial defiance.

5 Paul Revere's Ride (1775)

Revere rode to Lexington to warn revolutionaries Samuel Adams and John Hancock that British troops intended to arrest them. One of the bravest acts of the war, it would be immortalized in the Longfellow poem *The Midnight Ride of Paul Revere.*

6 Battle of Lexington (1775)

Revere's ride was followed by the first exchange of fire between the ragtag colonist army and the British at Lexington.

7 Fortification of Dorchester Heights (1776)

The British, caught off-guard by the colonists' tenacity at the battles of Lexington and Concord, entrenched themselves on this promontory south of the city.

George Washington

8 Battle of Bunker Hill (1776)

The colonists' fortification of Charlestown resulted in a full-scale British attack. Although defeated, the colonists' resolve was galvanized by this battle.

9 Washington Takes Command (1776)

The Virginia gentleman farmer, George Washington, led the newly-formed Continental Army south from Cambridge to face British troops in New York.

10 Declaration of Independence (1776)

On July 4, the colonies were absolved from all allegiance to the British Crown. Independence was declared from the Royal Governor's headquarters, known today as the Old State House.

For more information on Boston's history and figures in Boston history **See pp36–9**

Top 10 State House Features

1. 23-carat gold dome
2. Senate Chamber
3. House of Representatives
4. "Hear Us" Exhibit
5. Stained Glass Windows
6. Doric Hall
7. Hall of Flags
8. Nurses Hall
9. Sacred Cod
10. State House Pine Cone

The Sacred Cod

Bestowed on the House of Representatives by Boston merchant, Jonathan Rowe, the carving of the Sacred Cod has presided over the Commonwealth's legislative activities since 1784. It disappeared briefly in 1933, when Harvard's *Lampoon* magazine orchestrated a dastardly "codnapping" prank.

Massachusetts State House

The 1798 Massachusetts State House is Charles Bulfinch's masterwork, and among the nation's most mimicked – not to mention earliest – examples of public architecture. With its brash design details, imposing stature, and liberal use of fine materials, the State House embodies the optimism that ran through post-revolutionary America. The building is best understood in three distinct sections: the original Bulfinch front; the marble wings constructed in 1917; and the yellow-brick 1895 addition, known as the Brigham Extension after the architect who designed it. Just below Bulfinch's central colonnade, statues of famous Massachusetts natives strike poses for posterity; among them are the great orator, Daniel Webster, President J. F. Kennedy, and Civil War General Joseph Hooker (who possessed such a predilection for prostitutes that his last name eventually became synonymous with them). Directly below the State House's immense gilded dome is the Senate Chamber, which has hosted some of the most influential debates and speeches in US history. The government's larger legislature, the House of Representatives, convenes in the Brigham Extension. While the building's principal purpose remains governmental, the State House also functions as a working museum, boasting important murals, statues, and artifacts from Massachusetts history (see p75).

Massachusetts State House

Faneuil Hall Marketplace

Bostonians may bemoan its popularity with tourists, but this market complex deserves all the attention and accolades it has received since its revitalization in the mid-1970s. Once the pulsing center of Boston mercantile activity, the area fell into disrepair in the 1930s. Today, however, millions of visitors are testimony to its newfound vitality as a shopping and dining destination.

Exterior, Quincy Market

The soup crocks at Boston Chowda Co in Quincy Market are brimming with piping-hot seafood and veggie chowders.

The National Park Service conducts free historical lectures in Faneuil Hall's Great Hall every half-hour from 9am–5pm.

Purchase discounted day-of-performance theater tickets at the BosTix kiosk on Faneuil Hall's south side. Cash only. Open 10am–6pm Tue–Sat, 11am–4pm Sun.

- *Map: Q2*
- *"T" station: Government Center (green/blue line)*
- *617 523 1300*
- *Great Hall, Faneuil Hall: open 9am–5pm daily; free* • *Millennium Boston Hotel: 24 North St; 617 523 3600* • *Museum of the Ancient & Honorable Artillery Company: Faneuil Hall; 617 227 1638; open 9am–3:30pm Mon–Fri; free* • *Quincy Market: open 10am–9pm Mon–Sat, noon–6pm Sun*

Top 10 Attractions

1. Quincy Market
2. Faneuil Hall
3. Museum of the Ancient & Honorable Artillery Company
4. Millennium Bostonian Hotel
5. North & South Markets
6. Blackstone Block
7. Haymarket Square
8. Samuel Adams Statue
9. Holocaust Memorial
10. Boston Stone

1 Quincy Market

Quincy Market functioned from 1825 to the 1960s as the city's wholesale food distribution center. By the 1980s, the market had been revived, the grand atrium *(below)* restored, and a food court opened.

2 Faneuil Hall

Peter Faneuil, an influential French Huguenot merchant, donated the hall *(below)* to Boston in 1742. Today, the first floor is devoted to souvenir vendors, while the second floor is dominated by the Great Hall, where town meetings once took place.

3 Museum of the Ancient & Honorable Artillery Company

Assembled in 1638 to defend the Massachusetts Bay Colony, the company has held court on Faneuil Hall's fourth floor since 1746. The museum boasts war memorabilia dating from the Revolution to the War on Terrorism.

4 Millennium Bostonian Hotel

The many colonial-era artifacts unearthed during the hotel's construction in 1982 are now on display in the plush lobby area. And should your inner epicurean require sating, visit the hotel's exceptional Seasons restaurant.

Faneuil Hall and Quincy Market are both sights on the Freedom Trail **See pp8–11**

5 North & South Markets

Flanking each side of Quincy Market, these revitalized brick warehouses *(left)* are filled with name-brand shops and many unique restaurants.

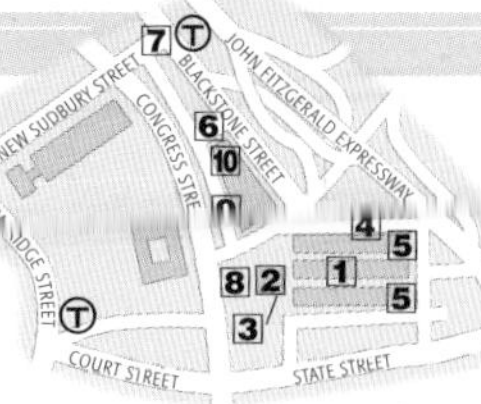

Around Faneuil Hall

6 Blackstone Block

Bounded by Congress, Hanover, Blackstone, and North streets, this block is as old world as Boston gets. The city's first commercial district, named after Boston's first settler, William Blaxton, took root here during the 17th century. Two of the country's oldest dining and drinking establishments – the Union Oyster House and Green Dragon Tavern – call the block home.

7 Haymarket Square

Every Friday and Saturday, vendors *(below)* hawk the day's bounty with unhinged abandon. Yet for all its boisterous chaos, the Haymarket handsomely rewards with cheap, fresh produce.

8 Samuel Adams Statue

The city's favorite brewer and patriot is immortalized in front of Faneuil Hall, where he delivered some of the Revolutionary era's most impassioned speeches *(see p10)*. Local sculptor Anne Whitney was commissioned to design the statue in 1880.

9 Holocaust Memorial

This 1995 memorial *(below)* comprises six glass columns, symbolizing the Nazis' principal death camps. Each column bears the numbers of one million victims, evoking the six million lives destroyed under Hitler.

10 Boston Stone

This curious landmark was once the measuring point from which all distances to and from Boston were calculated. The visibly unremarkable stone is embedded into a brick wall at the corner of Marshall Street and Salt Lane.

True Irish Pubs

The Quincy Market area boasts a bevy of Irish-style pubs. But if you're craving authentic Gaelic atmosphere to complement your black and tan, the choice is more limited than appearances might suggest. Two pubs that make the grade are Kitty O'Shea's (131 State St) and the Black Rose (160 State St; *see p102*) – both within two blocks of the marketplace.

For more on Boston's shopping experiences **See pp56–7**

Boston Common & Public Garden

Verdant Boston Common has hosted auctions, cattle grazing, and public hangings over its 350-year history, in addition to festivals and the requisite frisbee tosses. The adjacent Public Garden, opened in 1839, was the USA's first botanical garden. Its swan boats, weeping willows, and bridge are emblematic of Boston at its most enchanting. The French-style flowerbeds (center) *may only bloom in warmer months, but the garden exudes old-world charm year round.*

Sign for Boston Common

Quick, food court-style bites can be had inside the Corner shopping center, at Washington and Summer streets.

The Commonwealth Shakespeare Company stages free performances on the common during summer. Call 617 747 4468 for schedule.

- *Bounded by: Beacon, Park, Tremont, Arlington, & Boylston streets*
- *Map: M4, N4*
- *"T" station: Park Street (red/green line), Boylston, & Arlington stops (both green line).*
- *Open 24 hours*
- *Boston Common Visitors' Center: 147 Tremont St; 617 426 3115; open 8:30am–5pm Mon–Sat, 9am–5pm Sun*
- *Boston Parks & Recreation: 617 635 4505*
- *Swan boat rides: 617 522 1966; mid-May–mid Sep: noon–4pm Mon–Fri, 10am–4pm Sat–Sun; Adm: $2*

Top 10 Attractions

1. Shaw Memorial
2. Soldiers & Sailors Monument
3. Frog Pond
4. Parkman Bandstand
5. *Make Way for Ducklings* Statuettes
6. Founders' Memorial
7. Lagoon Bridge
8. Swan Boats
9. Bronze of George Washington
10. Ether Monument

1 Shaw Memorial

Augustus Saint-Gauden's lifelike bronze pays homage to the "Fighting 54th" – one of the only entirely African-American regiments in the Civil War. Led by Boston native Robert Shaw, the 54th amassed an impressive battle record.

2 Soldiers & Sailors Monument

Over 25,000 Union Army veterans remembered their fallen Civil War comrades at the 1877 dedication of Martin Milmore's impressive memorial. Bas-reliefs *(above)* depict the soldiers' and sailors' departure to and return from war.

3 Frog Pond

During summer, children splash under the iridescent spray of the pond's fountains. Come winter, kids of all ages lace up their skates and take to the ice. Skate rentals and hot chocolate are available at the nearby hut.

4 Parkman Bandstand

Built in 1912 to honor George Parkman, a benefactor of the park, the bandstand *(right)* is modeled after Versailles' *Temple d'Amour*. In summer it hosts everything from concerts to graduations.

For sights and attractions in neighboring Beacon Hill **See pp74–9**

5 *Make Way for Ducklings* Statuettes

Eight duckling statues have sprung from the pages of Robert McCloskey's kids' book and fallen in line behind their mother at the pond's edge.

6 Founders' Memorial

William Blaxton, Boston's first white settler, is depicted greeting John Winthrop *(see p38)* in John F Paramino's 1930 bronze. Note the word "Shawmut" – the Native American name for the land that would become Boston.

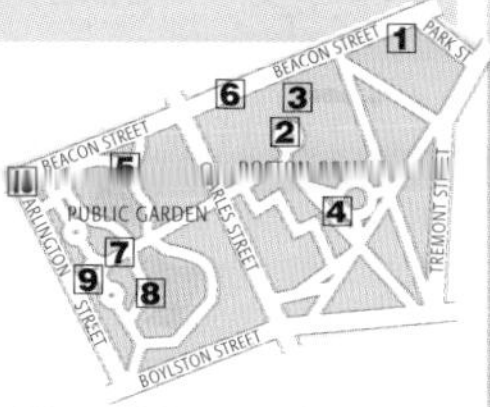

Plan of Boston Common & Public Garden

7 Lagoon Bridge

The world's smallest suspension bridge (1869) is a miniature-scale copy of New York's Brooklyn Bridge. The bridge is a favorite spot for staging wedding pictures.

8 Swan Boats

Summer hasn't officially arrived in Boston until the swan boats emerge from hibernation and glide onto the Public Garden pond. With their gracefully arching necks and brilliantly painted bills, each distinctive swan boat can accommodate up to 20 people.

Emerald Necklace

Boston Common and Public Garden may seem like solitary urban oases, but they are two links in a greater chain of green space that stretches all the way through Boston to the suburb of Roxbury. The Emerald Necklace, as this chain is called, was completed in 1896 by Frederick Law Olmsted, the man behind New York's Central Park.

9 Bronze of George Washington

The nation's first president cuts a stately figure at the western end of the Public Garden. Thomas Ball's 1869 bronze was the first to depict George Washington astride a horse.

10 Ether Monument

This 1868 statue commemorates the first etherized operation, which took place at Massachusetts General Hospital in 1846. Controversial from the outset, this is the West's only monument to the powers of a drug.

For sights and attractions in neighboring Downtown & the Financial District **See pp96–103**

TOP 10 Harvard University

America's most prestigious university – named in honor of its principal benefactor, John Harvard, in 1638 – has nurtured, tortured, and tickled some of the greatest minds of the past 350 years. It has hosted everything from global economic summits to kool-aid acid tests, and educated everyone from future US presidents to late-night talk show hosts. Visitors craving contact with the Harvard mystique are in luck, since much of the university is open to the public.

Memorial Hall

Students refuel on Campo de Fiori's delicious panini (1350 Massachusetts Av, 617 354 3805).

Harvard is planning to relocate the Fogg, Busch-Reisinger, and Sackler museums by 2006/7.

While on campus, pick up a copy of the student-run newspaper *The Crimson* to see what issues are exercising some of the world's greatest minds.

- *"T" station: Harvard (red line)*
- *617 495 1573*
- *www.harvard.edu/museums; www.ci.cambridge.ma.us/info*
- *Harry Widener Memorial Library: Harvard Yard; 617 495 2411; access only if accompanied by someone with valid Harvard ID*
- *Massachusetts Hall: Harvard Yard; open to the public but no tours*

Top 10 Features

1. Massachusetts Hall
2. John Harvard Statue
3. Memorial Hall
4. Harvard Yard
5. Harry Widener Memorial Library
6. Museum of Natural History
7. Fogg Museum
8. Busch-Reisinger Museum
9. Sackler Museum
10. Peabody Museum of Archaeology & Ethnology

1 Massachusetts Hall

The university's oldest building, constructed in 1720, acted as a meeting place for revolutionary soldiers. It continues to be a focal point of resistance movements, most recently in 2001, when students occupied the hall's administrative offices in an effort to secure a fair wage for the university's employees.

2 John Harvard Statue

The statue's *(right)* inscription "John Harvard, Founder 1638" conceals three deceptions, hence its nickname "The Statue of Three Lies". First, there is no known portrait of John Harvard, so the sculptor, Daniel French, used a model; second, John Harvard did not found the university – rather it was named after him; and last, the university was not founded in 1638, but in 1636.

3 Memorial Hall

Built over 14 years, Harvard's memorial to its fallen union army alumni was officially opened in 1878. Conceived as a multipurpose building, it has hosted graduation exercises, theatrical performances, and assemblies of all kinds.

4 Harvard Yard

Harvard's mixed residential and academic yard *(left)* became the standard by which most American institutions of higher learning modeled their campuses.

For more on Harvard University and Harvard's museums **See p119**

5 Harry Widener Memorial Library

The Widener *(left)* is the largest university library in the US. It houses a special collection of rare books, including a Gutenberg bible and early editions of Shakespeare's collected works (under renovation until 2004).

6 Museum of Natural History

Never mind George Washington's taxidermied pheasants, the ginormous Brazilian amethyst geode, or the world's only mounted Kronosaurus skeleton. Check out the glass flowers: 830 species of plants, painstakingly replicated in brilliant, colorful glass.

7 Fogg Museum

The world's largest, and most comprehensive, university art collection is housed here *(left)*. The focus is on Western art from the late Middle Ages to the present, with a fine selection of Impressionist works.

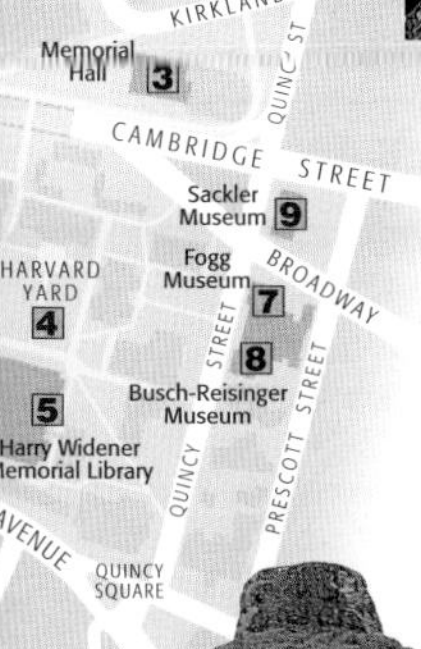

8 Busch-Reisinger Museum

Unlike the Fogg, its Impressionist-inclined downstairs neighbor, the Busch-Reisinger *(right)* leans toward German expressionism, the Bauhaus, and generally more contemporary art movements.

9 Sackler Museum

The university's Asian *(left)*, Egyptian, Islamic, and later Indian art collections are on display in the relatively modern Sackler. Don't forget to see what's showing in the special exhibition gallery, the largest at the university.

10 Peabody Museum of Archaeology & Ethnology

Housing one of the world's most comprehensive records of human cultural history, the Peabody caters for the Indiana Jones in all of us. Highlights include locally culled prehistoric artifacts, a permanent Mesoamerica exhibit, and a new gallery devoted to frequently rotating temporary exhibits.

Harvard Lampoon

Lampooners have made you laugh more than you might ever know. Aside from *The Harvard Lampoon* proper being the world's oldest humor magazine, nearly every successful contemporary American comedy to reach a TV or movie screen boasts an ex-Lampooner on its writing staff. One well known ex-Lampooner is Conan O'Brien of *The Simpsons* fame.

***Note:** Combined tickets for the Fogg, Busch-Reisinger, and Sackler museums cost $6.50*

Left **Leonard Bernstein** Right **T. S. Eliot**

TOP 10 Harvard Alumni

1 John Adams (1735–1826)
The nation's second president, although nervous upon entering the illustrious college as a freshman, eventually became enthralled by his studies.

2 Franklin Delano Roosevelt (1882–1945)
Apparently more of a social butterfly than dedicated academic, F.D.R. played pranks, led the freshman football squad, and earned a C average at Harvard before he became the 32nd president of the US.

3 W. E. B. Du Bois (1868–1963)
Founder of the National Association for the Advancement of Colored People (NAACP), Du Bois studied philosophy, and said of his experience, "I was in Harvard, but not of it".

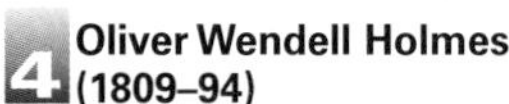

John Adams

4 Oliver Wendell Holmes (1809–94)
The 1861 grad and future Supreme Court Justice was also the class poet, delivering a stirring reading of original work at his Class Day exercises.

5 Henry Cabot Lodge (1850–1924)
Harvard's first Political Science PhD and future US senator earned notoriety for opposing American participation in the League of Nations, foreshadowing the isolationism that took hold in the US following World War I.

6 Leonard Bernstein (1918–90)
The country's greatest composer was firmly grounded in the arts at Harvard. He edited the *Advocate* – the college's estimable literary and performing arts journal.

7 T. S. Eliot (1885–1965)
The modernist poet of *The Waste Land* fame contributed much of his early work to the *Advocate*. He went on to edit many of those submissions for later publication.

8 Henry Kissinger (1923–)
The International Affairs and Government professor, who graduated from Harvard summa cum laude, became President Nixon's National Security Advisor in 1969 and Secretary of State in 1973.

9 Benazir Bhutto (1953–)
This class of 1973 alumna later became the first woman to lead a modern Muslim state when she was elected prime minister of Pakistan in 1988.

10 Henry James (1843–1916)
The master of the psychological novel sourced plenty of material at Harvard for his scathing 1886 work, *The Bostonians*.

Harvard's Top 10 Buildings

1. Memorial Hall, 45 Quincy St (Ware & Van Brunt, 1878)
2. Busch-Reisinger Museum, 32 Quincy St (Charles Gwathmey, 1991)
3. Massachusetts Hall, Harvard Yard (University Overseers, 1720)
4. Sackler Museum, 485 Broadway (James Stirling, 1984)
5. Fogg Museum, 32 Quincy Street (Coolidge, Bulfinch & Abbott, 1927)
6. University Hall, Harvard Yard (Charles Bulfinch, 1814)
7. Sever & Austin Halls, Harvard Yard & North Yard (H. H. Richardson, 1880 & 1883)
8. Harvard Graduate Center, North Yard (Walter Gropius, 1950)
9. Carpenter Center, 24 Quincy St (Le Corbusier, 1963)
10. Undergraduate Science Center, Cambridge St & Massachusetts Av (Jose Luise Sert, 1971)

Harvard's "Architectural Zoo"

Prominent modernist architect James Stirling described Harvard as an "architectural zoo" – and with a campus as aesthetically diverse as Harvard's, it's a well-deserved moniker. Stirling was himself responsible for the university's modernist Sackler Museum (see pp 17 & 119) *opened in 1985. The seemingly ubiquitous architect Charles Bulfinch, whose claim to fame is the Massachusetts State House* (see p11)*, left his mark on Harvard Yard with his 1814 University Hall, featuring an ingenious granite staircase that "floats" – supported solely by virtue of its interlocking steps. In complete contrast Walter Gropius, whose strongly linear residential buildings pepper college campuses throughout the northeast US, contributed the Harvard Graduate Center in 1950. Gropius strove to make his industry-informed projects seem welcoming for their inhabitants, but by most Harvard grad students' accounts, the austere-looking center doesn't exactly scream "Home Sweet Home." One of Harvard's more whimsical buildings is Le Corbusier's Carpenter Center. A wondrous collection of forms and materials, the center boasts entire walls made of glass and deeply grooved concrete. Surprisingly it is Le Corbusier's only design in North America.*

Sever Hall

Trinity Church *(see p26–7)* architect and 1859 Harvard alumnus H. H. Richardson designed Sever *(right)* and Austin halls. Both halls echo Richardson's distinctive Romanesque style found on his Copley Square masterpiece.

Carpenter Center

Around Newbury Street

Don't let the profusion of Prada-clad shoppers fool you: there's more to Newbury Street than world-class retail, people watching, and al fresco dining. One of the first streets created on the marshland known as Back Bay, Newbury has seen a myriad of tenants and uses over the past 150 years. Look closely and you'll glimpse a historical side to Newbury Street all but unseen by the fashionistas.

Newbury Street

Stock up at Deluca's Back Bay Market (239 Newbury St) and have a picnic.

View the schedule for Emmanuel Music, a highly respected chamber music society, at www.emmanuelmusic.org or call 617 536 3356.

• Map K5, L5, M5 • "T" station: Arlington, Copley, or Hynes/ICA • Boston Architectural Center: 320 Newbury St; 617 262 5000; open 9am–10pm Mon–Thu, 9am–5pm Fri–Sat, noon–5pm Sun • Church of the Covenant: 67 Newbury St • Emmanuel Church: 15 Newbury St; 617 536 3355 • French Library & Cultural Center: 53 Marlborough St; 617 266 4351; open 10am–8pm Tue–Thu, 10am–5pm Fri–Sat • New England Historical Genealogical Society: 101 Newbury St; 617 536 5740; open 9am–5pm Tue–Sat (until 9pm Wed–Thu) • Society of Arts & Crafts: 175 Newbury St; 617 266 1810; open 10am–6pm Mon–Sat, noon–5pm Sun • Trinity Church Rectory, 233 Clarendon St; closed to the public

Top 10 Sights

1. Emmanuel Church
2. Commonwealth Avenue
3. Church of the Covenant
4. Society of Arts & Crafts
5. Boston Architectural Center
6. Louis, Boston
7. Gibson House Museum
8. French Library & Cultural Center
9. New England Historical Genealogical Society
10. Trinity Church Rectory

1 Emmanuel Church

Architect Alexander Estey's impressive church (1860) was the first building to grace Newbury after the in-filling of Back Bay. The adjacent Lindsey Chapel (1924: *right*) is home to the renowned Emmanuel Music.

2 Commonwealth Avenue

A mall *(above)* running along the center of Commonwealth Avenue provides a leafy respite from the Newbury Street throngs. Benches and historical sculptures line the pedestrian path, where couples and a dog or two stake out their favorite spots.

3 Church of the Covenant

Although far more famous for his Trinity Church in New York, English-born architect Richard Upjohn also left his Neo-Gothic mark on Boston with the Church of the Covenant *(left)*, erected in 1865.

For more sights and attractions in Back Bay **See pp80–83**

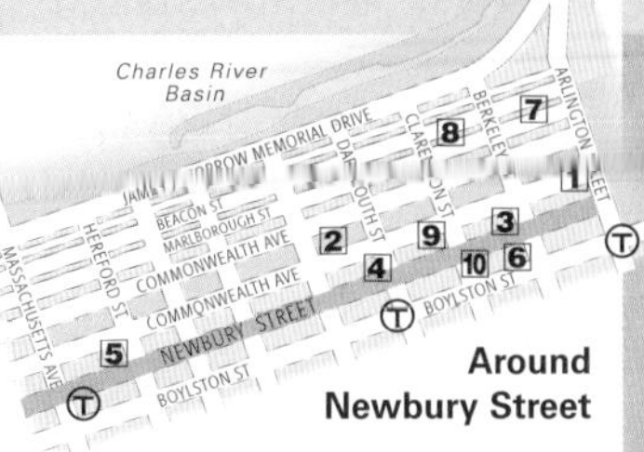

4 Society of Arts & Crafts

Formed in 1897, the Boston Society of Arts and Crafts was one of the earliest of its kind. Societies such as this helped to elevate the status of traditional arts.

5 Boston Architectural Center

For more than 100 years, aspiring architects have sought the counsel and workshops offered by the venerable BAC. The Cormick Gallery here displays architectural plans and designs.

6 Louis, Boston

Originally a natural history museum opened in 1864, this landmark building now offers the haughtiest couture shopping experience in town *(see p86)*.

7 Gibson House Museum

One of Back Bay's first private residences, Gibson House *(above)* was also one of the most modern houses of its day. Boasting gas lighting, indoor plumbing, and heating, it spurred a building boom in the area *(see p83)*.

8 French Library & Cultural Center

Housed in a grand Back Bay mansion, the French Library hosts everything from lectures in French to concerts and a legendary Bastille Day celebration. The library's lobby posts wire-service news reports from France.

9 New England Historical Genealogical Society

Members seek to make contact with their New England progenitors in one of the most extensive genealogical libraries in the US. For a fee, you too, can try your luck.

10 Trinity Church Rectory

H. H. Richardson, Trinity Church's principal architect, was commissioned to build this rectory *(left)* in 1879. His handiwork reflects the Romanesque style of his Copley Square masterpiece *(see p26–7)*.

Back Bay's Origins

Since its settlement by Westerners, Boston has been nipped, tucked, and reshaped to suit the needs of its inhabitants. Back Bay derives its name from the tidal swampland on which the neighborhood now stands. During the 19th century, hills were leveled to fill the marsh and create the foundations for the grand avenues and picturesque brownstones that now distinguish this highly sought-after area.

For more on Newbury Street shopping **See pp85–6**

TOP 10 Museum of Fine Arts

Over its 130 year-plus history, Boston's Museum of Fine Arts (MFA) has collected some 350,000 pieces from an array of cultures and civilizations, ranging from ancient Egyptian tomb treasures to stylish modern artworks. Today, the MFA boasts superlative collections of ancient Egyptian, Japanese, colonial New England, and Impressionist works, as well as contemporary and folk art.

Museum façade, Huntington Avenue

The MFA boasts a restaurant on each of its three levels, escalating in quality and price as you move from the courtyard level upward.

Boston's hottest singles meet for jazz and drinks at MFA First Fridays – call ahead for times and dates. Free entry with MFA general admission.

Free admission to the museum on Wednesdays from 4 to 9.45pm.

- *465 Huntington Av (Av of the Arts)*
- *Map D6*
- *617 267 9300*
- *www.mfa.org*
- *"T" station: Museum (green line/E train)*
- *Open: 10am–4:45pm Mon–Tue, 10am–9:45pm Wed–Fri (West Wing only after 5pm on Thu & Fri); 10am–4:45pm Sat–Sun.*
- *Adm: $15*

Top 10 Features

1. *La Japonaise*
2. Japanese Temple Room
3. John Singer Sargent Murals
4. John Singleton Copley Portraits
5. Egyptian Royal Pectoral
6. Tomb Treasure of King Aspelta
7. *Postman Joseph Roulin*
8. Silverwork by Paul Revere
9. *Dance at Bougival*
10. *Christ in Majesty with Symbols*

2 Japanese Temple Room

With its wood paneling and subdued lighting, the Temple Room evokes ancient Japanese shrines atop mist-enshrouded mountains. The statues, which date from as early as the seventh century, depict prominent figures from Buddhist texts.

1 *La Japonaise*

Claude Monet's 1876 portrait *(below)* reflects a time when Japanese culture fascinated Europe's most style-conscious circles. The model, interestingly, is Monet's wife, Camille.

3 John Singer Sargent Murals

Having secured some of Sargent's most important portraiture in the early-20th century, the MFA went one step further and commissioned the artist to paint murals and bas-reliefs on its central rotunda and colonnade *(left)*.

For more art, visit the neighboring Isabella Stewart Gardner Museum **See pp28–9**

4 John Singleton Copley Portraits

The self-taught, Boston-born Copley made a name for himself by painting the most affluent and influential Bostonians of his day, from pre-Revolutionary figures like John Hancock *(left)* to early American presidents.

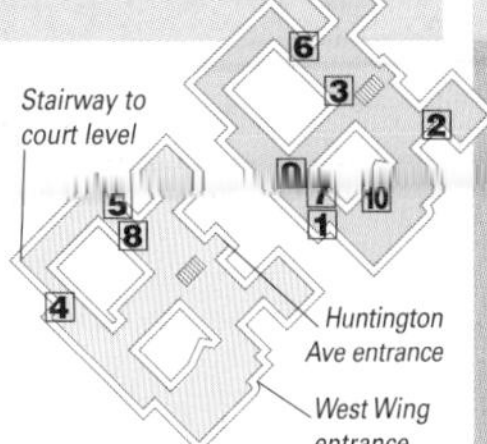

Key to Floorplan

First floor

Second floor

5 Egyptian Royal Pectoral

This extremely rare chest ornament *(below)* is nearly 4,000 years old. A vulture is depicted with a cobra on its left wing, ready to strike. This juxtaposition symbolized the union of Upper and Lower Egypt.

6 Tomb Treasure of King Aspelta

This assortment of artifacts belonging to a 6th-century BC Nubian king was recovered in 1920 at Nuri in present-day Sudan during a MFA/Harvard joint expedition.

7 *Postman Joseph Roulin*

The MFA boasts some of Vincent van Gogh's most important work, including this 1888 oil, which was painted during his stay in Arles, France.

8 Silverwork by Paul Revere

Famed for his midnight ride, Revere *(see p38)* was also known for his masterful silverwork. The breadth of his ability is apparent in the museum's 200-piece collection, including this Sons of Liberty bowl *(below)*.

9 *Dance at Bougival*

This endearing image (1883) of a couple dancing is among Renoir's most beloved works. It exemplifies the artist's knack for taking a timeless situation and modernizing it by dressing his subjects in the latest fashions.

10 *Christ in Majesty with Symbols*

Acquired in 1919 from a small Spanish church, this medieval fresco had an amazingly complex journey to Boston, which involved waterproofing it with lime and Parmesan for safe transport.

Gallery Guide

Many of the East Wing's holdings will be on tour during the MFA's multi-year, $425-million expansion project but the MFA should still remain high on any visitor's must-see list. Middle Eastern, Egyptian, Nubian, and Asian galleries, as well as a superb collection of American decorative arts and sculpture, are all on the first floor. Stop to admire the Sargent murals on the rotunda en route to the second floor galleries where you'll find the Chinese, Japanese, Impressionist, and European art collections.

Left **Textile and Fashion Arts Collection** Right **Coffins, Art of Egypt Collection**

Top 10 Museum of Fine Arts Collections

1 Art of Asia

For Japanese art connoisseurs, the museum offers a dizzying overview of Japan's multiple artistic forms. In fact, the MFA holds the largest collection of ancient Japanese art outside of Japan. In addition to the tranquil Temple Room *(see p22)*, with its centuries-old Buddhist statues, visitors should admire the beautiful hanging scrolls and woodblock prints, with their magical, dramatic landscapes and spirited renderings of everyday life. Kurasawa fans will be enthralled by the menacing samurai weaponry and flamboyant uniforms. Additionally, the Art of Asia collection boasts exquisite objects from 2,000 years of Chinese, Indian, and Southeast Asian history, including sensuous ivory figurines, pictorial carpets, and vibrant watercolors.

2 Art of Egypt, Nubia, & the Ancient Near East

This collection is a treasure trove of millennia-old Egyptian sarcophagi, tomb finds, and Nubian jewelry and objects from everyday life. The assemblage of Egyptian funerary pieces, including beautifully-crafted jewelry and intact ceramic urns is awe-inspiring. Ancient Near Eastern artifacts, with their bold iconography and rich materials, illustrate why the region was known as the Cradle of Civilization.

Marble busts, Classical Art Collection

Plan of the Collections

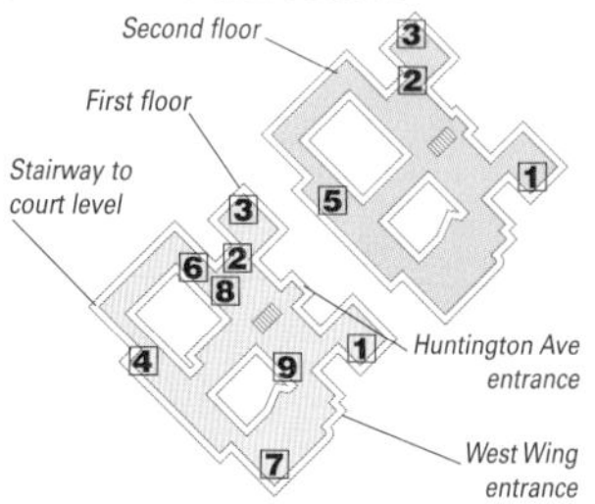

3 Classical Art

The remarkable Classical Art Collection has a hoard of gold bracelets, glass, mosaic bowls, and stately marble busts. One of the earliest pieces is a c.1500 BC gold axe, inscribed with symbols from a still-undeciphered Cretan language.

4 American Art to 1900

The MFA houses the world's finest collection of colonial New England furniture. The museum also showscases rare 17th-century American portraiture and works from the country's own "Old" Masters including Copley, Stuart, Cole, Sargent, Cassat, Homer, and many others.

Grand piano, Musical Instruments Collection

5 European Art to 1900

From 12th-century tempera baptism scenes to Edvard Munch's *Melancholy*, the MFA's European collection is staggeringly diverse. Painstakingly transferred medieval stained-glass windows, beautifully illuminated bibles, and delicate French tapestries are displayed alongside works by Old Masters: Titian, El Greco, Rembrandt, and Rubens. The superlative Impressionist collection boasts the likes of Monet, Renoir, Degas, and Cézanne.

6 Textile & Fashion Arts

Quaint pictorial quilts, period fashions, fine Persian rugs, and pre-colonial Andean weavings are on display in the Loring Gallery. Particularly interesting are the museum's holdings of textiles and costumes from the Elizabethan and Stuart periods – an unprecedented 1943 donation from the private collection of Elizabeth Day McCormick.

African mask, Art of Africa Collection

7 Contemporary Art

Given Boston's affinity for the traditional, you might be surprised by the museum's world-class contemporary art collection. The Cubists, Matisse, Pollock, O'Keefe, and Warhol are all represented.

8 Musical Instruments

Priceless 17th-century guitars, ornately inlaid pianos, and even a mouth organ are on view in the Musical Instruments gallery. Among the more distinctive pieces is the c.1796 English grand piano – the earliest extant example of a piano with a six-octave range – and a 1680 French guitar by the Voboam workshop.

9 Art of Africa, Oceania, & the Ancient Americas

Pre-colonial artifacts from these collections include Melanese canoe ornaments, dramatic Congolese bird sculptures, and Mayan burial urns. The African art collection's most popular display is the powerful looking 19th- and 20th-century wooden masks. The Ancient Americas gallery shows hieroglyphic texts painted on Mayan ceramics.

10 "Please be Seated!" Installations

One of the country's most comprehensive collections of American contemporary furniture is interspersed throughout the MFA's galleries. The museum encourages visitors to not only admire these furniture pieces, but to sit on them, too. Take a break on fine American handiwork by designers such as Maloof, Castle, and Eames.

Top 10 Trinity Church

Boston has a knack for creating curious visual juxtapositions, and one of the most remarkable is in Copley Square, where H. H. Richardson's 19th-century Romanesque Trinity Church reflects in the blue-tinted glass of the decidedly 20th-century John Hancock Tower. The breathtakingly beautiful church was named a National Historic Landmark in 1971 and has earned the American Institute of Architects' distinction of being among the ten greatest buildings in the country.

Trinity Church façade

Grab a quick bite at the Prudential Center food court, just two blocks away (800 Boylston St).

Although currently in the midst of a multi-year preservation project, Trinity remains open to the public.

Vistors are asked to respect the fact that Trinity Church is primarily a place of worship.

Tours of the church are available and begin in the bookstore on the Boylston Street side of the complex.

- *206 Clarendon St*
- *Map L5*
- *"T" station: Copley Sq (green line) & Back Bay (orange line)*
- *617 536 0944 (church)*
- *617 927 0038 (store)*
- *www.trinityboston.org*
- *Church open 8am–6pm daily*
- *Bookstore open 9am–6pm Mon–Sat, 10am–6pm Sun*
- *Adm: $3 (tours: $5)*

Top 10 Features

1. La Farge Windows
2. Burne-Jones Windows
3. Central Tower
4. Front Façade & Side Towers
5. Organ Pipes
6. Phillips Brooks' Bust
7. Pulpit Carving
8. Embroidered Kneelers
9. Bookstore
10. The Foundation

1 La Farge Windows

A newcomer to stained glasswork at the time, John La Farge approached his commissions (like *Christ in Majesty, below*) with the same sense of daring and vitality that Richardson employed in his Trinity design.

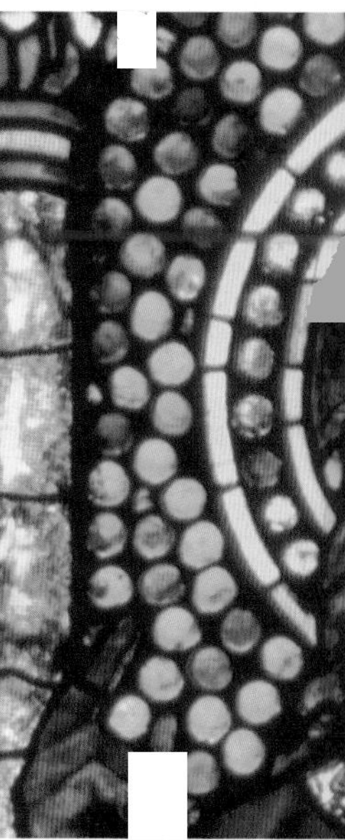

2 Burne-Jones Windows

Edward Burne-Jones' windows – on the Boylston Street side – was inspired by the burgeoning English Arts & Crafts Movement for inspiration. Its influence is readily apparent in his *David's Charge to Solomon (below)*, with its bold patterning and colors.

3 Central Tower

The church's central tower borrows its square design from the Cathedral of Salamanca, Spain. On the interior, wall paintings by La Farge depicting biblical figures in vibrant hues are in sharp contrast to the austere church interiors of the artist's day.

4 Front Façade & Side Towers

Inspired by the Romanesque church of St Trophime in Arles, France, Richardson redesigned Trinity's front portico as well as two new side towers. The additions were implemented by his firm of architects some years after his death in the 1890s.

For more on attractions in Back Bay **See pp80–83**

5 Organ Pipes

The beautiful organ pipes frame the church's west wall *(left)*. Exquisitely designed, ornately painted, and – of course – very sonorous, the pipes seem to hug the church's ceiling arches.

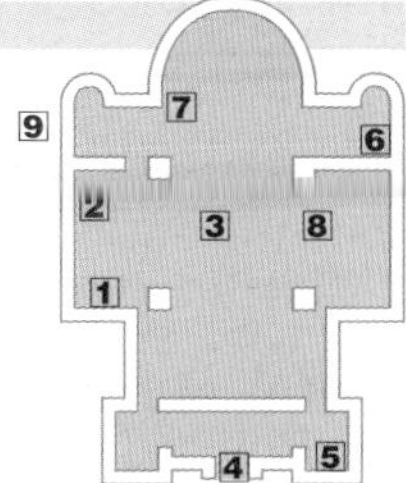

Church Floorplan

6 Phillips Brooks' Bust

Keeping watch over the baptismal font is Rector Brooks. Renowned for his sermons – bold, forthright, and fresh for their time – he was rector at Trinity from 1869–91.

7 Pulpit Carving

Early preachers throughout the ages, including St Paul, Martin Luther, and Philip Brooks of Trinity *(right)*, are depicted in high relief on the pulpit designed by Charles Coolidge.

8 Embroidered Kneelers

Trinity's colorful kneelers have been stitched by parishioners in memory of people and events past. They serve as an informal, folk history of the congregation.

9 Bookstore

Apart from the requisite Christian literature and Bibles, the bookstore also sells high-quality replicas of designs that appear throughout the church.

Trinity Sings "Hallelujah"

One of Boston's most cherished traditions is the singing of Handel's *Messiah* and its unmistakable "Hallelujah Chorus" at Trinity during the Christmas season. Hundreds pack the sanctuary to experience the choir's ethereal, masterful treatment of the piece. Call 617 536 0944 for performance information.

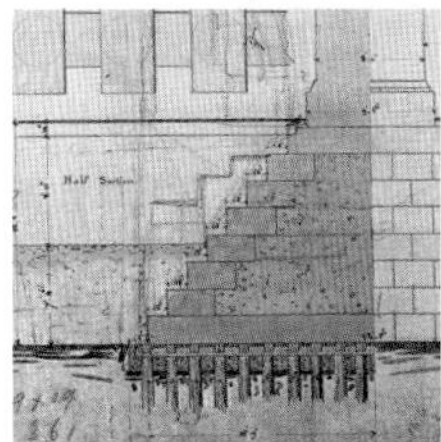

10 The Foundation

It was in 1873 that Richardson, aged only 34, drove 4,500 wooden foundation-pilings for the new church into the spongy Back Bay. Building costs were originally estimated at around $640,000.

For more H. H. Richardson buildings **See p19**

Isabella Stewart Gardner Museum

One needn't be a fervent patron of the arts to be wowed by the Gardner Museum. Its namesake, who traveled tirelessly to acquire the pieces now housed here, opened the museum in 1903 to befit (some would say to rival) her staggering collection. The 15th-century, Venetian-style palazzo is a veritable feast of artifacts, art, and architecture in which flowers bloom, sculpted nudes pose in hidden corners, and entire ceilings reveal their European origins.

Isabella Stewart Gardner

Light salads and sandwiches are served in the museum's café. Weather permitting, request a table on the gorgeous outdoor patio.

The museum's Tapestry Room hosts a concert series in the spring and fall. See museum website for more information.

No photography or filming is permitted in the museum.

Guided tours available by appointment.

- *"T" station: Museum (green line/E train)*
- *280 The Fenway*
- *Map D6*
- *617 566 1401*
- *www.gardnermuseum.org.*
- *Open 11am–5pm Tue–Sun.*
- *Adm: $10 ($11 Sat–Sun)*

Top 10 Features

1. The Courtyard
2. Dutch Room
3. Gothic Room
4. Titian Room
5. Long Gallery
6. Raphael Room
7. Tapestry Room
8. Macknight, Yellow, & Blue Rooms
9. Spanish Cloister
10. Veronese Room

1 The Courtyard

Gardner integrated Roman, Byzantine, Romanesque, Renaissance, and Gothic elements in the magnificent courtyard *(below)*, which is out of bounds but can be viewed through the graceful arches surrounding it.

2 Dutch Room

The space that houses some of Gardner's most impressive acquisitions *(below)* was the scene of of an incredible art heist in 1990: among the 13 works stolen were a Vermeer and two Rembrandts.

3 Gothic Room

Appreciate John Singer Sargent's splendid and somewhat risqué 1888 portrait of Mrs Gardner as well as medieval liturgical artwork from the 13th century.

4 Titian Room

The most artistically significant gallery was conceived by Gardner as the palazzo's grand reception hall. It has a distinctly Italian flavor and showcases Titian's *Europa (left)*, one of the greatest masterpieces in the US.

For more art, visit the neighboring Museum of Fine Arts
See pp22–5

5 Long Gallery

Roman sculptural fragments and busts line glass cases crammed with unusual 15th- and 16th-century books and artifacts. One such rare tome is a 1481 copy of Dante's *The Divine Comedy*, featuring drawings by Botticelli.

10 Veronese Room

With its richly gilded and painted Spanish-leather wallcoverings, it's easy to miss this gallery's highlight: look up at Paolo Veronese's 16th-century masterwork *The Coronation of Hebe*.

6 Raphael Room

Gardner was the first collection to bring works by Raphael to the US; three of the artist's major works are on display here *(left)*, alongside Botticelli's *Tragedy of Lucretia* and Crivelli's *St. George and the Dragon*.

8 Macknight, Yellow, & Blue Rooms

Fans of the Impressionists need look no further than these rooms *(above)*, which house portraits and sketches by the likes of Manet, Matisse, Degas, and Sargent. Of particular note is Sargent's *Mrs. Gardner in White*.

9 Spanish Cloister

With stunning mosaic tiling and a Moorish arch, the Spanish Cloister looks like a hidden patio at the Alhambra. But Sargent's sweeping *El Jaleo* (1882, *below*), all sultry shadows and rich hues, gives the room its distinctiveness.

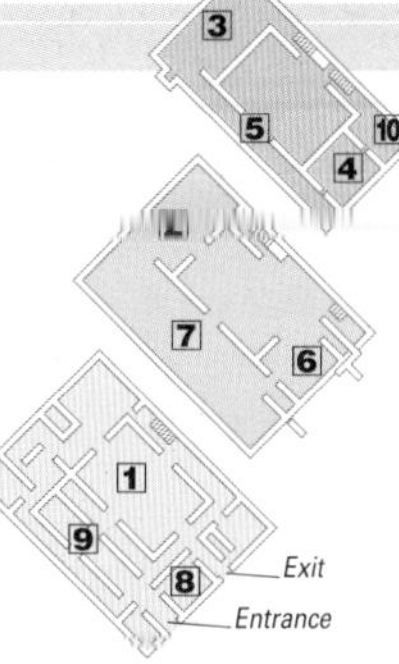

Key to Floorplan

- First floor
- Second floor
- Third floor

7 Tapestry Room

This room houses two series of 16th-century Belgian tapestries, each comprised of five individual works: one depicts *Scenes from the Life of Cyrus the Great* and another *Scenes from the Life of Abraham*.

Fenway Court

Before Isabella Stewart Gardner died in 1924 she stipulated in her will that Fenway Court (as it was then known) and her collection become a national museum. She believed that works of art should be displayed in a setting that would fire the imagination.
So the collection, exhibited over three floors, is not arranged chronologically or by country of origin but organized purely to enhance the viewing of the individual treasures. To encourage visitors to respond to the artworks themselves many of the 2500 objects – from ancient Egyptian pieces to Matisse's paintings – are left unlabeled, as Gardner had requested.

TOP 10 Charlestown Navy Yard

Some of the most storied battleships in American naval history began life at Charlestown Navy Yard. Established in 1800 as one of the country's first naval yards, Charlestown remained vital to US security until its decommissioning in 1974. From the 200-year-old wooden-hulled USS Constitution *to the World War II-era steel destroyer USS* Cassin Young*, the yard gives visitors an all-hands-on-deck historical experience unparalleled in America.*

Defensive guns

Try some pub grub at the atmospheric 18th-century Warren Tavern (2 Pleasant St).

Expect long lines for USS *Constitution* on afternoons in summer.

- *Visitors' Center: 55 Constitution Rd*
- *Map H2*
- *617 242 5601*
- *www.nps.gov/bost*
- *"T": North Station (green & orange lines)*
- *Water shuttle from Long Wharf, www.mbta.com for boat schedules*
- *Bunker Hill Monument: Visitor Lodge: open 9am–5pm daily; Monument: open 9am–4.30pm daily*
- *Naval Yard Visitors' Center: open 9am–5pm daily* • *USS* Cassin Young*: open 10am–4pm daily (to 5pm summer)* • *USS* Constitution*: 10am–4pm daily* • *USS* Constitution *Museum: open 10am–5pm daily (9am–6pm summer)* • *"Whites of Their Eyes": open Apr–Nov: 9am–5pm daily*

Top 10 Sights

1. USS *Constitution*
2. Bunker Hill Monument
3. Navy Yard Visitors' Center
4. "Whites of Their Eyes"
5. USS *Constitution* Museum
6. Ropewalk
7. Dry Dock #1
8. Commandant's House
9. Muster House
10. USS *Cassin Young*

1 USS *Constitution*

First tested in action during the War of 1812, the USS *Constitution* *(below)* is the world's oldest warship still afloat. A tugboat helps her perform an annual turnaround cruise on July 4th.

2 Bunker Hill Monument

Ten minutes' walk from the yard is this 220-ft (67-m) granite obelisk *(below)*, which has towered over Charlestown since 1842. It commemorates the first major battle of the American Revolution *(see p10)*.

3 Navy Yard Visitors' Center

Begin your stroll through the Yard at the National Park Service-operated Visitors' Center, where you can pick up literature about the site's attractions and purchase tickets for the "Whites of Their Eyes" show.

4 "Whites of Their Eyes"

This multimedia show places viewers in the thick of the Battle of Bunker Hill. More than 1,000 slides and seven sound channels bring history to heart-pumping life.

***Note:** All sights, with the exception of the "Whites of Their Eyes" show, are free*

5 USS *Constitution* Museum

With enough activities to keep kids entertained and plenty of nautical trivia to satisfy a naval historian, this museum brings USS *Constitution*'s 200 years to life. This watercolor *(left)* on ivory is of 19th-century naval hero Commodore William Bainbridge.

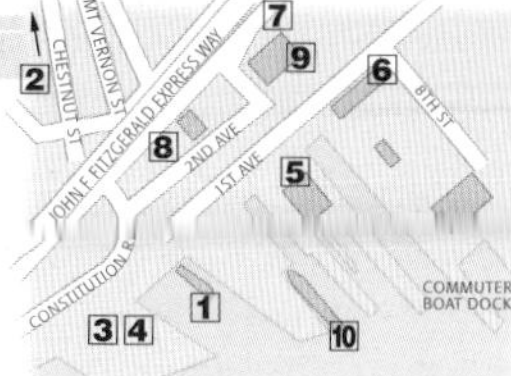

Charlestown Navy Yard

6 Ropewalk

This quarter-mile-long (0.5 km) building (1837) houses steam-powered machinery that produced rope rigging for the nation's warships.

7 Dry Dock #1

To facilitate hull repairs on the navy's ships, Dry Dock #1 *(right)* was opened in 1833. The granite dock was drained by massive steam-powered pumps. USS *Constitution* was the first ship to be given an overhaul here.

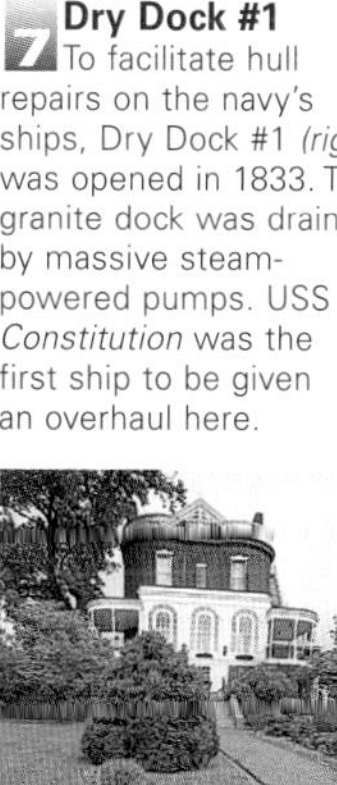

8 Commandant's House

The oldest building in the yard (1805) housed the commandants of the First Naval District. With its sweeping harbor views and wraparound porch, this elegant mansion *(left)* was ideal for entertaining dignitaries from all over the world.

9 Muster House

This octagonal brick building was designed in the Georgian-revival style popular in the northeast in the mid-19th-century. The house served as an administration hub, where the Yard's clerical work was carried out.

10 USS *Cassin Young*

Never defeated, despite withstanding multiple kamikaze bomber-attacks in the Pacific, this World War II era destroyer *(left)* could be considered USS *Constitution's* 20th-century successor.

Old Ironsides

Given her 25-inch (63-cm) thick hull at the waterline, it's easy to imagine why USS *Constitution* earned her nickname "Old Ironsides." Pitted against HMS *Guerriere* during the War of 1812, the ship engaged its enemy in a shoot-out that left *Guerriere* all but destroyed. Upon witnessing British cannon balls "bouncing" off USS *Constitution's* hull, a sailor allegedly exclaimed, "Huzzah! Her sides are made of iron." The rest is history.

Note: *Muster House, Commandant's House, and the Ropewalk are closed to the public*

TOP 10 New England Aquarium

The sea pervades nearly every aspect of Boston life, so it's appropriate that the New England Aquarium is one of the city's most popular attractions. What sets this aquarium apart from similar institutions is its commitment to presenting not only an exciting environment to learn about marine life, but also to conserving the natural habitats of its gilled, feathered, and whiskered inhabitants.

Aquarium façade

If the aquarium has not convinced you to eliminate fish from your diet, visit Legal Sea Foods for a leisurely, moderately priced meal *(see p42)*. Quick, quality bites from around the globe can also be had at the Quincy Market food hall, three blocks away.

Admission to the aquarium includes one sea lion show plus discounts on an IMAX feature and whale-watching tours.

- *"T" station: Aquarium (blue line).*
- *Central Wharf*
- *Map R3*
- *617 973 5200*
- *www.neaq.org for general info, including current IMAX features.*
- *Open 9am–5pm Mon–Fri, 9am–6pm Sat & Sun*
- *Adm: $13.50*
- *Whale Watch: 617 973 5281 for reservations and rate information*
- *IMAX: open 10am–9:30pm daily; Adm: $8*

Top 10 Features

1. Penguin Pool
2. Tropical Gallery
3. Giant Ocean Tank
4. IMAX Theater
5. Harbor Seal Tanks
6. Changing Exhibition Gallery
7. Whale Watch
8. Sea Lion Shows
9. Freshwater Gallery
10. Edge of the Sea

1 Penguin Pool

Three species of penguins – Rockhopper *(above)*, Little Blue, and African – compete for space on the central island and take dips in the surrounding pool.

2 Tropical Gallery

A vibrant Pacific coral reef *(right)* thrives beneath intense lighting that ensures the fragile coral's survival. Corals house small plants in their tissues that require light to carry out photosynthesis.

3 Giant Ocean Tank

Offering a veritable cross-section of a Caribbean reef, the Giant Ocean Tank packs tortoises, sharks, moral eels, brightly colored tropical fish *(above)* and scores of other species into the 200,000-gallon (900,000 liter) tank.

4 IMAX Theater

The Simons IMAX Theater shows large-format 3D documentaries, featuring digital surround sound and plenty of breathtaking, you-are-there cinematic moments. Education with an adrenalin rush.

5 Harbor Seal Tanks

Harbor seals swim, feed, and play in specially designed tanks outside the aquarium. All have either been born in captivity or rescued and deemed unfit for release into the wild.

For more information on Whale Watch excursions **See p137**

6 Changing Exhibition Gallery

Temporary exhibitions on the ground floor highlight a particular region of the aquatic world. Exhibitions have included "Living Links", which features species from a South Pacific coral reef.

7 Whale Watch

The aquarium's extremely popular whale watch ships (Apr–Oct only) provide an unparalleled glimpse into the life cycles of the world's largest mammals *(left)*. *Voyager II* and *III* steam well outside Boston Harbor to the Stellwagen Bank, a prime feeding area for pods of whales.

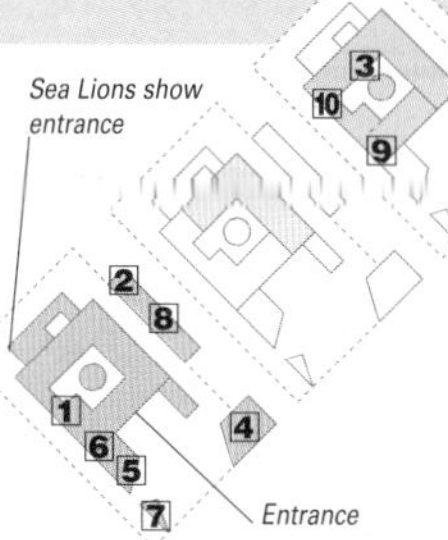

Key to Floorplan

▒	Ground Floor
▒	Mezzanine
▒	First Floor

8 Sea Lion Shows

For about half an hour you can witness these 850-pound (385-kilo) behemoths whipping through the water, jumping onto the pool deck, and even kissing lucky onlookers.

9 Freshwater Gallery

Providing an interesting counterbalance to the aquarium's seaward slant, this exhibit gives freshwater fish their due. In addition to piranhas, electric eels, and local salmon, it boasts intriguing studies of endangered freshwater habitats from the Amazon to North American temperate forests.

10 Edge of the Sea

For those not content to merely gaze at fish behind glass, the Edge of the Sea tidepool exhibit puts marine life at visitors' fingertips – literally *(below)*. Inside a ground-level fiberglass tank, the New England seashore is recreated in all its diversity.

The Aquarium's Mission

The aquarium's aim, first and foremost, is to instigate and support marine conservation. Its Conservation Action Fund has fought on behalf of endangered marine animals worldwide, helping to protect humpback whales in the South Pacific, sea turtles in New England, and dolphins in Peru.

Following pages **Swan Boats, Boston Common**

Battle of Concord Bridge

Top 10 Moments in Boston History

1 1630: Boston Founded
Under the leadership of John Winthrop *(see p38)*, English Puritans moved from overcrowded Charlestown and colonized the Shawmut Peninsula. Permission was granted from its sole English inhabitant, Anglican cleric William Blaxton. Their city on the hill was named Boston in honor of the native English town of their leaders.

2 1636: Harvard Created
Boston's Puritan leaders established a college at Newtowne (later Cambridge) to educate future generations of clergy. When young Charlestown minister John Harvard died two years later and left his books and half his money to the college, it was renamed Harvard *(see p16)*.

3 1775: American Revolution
Friction between colonists and the British crown had been building for more than a decade when British troops marched on Lexington to confiscate rebel weapons. Forewarned by Paul Revere *(see p38)*, local militia, known as the Minute Men, skirmished with British regulars on Lexington Green. During the second confrontation at Concord, the shot heard round the world marked the beginning of the Revolution, which ended in American independence with the 1783 Treaty of Paris.

Detail, Boston Library

4 1845: Irish Arrived
Irish fleeing the potato famine arrived in Boston in tens of thousands, many eventually settling in the south of the city. By 1900, the Irish were the dominant ethnic group in Boston. They flexed their political muscle accordingly, securing the election of John F. Kennedy *(see p39)* as president in 1960.

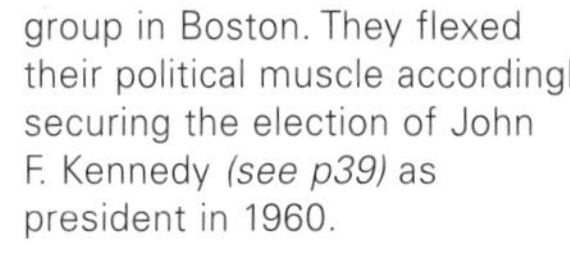

5 1848: Boston Public Library Founded
The Boston Public Library was established as the first publicly supported municipal library in the US. In 1895 the library moved into the Italianate "palace of the people" on Copley Square *(see p81)*.

6 1863: Black Boston Went to War
Following decades of agitation to abolish slavery, the city sent the country's first African-American

Gates, Harvard University

regiment to join Union forces in the Civil War. The regiment was honored by the Shaw Monument on Boston Common *(see p14)*.

7 1886: City Expanded

Boston assumed its modern form with the filling in of Back Bay *(see p21)* and the completion of Franklin Park, the final link in the Emerald Necklace *(see p13)*.

8 1897: Subway Opened

The Tremont Street subway, the first underground in the US, was opened on September 1 to ease road congestion. It cost $4.4 million to construct and the initial fare was five cents. This single line grew into the Metropolitan Boston Transit Authority (MBTA) with 181 routes and 252 stations.

The Big Dig

9 1958: Freedom Trail Opened

This historical walking tour was established, with its familiar red brick and paint connecting the city's sights. It was based on a 1951 *Boston Herald Traveler* column by William Scofield, and was the first of its kind in the US.

10 1991–: The Big Dig

The central artery/tunnel project, aka the Big Dig, is the most technologically challenging highway project in the country. The $15 billion project plans to alleviate Boston arterial traffic congestion by 2005.

Top 10 Innovations

1 Sewing Machine

Elias Howe invented the sewing machine in Cambridge in 1845, but spent decades securing patent rights.

2 Surgical Anesthesia

Ether was first used for surgical anesthesia at Massachusetts General Hospital in 1846.

3 Telephone

Alexander Graham Bell invented the telephone in his Boston laboratory in 1876.

4 Safety Razor

Bostonian King Camp Gillette invented the safety razor with disposable blades in 1901.

5 Baby Formula

The New England Medical Center devised nutritionally enhanced baby formula in 1919.

6 Mutual Fund

Massachusetts Investors Trust opened in 1924 as the first modern mutual fund that pooled investor's money to purchase portfolio stocks.

7 Programmable Digital Computer

A Harvard team built the first programmable digital computer, Mark 1, in 1946. Its 750,000 components weighed about 10,000 lb (454 kg).

8 Microwave Oven

A Raytheon company engineer placed popcorn in front of a radar tube in 1946 and discovered the principle behind the microwave oven.

9 Instant Film

Cambridge inventor Edwin Land devised the Polaroid camera, launched in 1948.

10 E-mail

Ray Tomlinson, an engineer at Bolt, Beranek, and Newman in Cambridge, sent the first e-mail message in 1971.

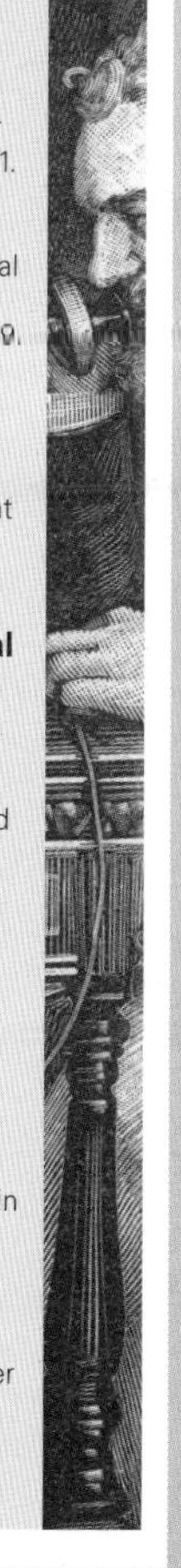

Note: *Innovation Odyssey, a bus tour with actors, makes Saturday afternoon tours of innovation sites. Call 617 350 0358*

Left **John F. Kennedy** Right **James Michael Curley (seated)**

Top 10 Figures in Boston History

1 John Winthrop (1587–1649)

Acting on a daring plan put together by English Puritans in 1629, Winthrop led approximately 800 settlers to the New World to build a godly civilization in the wilderness. He settled his Puritan charges at Boston in 1630 *(see p36)* and served as the governor of the new Massachusetts Bay Colony until his death.

2 Increase Mather (1639–1723)

Educated at Harvard, preacher Increase Mather solidified the hold of Puritan theologians on the Massachusetts government. When William took the English crown, Mather persuaded the king to grant a charter that gave the colony the right to elect the council of the governor in 1691. His influence was later undermined by his support of the 1692 Salem witch trials.

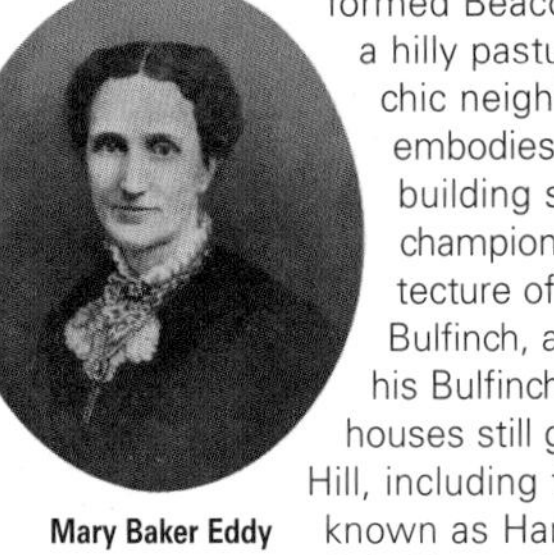

Mary Baker Eddy

3 Samuel Adams (1722–1803)

Failed businessman Samuel Adams became Boston's master politician in the tumultuous years leading up to the revolution *(see p10)*. Adams signed the Declaration of Independence and served in both Continental Congresses. As governor of Massachusetts, he joined Paul Revere in laying the cornerstone of the State House *(see p11)* in 1795.

4 Paul Revere (1735–1818)

Best known for his "midnight ride" to forewarn the rebels of the British march on Concord, Revere served the American Revolution as organizer, messenger, and propagandist. A gifted silversmith with many pieces in the Museum of Fine Arts *(see p22–5)*, he founded the metal-working firm that gilded the State House dome and sheathed the hull of the USS *Constitution*.

5 Harrison Gray Otis (1765–1848)

In the 1790s, Harrison Gray Otis and James Mason transformed Beacon Hill from a hilly pasture into a chic neighborhood that embodies the Federal building style. Otis championed the architecture of Charles Bulfinch, and three of his Bulfinch-designed houses still grace Beacon Hill, including the one now known as Harrison Gray Otis House *(see p76)*.

6 Donald McKay (1810–1880)

McKay built the largest and swiftest of the clipper ships in his East Boston shipyard in 1850. The speedy vessels revolutionized long-distance shipping at the time of the California gold rush and gave Boston its last glory days as a mercantile port before the rise of rail transport.

7 Mary Baker Eddy (1821–1910)

After recovering from a major accident, Eddy wrote *Science and Health with Key to the Scriptures*, the basis of Christian Science. She founded a church in Boston in 1879, and in 1892 reorganized it as the First Church of Christ, Scientist *(see p82)*. Eddy also established the Pulitzer prize-winning *Christian Science Monitor* newspaper in 1908.

8 James Michael Curley (1874–1958)

Self-proclaimed champion of "the little people," Curley used patronage and Irish pride to retain a stranglehold on Boston politics from his election as mayor in 1914 until his defeat at the polls in 1949. Known as "the rascal king" he embodied political corruption but created many enduring public works.

9 John F. Kennedy (1917–1963)

Grandson of Irish-American mayor John "Honey Fitz" Fitzgerald and son of ambassador Joseph Kennedy, John F. Kennedy represented Boston in both houses of the US Congress before he became the first Roman Catholic elected president of the United States. The presidential library at Columbia Point exhibits his brief, but intense, period in office *(see p129)*.

10 W. Arthur Garrity, Jr. (1920–1999)

In 1974, US District Court judge Garrity ruled that African-American students had been denied their constitutional rights to the best available education. He ordered a desegregation plan for Boston's 200 schools, setting off protests, some violent, in predominantly white neighborhoods.

Literary Bostonians

1 Anne Bradstreet
Bradstreet (c.1612–72) was America's first poet, publishing *The Tenth Muse, Lately Sprung Up in America* in 1650.

2 Ralph Waldo Emerson
Poet and philosopher, Emerson (1803–82) espoused transcendentalism and pioneered American literary independence.

3 Henry Wadsworth Longfellow
Known for epic poems such as *Hiawatha*, Longfellow (1807–82) also translated Dante.

4 Louisa May Alcott
Little Women sealed Alcott's (1832–88) literary fame, but she also acted as a nurse in the Civil War.

5 Henry James
Master of sonorous prose, James (1843–1916) is considered one of the creators of the psychological novel.

6 Dorothy West
African-American novelist and essayist West (1907–98) made sharp observations about class and race conflicts.

7 Robert Lowell
Lowell's (1917–77) "confessional poetry" influenced a generation of writers.

8 Robert Parker
Scholar of mystery literature, Parker (b.1932) is best known for his signature detective Spenser.

9 Robert Pinsky
Poet, critic, and translator Pinsky (b.1940) served as US poet laureate and now teaches at Boston University.

10 David Mamet
Playwright and screenwriter Mamet (b.1947) brings a gift for gritty language to explorations of lost morality.

***Note:** Portraits of many famous Bostonians painted 1760–1820 are displayed at the Museum of Fine Arts* **See p22–5**

Left **Salts** Right **L'Espalier**

Top 10 Restaurants

1 L'Espalier

Set in a gracious townhouse, lit by candles, and staffed by impeccable waiters and brilliant cooks, romantic L'Espalier serves Boston's finest contemporary French cuisine. Chef-owner Frank McClelland's vegetarian entrées are every bit as sophisticated as those with meat. *30 Gloucester St • Map K5 • 617 262 3023 • Closed lunch & Sun • $$$$$*

2 Rialto

Chef Jody Adams takes a luscious approach to Mediterranean cuisine, working magic with a simple basil cream soup, or using grilled tomatoes to give extra depth to her gazpacho. A green olive and balsamic vinegar sauce perfectly balances the unctuousness of her signature roasted marinated duck. The comfortable and soothing dining room is ideal for special occasions. *Charles Hotel, 1 Bennett St, Cambridge • Map B2 • 617 661 5050 • Closed lunch • $$$$$*

3 Hamersley's Bistro

Chef-owner Gordon Hamersley presides over this defining South End restaurant. The menu is inspired by French provincial cooking but features the best of mostly local produce (don't miss the lemon-infused broiled chicken). The bar scene is lively, and the outdoor dining tables provide one of the neighborhood's prime social settings in summer. *553 Tremont St • Map F5 • 617 423 2700 • Closed lunch • $$$*

4 Clio

One of the country's most-lauded young chefs, Ken Oringer is dedicated to innovation. With an ever-changing menu he always looks for new flavor sensations. Few Boston chefs would dare to serve bone marrow custard with nougats of wild mushrooms and black truffles. *Eliot Hotel, 370 Commonwealth Ave • Map J5 • 617 536 7200 • Closed lunch & Mon • $$$$$*

5 Locke-Ober

Everything old is new again since über-chef Lydia Shire took over Boston's oldest gourmet restaurant (c.1875) and breathed new life into the classic *haute cuisine* dishes. Her crisped duck with elderberries and ginger achieves the perfect crackling over succulent meat. The city's most established families dine here. *3 Winter Pl • Map P4 • 617 542 1340 • Closed Sun & lunch Sat • $$$$$*

6 Salts

Chef Steven Rosen has mined the culinary traditions of central and eastern Europe to spectacular effect. He's a fanatic about making his own ingredients, even curing his own trout gravlax, which he serves with roasted beets, watercress, and pickled onions. The warmly contemporary room is small so reserve ahead to beat the slew of Cambridge professionals who consider Salts their secret. *798 Main St, Cambridge • Map D3 • 617 876 8444 • Closed lunch Sun & Mon • $$$*

***Note:** For more restaurants and key to price categories* **See pp89, 95, 103, 111, 117, 125, 131**

7 Ambrosia on Huntington

High ceilings and huge windows give the room a triumphal quality. Chef-owner Anthony Ambrose's dishes (such as an appetizer of half a lobster on buckwheat crepe) apply subtle shadings of Indonesian and Chinese spices to classic French combinations. *116 Huntington Ave • Map L6 • 617 247 2400 • Closed lunch Sat & Sun • $$$*

8 Olives

Olives is home base for the city's most famous chef, Todd English, and a no-reservations policy means lines form as early as 4pm. Many feel the wait is worthwhile. English cooks with panache, piling plates high with delights such as roasted pork chop on garlic mashed potatoes topped with a caramelized mushroom sauce. Huge and loud, Olives is a temple to bravura cookery. *10 City Sq, Charlestown • Map G2 • 617 242 1999 • Closed lunch & Sun • $$$$*

9 Mantra

Chainmail curtains dividing the cavernous room and a hookah lounge enclosed in a bamboo "tent" give Mantra definite drama. Chef Thomas John mixes his native Indian spices with French

Radius

technique, like encasing lamb in a crust of poppy seed and carda–mom. *52 Temple Pl • Map P4 • 617 542 8111 • Closed Sun & lunch Sat • $$$$$*

10 Radius

Chef Michael Schlow blends multiple flavors for a single, clear taste fusion in his own version of New American cuisine. You'd think seared Maine scallops might get lost when combined with wild mushrooms, potato puree, leeks, and a truffle emulsion, but the woodsy flavors just enhance the sweet, salty taste of the sea. The restaurant is regularly mobbed by successful CEOs and their more glamorous stockholders. *8 High St • Map Q4 • 617 426 1243 • Closed lunch Sat & Sun • $$$$$*

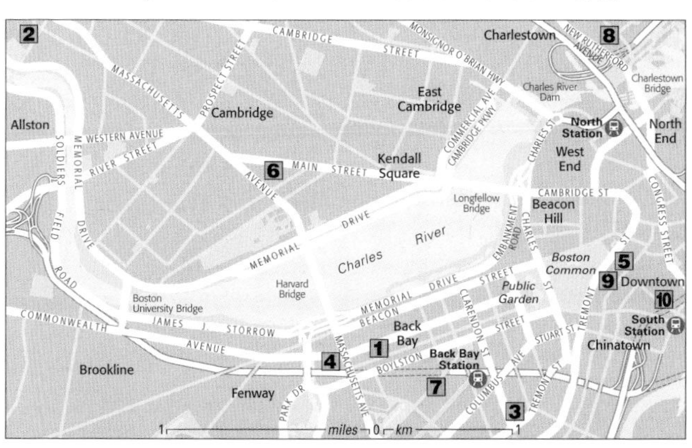

Note: *Even restaurants that are booked weeks ahead will often have seats available for diners willing to eat at 6pm or earlier*

Left **Barking Crab** Right **East Coast Grill**

Top 10 Spots for Seafood

1 Barking Crab

This colorful fish shack is most congenial in the summer, when diners sit outdoors at picnic tables. Most of the local fish – cod, haddock, tuna, halibut plus clams and crab – are so fresh that they only need the most basic of preparation. *88 Sleeper St • Map H4 • 617 426 2722 • $*

2 Legal Sea Foods

Legal is a Boston chain where diners can always count on getting immaculately fresh local fish in a fine-dining setting. The clam chowder is legendary; raw clams and oysters are impeccable. Legal's only shortcoming is that it doesn't take reservations. *Long Wharf & other locations • Map H3 • 617 742 5300 • $$$*

3 East Coast Grill

Chef-owner Chris Schlesinger was among the first Boston chefs to perfect the art of cooking seafood with the smoke and heat of an open fire. Schlesinger is also an aficionado of hot spices, often perking up a more bland fish with a peppery basting sauce or toning down an oily fish with a citrus marinade. The simple, unfussy dining room allows the food to shine. Reservations are not accepted so arrive early, and be prepared to wait. *1271 Cambridge St, Cambridge • Map E2 • 617 491 6568 • Closed lunch Mon–Sat • $$$*

Lobster, Jimbo's Seafood

4 Jimmy's Harborside & Jimbo's Seafood

Don a sports coat for the more formal Jimmy's Harborside, or lounge in shorts and sandals on the outside deck of Jimbo's Seafood with its great harbor views. In either case, opt for the simplest preparations, as sauces don't always measure up to the fish. See if you can recognize any of the celebrities in the glossy photos. *242 Northern Ave • 617 423 1000 • Closed lunch Sun • $$$*

5 No Name Restaurant

As Fish Pier's only restaurant, No Name has an intimate relationship with the fishermen who both sell their catch to, and eat at, this bare-bones restaurant. The very basic menu consists mostly of fried fish. The outstanding chowder is what fishermen call "trim" chowder – full of hunks of whatever has been boned and trimmed that day. *15½ Fish Pier • 617 423 2705 • $*

6 Turner Fisheries

The elegant space in the street-level corner of the Westin Copley Place is for smart dining, with an emphasis on large portions of select fish in season. Start with a Caesar salad laden with anchovies, then tuck into a bluefin tuna steak so large it hangs off the plate. Opt for either the airy outer room with

For more restaurants and key to price categories **See pp89, 95, 103, 111, 117, 125, 131**

windows onto Copley Square or the cozier lounge near the bar where there's live jazz on weekends. *10 Huntington Ave • Map F5 • 617 424 7425 • Closed lunch Sun • $$$$*

7 James Hook & Co.

Located right on Fort Point Channel, Hooks is primarily a broker that supplies lobster to restaurants throughout the US. But they also cook lobster, clams, crab, and some fin fish on the spot. Take your order, sit on the sea wall, and chow down. *15 Northern Ave • Map H5 • 617 423 5500 • Closed evenings • $*

8 Topacio

The Central American flavor of this area of East Boston really comes through at this casual storefront Salvadoran restaurant. The *sopa de mariscos* is filled with calamari, shrimp, scallops, and clams in their shells and is served with a lobster tail and claws draped over the bowl. Redolent of cilantro (coriander), the soup is accompanied by a stack of thick, homemade corn tortillas. *120 Meridian St, East Boston • 617 567 9523 • No DA • $*

Jumbo Seafood

9 Jumbo Seafood

Replicating the complex seafood cuisine of China's Guandong province isn't easy in Boston, but Jumbo manages to import the requisite dried shrimp and jellyfish, gets hold of specialties such as sea squirt, and buys wonderfully fresh seafood from the boats on Fish Pier. *5 Hudson St • 617 542 2823 • $–$$*

10 Morse Fish

Morse is principally a South End fish monger. But they also cook fish to order for great sandwiches or fried fish dinners at a relative pittance. There are a few tables in this cheery shop, or they'll pack dinner for a picnic in nearby Blackstone Park. No lobster. *1401 Washington St • Map F6 • 617 262 9375 • Closed Sun • $*

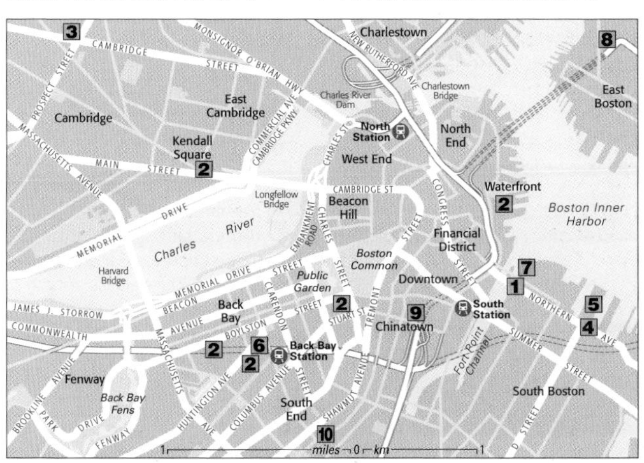

Note: *At 6:30am on weekdays, the catch from Boston-based boats is auctioned in 1,000-lb (453-kilo) lots from Fish Pier*

Left **Trident Booksellers & Café** Center **Cappuccino, Café 300** Right **Sonsie**

Top 10 Cafés

1 Café Pamplona

Pamplona evokes the beatnik cafés of the 50s. Smokers sit outside on the sidewalk terrace while tobacco-free hipsters favor the low-ceilinged basement room. There's a Basque influence to the menu and the coffee is as dense and dark as a Baudelaire poem. *12 Bow St, Cambridge • Map B2 • Closed Sun • No DA*

2 Caffè Vittoria

The jukebox at the largest of North End's Italian cafés has nearly every song ever recorded by Frank Sinatra, Tony Bennett, and Al Martino. The menu is long on short coffees and short drinks, including at least seven varieties of grappa, as well as a fair selection of Italian ices. *296 Hanover St • Map Q1*

3 Diesel Café

Diesel is the quintessential Davis Square gathering spot where the tragically hip rub shoulders with lesbian couples and scruffy Tufts students. The spacious café has old-fashioned booths, couches, and a pair of pool tables out back. The coffee menu includes a double-caffeine "High Octane" brew plus teas and tisanes. *257 Elm St, Somerville*

4 Trident Booksellers & Café

Bibliophiles make pilgrimages to this fine bookstore. The in-store café and bar serves light and casual meals ranging from breakfast eggs to lunch wraps as well as dinner dishes like lasagna. *338 Newbury St • Map J5*

5 Sonsie

Although continental breakfast is served, the scene doesn't really kick in until lunch time. By dusk, Sonsie is full of folks who just stopped in for a post-work drink and ended up making an evening of it. The food – pizza, pasta and fusion-tinged entrées – deserves more attention than most café-goers give it. *327 Newbury St • Map J5*

6 Mama Gaia's Café

There's a distinctive Latin flavor to Mama Gaia's menu, which flits among South American and Central American cuisines. Both the coffee and the clientele tend to be mellow, with 60s, New Age, and nuevo-Latino sensibilities ensuring a peaceful co-existence. Poetry, politics, and Cuban jazz often fill the stage. *401 Massachusetts Ave, Cambridge • Map D3*

Garden of Eden Café

7 1369 Coffee House

The 1369 Coffee House is as community-based as Starbucks is corporate. The original Inman Square branch has a more interesting cross section of ages and ethnicities but Central Square has sidewalk seating. Both branches serve mostly caffeine drinks and sweets – with sandwiches at lunch. *1369 Cambridge St, Cambridge • Map D2 • 757 Massachusetts Ave, Cambridge • Map D3*

8 Garden of Eden Café

The best-dressed, most buff South Enders patronize this gem of a café for tasty dishes like duck pâté with bits of pistachio and orange or classic French onion soup. Prepare to wait in line at lunch time for the sandwiches or stop by mid-afternoon to savor a large molasses cookie with a cappuccino. *571 Tremont St • Map M6*

9 Café 300

Located next to an art gallery in the central atrium of an artists' studio building, Café 300 is a magnet for architects and artists. They come for the laid-back vibe, pasta of the day, and tasty sandwich combos like grilled eggplant, tomato, basil, and mozzarella. *300 Summer St • Map R5 • Closed Sun*

10 Parish Café

During warm weather, the tables outside Parish Café offer a terrific view of the lower Back Bay street scene. Parish has some of the most creative sandwiches in the city – designed by chefs of Boston's top restaurants. Comfort food dishes (meatloaf with mashed potatoes, fishcakes with Pommery mustard) are also excellent. *361 Boylston St • Map M5*

Top 10 Spots to Break your Diet

1 Finale
End the evening with molten chocolate gateau or rich crème brûlée. *1 Columbus Ave • Map M5*

2 L. A. Burdick Chocolatiers
Sinful bonbons and Boston's best hot chocolate. *52D Brattle St, Cambridge • Map B1*

3 Dairy Fresh
An old-fashioned shop jammed with candy, nuts, and treats. *57 Salem St • Map Q1*

4 Toscanini's Ice Cream
Bold but simple flavors make the ice cream here a favorite. *899 Main St, Cambridge • Map D3*

5 Flour Bakery & Café
Delectable cakes, satisfying cookies, and perfect cups of coffee. *1595 Washington St • Map F6*

6 Rosie's Bakery
Rosie's invented the "chocolate orgasm," a devilishly dense brownie. *243 Hampshire St, Cambridge • Map D1*

7 Eldo Cake House
Western-style iced cakes and downhome Chinese treats such as sweet red bean buns. *36 Harrison Ave • Map P4*

8 Herrell's
Chopped candy bars and sundae toppings folded into super-rich ice cream. *15 Dunster St, Cambridge • Map B2*

9 Le Méridien Chocolate Dessert Buffet
A showcase of French chocolate pastry and confectionery. *250 Franklin St • Map Q4 • Open Oct–May: Sat*

10 Denise's Homemade Ice Cream
No-frills ice cream shop. *4 College Ave # A, Somerville*

Note: *Cafés serious about their coffee do not offer "flavored" coffees, but may offer a choice between light and dark roasts*

Left **Miracle of Science** Right **The Littlest Bar**

Top 10 Bars

1 Matt Murphy's

Matt Murphy's is the rarest of stateside Irish pubs. Unlike most of its Boston brethren, which rely on bar mirrors and Guinness signage to create Irish atmosphere, Murphy's allows its hearty stews, sharp-witted publicans, rustic furnishings, and perfectly-drawn pints to do the talking. *14 Harvard St, Brookline*

2 The Oak Bar

Exuding class from every polished wooden fiber, the Copley Plaza hotel bar exists in a sumptuous Edwardian fantasy world. Refreshingly, its patrons would just as well be seen in jeans as in Galliano. Most glasses at the bar are filled with the house's signature martini. *138 St James Ave • Map L6*

Beer selection

3 Miracle of Science

MIT students' favorite watering hole boasts one of the city's most original decorative concepts. How many bars display the day's menu items and on-tap beers on a periodic table, serve salad dressing in a test tube, or claim Einstein as a patron saint? *321 Massachusetts Ave, Cambridge • Map D3*

4 Delux Café

The kind of place that is so unique, you want to keep it a secret. The South End's intimate Delux Café attracts a one-of-a-kind mix of professionals, bike messengers, and gay boys and girls, all suckers for the bar's kitschy Elvis motif, extensive on-tap beers, and perpetual broadcast of the Cartoon Network. *100 Chandler St • Map M6 • Closed Sun*

5 Good Life Downtown

A favorite after-work spot for the Financial District's young executives, the Good Life feels like the kind of place the Rat Pack would have spent many an hour in. Dim lighting, red vinyl booths, be-bop on the hi-fi, and a long cocktail menu round out the swingin' scene. *28 Kingston St • Map P4*

6 Les Zygomates

The dinner crowd at Les Zygomates (the French term for the facial muscles that make you smile) is lured by reasonably priced French bistro fare. Come 9pm, the sleek, whimsically designed bar area comes alive with young professionals intent on flexing their smile muscles and appreciating the nightly live jazz performances. *129 South St • Map Q5 • 617 542 5108 • Closed Sun*

7 Whiskey Park

Anchoring the Park Plaza Hotel, Whiskey Park more closely approximates the trendy Manhattan cocktail-lounge concept than any bar in Boston. The gorgeous, black-clad wait staff serves all the classics – sidecars, martinis, cosmopolitans, et al. The bar is owned by "Mr Cindy Crawford", nightlife mogul Rande Gerber. *64 Arlington St • Map M5*

8 Regattabar
The giants of jazz frequently stop at this nautical-theme lounge in Cambridge's Charles Hotel. Drinks may not be extraordinary but the talent is; recent visitors have included McCoy Tyner, Ron Carter, and local favorite the Charlie Kolhase Quintet. Shows sell out quickly. *1 Bennett St, Cambridge • Map B2 • Closed Sun–Mon*

9 Beacon Hill Pub
Serving cheap, plentiful beer to recent college grads is the BHP's *raison d'être*. The delightfully incongruous location at the foot of blue-blooded Beacon Hill only adds to the bar's gritty appeal. Should you find drinking games and vacuous conversation stultifying, there are classic video games and a shoot-out basketball machine toward the back. *149 Charles St • Map M3*

10 The Littlest Bar
Licensed to hold no more than 38 patrons, the Littlest amply deserves its distinction as Boston's most intimate Irish pub. Located just across from the State House, it is popular with politicians and local professionals. *47 Province St • Map P3*

Les Zygomates

Top 10 Locally-Brewed Beers

1 Tremont Ale
An English-style pale ale with the delicious, malty middle of its forbearers.

2 Harpoon IPA
Ranked among the top domestic and imported India pale ales by *Beer Connoisseur Magazine*.

3 John Harvard's Coffee Stout
Try this novel, rich stout at John Harvard's Brewhouse (33 Dunster St, Cambridge).

4 Samuel Adams Octoberfest
Sam's finest – available only during the autumn – with deep amber coloring and a warm, spicy smoothness.

5 Boston Beer Works Fenway Pale Ale
Don your Red Sox cap and sip a light Fenway Pale at Beer Works *(see p116)*.

6 Samuel Adams Boston Lager
The beer that put Sam back on the brewing map after a 200-year hiatus.

7 Buzzards Bay Old Buzzards Lager
A sweet, fruity, Export-style lager; available in bottles at most agency liquor stores.

8 Samuel Adams Cherry Wheat Ale
Like a hybrid between champagne and cherry soda; available at most liquor stores.

9 Harpoon UFO Hefeweizen
Unfiltered, Belgian-style brew, with fruity undertones.

10 Tremont Winter Ale
Robust, strong ale for those cold winter nights (on tap October to April).

Note: *Unless otherwise specified, locally-brewed beers listed here are available citywide*

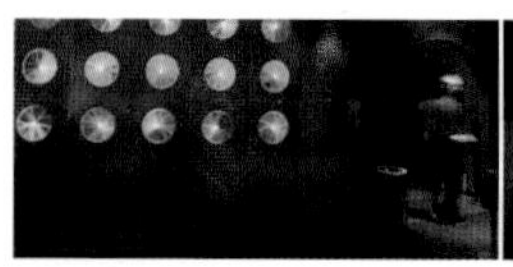

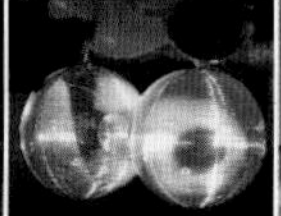

Left **Club on Lansdowne Street** Center **Roxy** Right **Ryles**

Top 10 Dance & Live Music Venues

1 Avalon

Lansdowne Street clubs come and go, but Avalon perennially ranks among New England's best dance and live music venues. Its Sunday night gay parties are the stuff of Boston legend *(see p50)*. Local band showcases and national touring acts bring lines that extend around the block. And its state-of-the-art sound and light systems rival any in New York or LA. *15 Lansdowne St • Map D5 • 617 262 2424 • Closed Mon–Wed • Adm*

2 The Middle East

The region's alternative rock scene can trace its genesis to this Central Square landmark. Seminal local bands like the Pixies, Mighty Mighty Bosstones, and Morphine all honed their chops on the Middle East's three stages. Today, the club continues the tradition, openly embracing musicians operating just under the mainstream radar. *472–480 Massachusetts Ave, Cambridge • Map D3 • 617 864 3278 • Adm*

3 House of Blues

The national chain's original location rocks Harvard Square seven nights a week. This is the city's premier venue for live R&B and straight blues, and the amazing acoustics make it a favorite among musicians and audiences alike. Its Sunday Gospel Brunch – which pairs a live gospel choir with rich Southern cooking – adds new meaning to the term, "soul food." *96 Winthrop St, Cambridge • Map B2 • 617 491 2583 • Adm*

4 Pravda 116

Like a modern-day Moscow speakeasy, Pravda seduces with its sumptuous red interior, exhaustive vodka menu, and chic clientele. Weekends bring out a mix of black-clad Euros intent on striking fetching poses with vodka martinis in hand, and international students hell-bent on having a decadent night out. DJs spin an infectious mix of house and electro. *116 Boylston St • Map N5 • 617 482 7799 • Closed Sun–Mon • Adm*

5 Good Life Cambridge

The Good Life's Central Square outpost retains the same classic cocktails and jazzy atmosphere that made the downtown original such a hit. But the Cambridge location is the one frequented by serious jazzbos, who come to see some of the region's best acts jump, jive, and wail (Thu–Sat). *720 Massachusetts Ave, Cambridge • Map C2 • 617 868 8800*

Avalon

***Note:** Nightlife and live music venues usually close at 1 or 2am*

6 Ryles

One of Inman Square's great-est assets, where murals of Duke, Dizz, and Lady Day inspire top jazz bands to go, go, go. Call ahead to learn if samba or swing lessons are scheduled. And don't miss the good value Sunday jazz brunch: no cover, live jazz, bois-terous crowds, and hearty entrees that rarely venture above $8. *212 Hampshire St, Cambridge • Map D2 • 617 876 9330 • Closed Mon • Adm*

7 Roxy

Housed in an ornate, bilevel theater, the Roxy can accommodate more nightlife denizens than any other Boston club. Top 40, '80s, Latin, and house blare through the powerful sound system, while a mixed crowd lounges around on cushy ban-quettes or keeps the beat on the mammoth dance floor. *279 Tremont St • Map P5 • 617 338 7699 • Closed Sun–Wed • Adm*

Sign, Ryles

8 Johnny D's

World-music aficionados from all over the city have been flocking here for years to hear live funk, zydeco, folk rock, and – in the case of Babalu, Johnny D's multiculty band [illegible] punk mambo hardcore juju. *17 Holland St, Somer-ville • 617 776 2004 • Adm*

9 Paradise Rock Club

Although it's no longer in its original downtown location, the Paradise is the oldest name among Boston rock venues. Icons Van Halen, the Police, and Blondie from the '70s and '80s first put the club on the map. Today, the Paradise remains true to its rock 'n' roll roots, welcoming nationally recognized acts that favor volume levels north of ten. *967 Commonwealth Ave • Map C5 • 617 562 8800 • Adm*

10 Cantab Lounge

At first glance, this unas-suming Central Square bar might seem an unlikely home for a legendary local Rhythm & Blues man. Yet therein lies the Cantab's inimitable appeal. "Little" Joe Cook has been Boston's ambas-sador of the blues for years, holding court at the Cantab on Friday and Saturday nights. *738 Massachusetts Ave, Cambridge • Map C3 • 617 354 2685 • Adm*

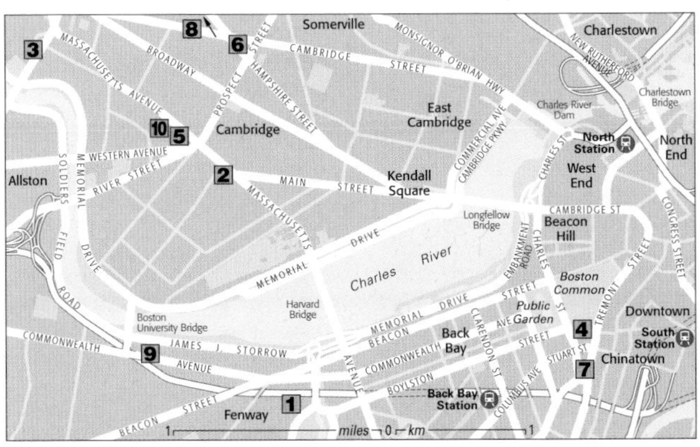

Left **Buzz Party @ Club Europa** Right **Sign, Machine**

Top 10 Gay & Lesbian Hang-Outs

1 Club Café

Live jazz (Thu–Sat) and a popular Sunday brunch infallibly bring out the beautiful boys at this multifunction South End meeting spot. Choose from the casually elegant restaurant, which puts inspired twists on classic continental fare, the mirrored bar area – perfect for scoping the room – and the sleek cocktail lounge out the back. *209 Columbus Ave • Map M6*

2 Midway Café

Having offered its stage to rockabilly, punk, swing, reggae, and hip-hop acts since 1987, the Midway Café is partially responsible for the youth-driven renaissance in Jamaica Plain *(see p129)* in recent years. Most nights bring an eclectic, edgy mix of music lovers, both gay and straight. The club's Thursday Dyke Night is the most popular lesbian club night in town. *3496 Washington St, Jamaica Plain • Adm*

3 Avalon Sundays

As if commanding the best lights, best sound, and best DJs in New England was not enough, Avalon compels the finest gay men in the city to strut through its door every Sunday for five hours of serious booty shaking. Boston's longest running gay club night brings the world's leading circuit DJs along with special guests like drag queen extraordinaire, Lady Bunny. *15 Lansdowne St • Map D5 • Adm*

Jacque's

4 Buzz Party @ Club Europa

This Saturday party at Club Europa is quickly becoming the hottest gay club night in town for the post-grad twentysomething crowd. Dressing down is the order at Buzz, where hard-bodied studs crowd the bi-level dancefloors for high-energy dance. Should you wish to take a break, there are comfortable multiple lounge areas all over the club, a billiard room, and bars on each side of every room. *51 Stuart St • Map N5 • Closed Sun–Tue • Adm*

5 Jacque's

One of the oldest names on the Boston gay club scene, Jacque's has been welcoming queer rock bands, drag queens, and their adoring fans long before being "out" was "in." Garage rock and beer fuel the downstairs scene, while up above, cabaret acts, rockers, and transvestites perform. Queens generally command the stage Tuesday through Friday and bands play mostly on weekends. *79 Broadway • Map N5 • Adm*

6 Machine

Downstairs from its older brother Ramrod, Machine keeps things loose and relaxed. A billiard room, video games, and a comfy lounge area ensure plenty of diversions for gay men other than the pulsing, sunken dance-floor, and four bars. Male strippers often appear on Saturdays, supplying plenty of eye candy to supplement the beautiful crowd.
1254 Boylston St • Map E5 • Adm

7 Ramrod

Thursday through Saturday, club goers must wear black leather (no brown leather or suede, please), full Western wear (think John Travolta in *Urban Cowboy*) – or go shirtless. That's right, guys: no gear, no beer. Fortunately, the prohibitive dress code is well worth it, with weekend fetish shows and throbbing techno music. Country and western two-stepping on Tuesdays brings the cowboys out in droves.
1254 Boylston St • Map E5

8 ManRay

ManRay's face changes dramatically according to the day of the week. The minimal, quasi-industrial layout works perfectly for Wednesday night's "Crypt," when DJs spin Goth and Industrial. Thursday brings the club's most popular party, Campus, which caters to the city's queer student body with '80s New Wave and Britpop. And Fetish Fridays beckons an outrageous crowd.
21 Brookline St, Cambridge • Map D3 • Closed Sun–Tue (Sat night is straight) • Adm

Buzz Party @ Club Europa

9 Vapor

Vapor's Saturday party, Evolution, is a New York City caliber gay-dance night – complete with top circuit DJs, a deafening sound system, and pulsing lights – but without the drama or attitude. Much of the Evolution crowd returns for the Sunday T Dance where the beat goes on through the morning. *100 Warrenton St • Map N5 • Closed Mon • Adm*

10 Boston Eagle

A doorway-mounted wooden eagle has welcomed gay men to this subterranean South End bar for years. Having no qualms about simply being a gay bar, the Eagle is not a place to dance. The dimly lit bar area is roomy and comfortable; in the back, a mirrored wall captures pool sharks and pinball wizards at work.
520 Tremont St • Map F6

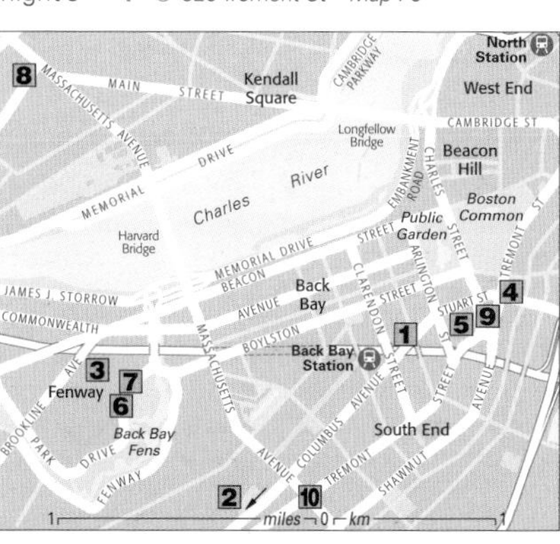

Note: Unless otherwise specified, venues are open nightly

Left **Somerville Theatre** Center **Hatch Shell** Right **Concert, Symphony Hall**

TOP 10 Performing Arts Venues

1 Symphony Hall

The storied home of the internationally renowned Boston Symphony Orchestra, Symphony Hall is one of the world's most acoustically perfect concert venues. Its recent 100th anniversary season brought such notables as Tony Bennett and André Previn to town. The BSO also frequently hosts sought-after guest conductors and soloists. *301 Massachusetts Ave • Map E6 • 617 266 1492*

2 Wang Center

Capturing the gilded and marbled opulence of its muse, Versailles, the Wang ranks among the city's most beautiful buildings. Touring productions from London's West End often perform here and the Boston Ballet consistently fills all 3,600 seats for its Christmas *Nutcracker* performances. *270 Tremont St • Map N5 • 617 482 9393*

Detail, Wang Center

3 Hatch Shell

The Esplanade's biggest attraction is this semi-enclosed concert venue. Every July 4th *(see p54)* the Boston Pops orchestra rings in Independence Day here. Additionally, Free Friday Flicks brings family faves such as *The Wizard of Oz* to the screen, while countless dance and music events occur almost nightly during summer. *The Esplanade • Map M3 • 617 722 5430*

4 Boston Center for the Arts

Home to ten independent theater companies and three galleries, the BCA is the cornerstone of the South End arts scene. The artists who perform and exhibit here are generally cutting edge, presenting work every bit as provocative as you might find in New York. *539 Tremont St • Map F5 • 617 426 5000*

5 Sanders Theatre

Located in Harvard's splendid Memorial Hall *(see p18)*, this theater has hosted many luminaries over its 120 plus years. Great performers of the past century have graced its intimate stage, including mime artist Marcel Marceau, and the theater has counted Longfellow, Oliver Wendell Holmes, and Ralph Wardo Emerson among its early audiences. *45 Quincy St, Cambridge • Map B1 • 617 496 2222*

6 New England Conservatory, Jordan Hall

Dozens of local orchestral and choral ensembles call the NEC's Jordan Hall home. Built at the turn of the 20th century and renowned for its intimacy and beautiful acoustics, the space was recently added to the National Registry of Historic Landmarks. The NEC's students participate in more than 100 recitals each year, which are free and open to the public.

Note: *Box offices are usually open 10am–6pm Mon–Sat*

Five Week Singers, Berklee Performance Center

Tickets are available two hours before the performance. ✆ *30 Gainsborough St • Map E6 • 617 536 2412*

7 Loeb Drama Center

Harvard's Loeb Drama Center trains the university's performing arts students and houses one of New England's best theater companies, the American Repertory Theatre. The ART constantly balances the familiar with the new, presenting unorthodox stagings of Shakespeare, work by up-and-coming playwrights, and spirited plays for children. ✆ *64 Brattle St, Cambridge • Map B1 • 617 547 8300*

8 ImprovAsylum

Expect a party just as much as a performance at this North End favorite. Public participation is an integral part of the Improv's frenetically paced productions, which usually leave the audience applauding raucously. ✆ *216 Hanover St • Map Q2 • 617 263 6887*

9 Berklee Performance Center

Berklee, the world's largest independent music college, boasts this premier venue. The great acoustics ensures that some of the most highly distinguished jazz, folk, and world musicians play here. ✆ *136 Massachusetts Ave • Map J6 • 617 747 8890*

10 Somerville Theatre

Extensive renovation has returned this Davis Square landmark to its original, ornate glory. When it isn't hosting some of the country's finest jazz, world music, and underground rock acts, the Somerville packs audiences in for great value, second-run movies. ✆ *55 Davis Sq, Somerville • 617 625 5700*

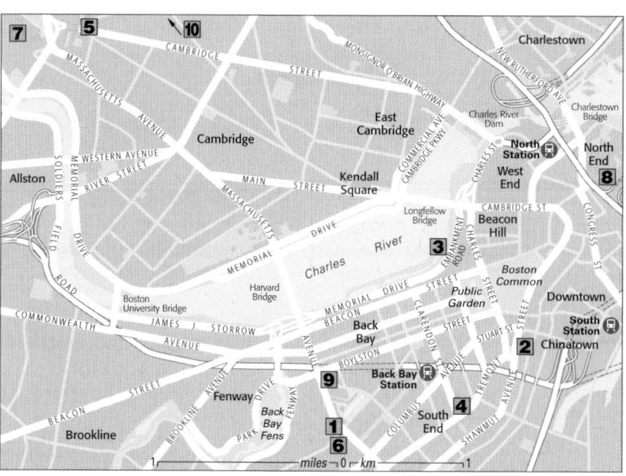

For more on Boston's Theater District **See pp104–111**

Left **Fourth of July** Right **First Night**

Top 10 Festivals & Events

1 Fourth of July

Given Boston's indispensable role in securing independence for the original 13 colonies, Independence Day adopts a certain poignancy here. With beer-fueled barbecues and a fireworks display on the Charles River banks, Boston throws the nation a rousing birthday party.

2 Chinese New Year

Chinatown *(see pp104–11)* buzzes with the pageantry of the Chinese New Year every February. Streets are transformed into frenzied patchworks of color, while sidewalk vendors peddle steamed buns, soups, and other Chinese delights. Don't miss the annual parade, held the Saturday following the Lunar New Year.

3 New England Flower Show

For one week in March, more than 150,000 visitors descend on this indoor exhibition to forget their winter blues and enjoy the bright blooms and fragrant aromas.

Bayside Exposition Center, 200 Mount Vernon St • Map M3

4 First Night

Despite being plagued in recent years by staggeringly cold weather, the New Year's Eve festivities remain among the most highly anticipated events of Boston's year. A $10 pass grants access to countless concerts, performances, and museum exhibits throughout the city, not to mention a dazzling midnight fireworks display over Boston harbor.

5 Boston Globe Jazz & Blues Festival

For nearly 40 years, Boston's squares, parks, and bandstands have staged the greatest names in jazz and blues for one week in June. All the shows – save the marquee acts like Harry Connick Jr., Branford Marsalis, and Natalie Cole – are free.

Plaque celebrating Boston Marathon

6 Feast of St. Anthony

The Feast of St. Anthony caps an entire summer of feast holidays in the North End *(see pp90–5)*. On the last weekend in August, from morning well into the night, Hanover Street bulges with revelers, parades, and food vendors giving a vibrant display of the area's old world Italian spirit.

7 St. Patrick's Day

Boston's immense Irish-American population explains why few, if any, American cities can match Boston's Irish pride. Come St. Paddy's, pubs host live Irish bands and increasingly raucous crowds. The South Boston St. Patrick's Day Parade, with its famous drum corps, is a tradition that starts off from Broadway "T" station.

***Note:** Contact the Boston Convention & Visitors Bureau for information on festivals and events (1 888 733 2678; www.bostonusa.com)*

8 August Moon Festival

In late August, Chinatown *(see p104–11)* commemorates the summer's fullest moon – signifying the beginning of the harvest season – with a jubilant, unique festival. A dragon dance snakes through the area and vendors line the streets hawking everything from hand-painted fans and herbal remedies to the festival's official food, the semisweet mooncake.

9 Spinazzola Gala

Every winter, dozens of the city's top chefs convene at Boston's World Trade Center to create one night of outrageously inventive cuisine. Funds raised support the Spinazzola Foundation, which aids food banks and homeless shelters citywide. The gala runs concurrently with the equally luxe Boston Wine Expo.

10 Lilac Sunday

While the Arnold Arboretum *(see p127)* counts 4,463 species of flora, one plant deserves particular celebration. When its 500 lilac plants are at their fragrant, color-washed peak, garden enthusiasts arrive in droves for a May Sunday of picnics, folk dancing, and tours of the lilac collections.

August Moon Festival

Top 10 Sporting Traditions

1 Boston Marathon

The country's oldest marathon beckons sports lovers. ✆ *3rd Mon/Apr • 1 508 435 6905*

2 Head of the Charles Regatta

Rowing crews race down the Charles while the banks teem with boisterous onlookers. ✆ *3rd Sat & Sun/Oct • 617 868 6200*

3 Red Sox vs Yankees

The most heated rivalry in US sports flares up every time the Yanks visit Fenway Park *(see p113)*. ✆ *617 267 1700*

4 Boston Celtics

The Celts keep basketball playoff dreams alive at the Fleet Center. ✆ *617 624 1000*

5 Boston Bruins

Energetic crowds cheer this ice hockey team at the Fleet Center. ✆ *617 624 1000*

6 Patriots

CMGI Field is the massive new home of the Patriots, the National Football League's 2002 champs. ✆ *1 800 543 1776*

7 Harvard vs Yale

"The Game" sees these Ivy League football toughs butt helmets at Harvard Stadium in the fall. ✆ *617 495 4848*

8 Beanpot Hockey Tournament

A February tradition pits Boston's top collegiate hockey teams against each other at the Fleet Center. ✆ *617 624 1000*

9 The Revolution

New England's entry in Major League Soccer is an annual playoff threat at the CMGI Field. ✆ *1 800 543 1776*

10 Halloween Hustle

A 3 mile (5 km) run in Newton with prizes for top Halloween costumes. ✆ *31 Oct • 617 964 2039 ext. 169*

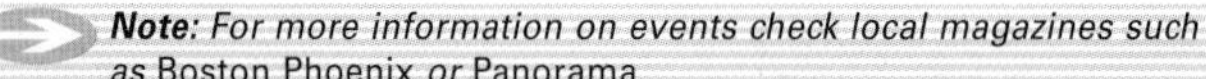

***Note:** For more information on events check local magazines such as* Boston Phoenix *or* Panorama

Left & Center **Stores, Newbury Street** Right **Stall, Faneuil Hall Marketplace**

Top 10 Essential Shopping Experiences

1 Newbury Street

Try as it might, Back Bay's most famous street cannot escape comparisons to Beverly Hills' Rodeo Drive. True, both offer stupendous people-watching, sophisticated shopping, chic dining, and prestigious galleries. Yet with its 19th-century charm and convenient subway stops, Newbury Street outclasses its built-yesterday Left Coast counterpart by far. *See pp80–9.*

Filene's Department Store and Basement

2 Filene's Basement

Discount fashion outlets nationwide owe Filene's Basement an immense debt of gratitude. Since 1908, this sprawling subterranean department store has championed the "name-brand shopping for less" retail philosophy. Some items are well priced, while others see their prices plummet the longer they sit on the shelves – illustrating Filene's markdown concept. The store inspires severe cases of bargain-hunting hysteria, especially during the bridal gown sale *(see p59)*. *426 Washington St • Map P4*

3 Charles Street

Charm abounds on this bluest of blue-blooded street, which is studded with antique dealers *(see p78)*, specialty grocers, and modern houseware boutiques. Come nightfall, wrought-iron gaslamps illuminate the brick sidewalks, residents hurry home with wine and fresh flowers, and sleek bistros buzz with excitement. *Map M3*

4 Dairy Fresh

The waft of enticing aromas floating from this treasure could send even the most resolute dieter into a tailspin. Candied fruits, chocolate-covered nuts, imported hard candies – all sold in bulk – taste as heavenly as they smell. But don't overlook the extensive inventory of imported Italian foods, and quality teas and coffees. *57 Salem St • Map Q1*

5 Harvard Coop

Next to a Red Sox baseball cap, no other clothing item is as fundamentally Bostonian as a Harvard sweatshirt. The Coop, in Harvard Square, is your one-stop shop for Harvard-related merchandise with a dizzying array of clothing, books, posters, prints, and even specially engraved Tiffany silver jewelry. *1400 Massachusetts Ave, Cambridge • Map B1*

6 Copley Place

This was among the country's first upscale urban shopping malls. It counts such *du mode* tenants as Armani Exchange, Tiffany, Neiman Marcus, and Bebe plus locally owned shops such as the arts and crafts boutique, Pavo Real. *100 Huntington Ave • Map L6*

7 The Haymarket

Being presented with a grilled salmon fillet may be more appealing than cooking one yourself, but this 350-year-old outdoor produce market still holds undeniable charm for visitors. Witness the feeding frenzy as fishmongers try to undercut each other on the day's catch. *Map Q2 • Open 7am–7pm Fri–Sat*

8 Harvard Square Bookstores

Harvard Square's bookstores are some of the most distinguished in the country. The intimate Globe Corner Bookstore (28 Church St) boasts a mind-boggling inventory of travel books and maps. The c.1932 Harvard Book Store (1256 Massachusetts Ave) stocks countless new and used titles. And the irrepressible Revolution Books *(see p122)* keeps the red flag waving with socialist and communist literature. *Map B1*

Fish stall, The Haymarket

9 Faneuil Hall Marketplace

With its millions of visitors every year, Faneuil Hall Marketplace would not be found on any best-kept secret list. However, with its central location and rich colonial history, it offers a unique shopping environment. Choose from name-brand stores such as the Gap, Banana Republic, and Abercrombie & Fitch plus a plethora of food stalls. *See pp12–13.*

10 Downtown Crossing

Here you'll find large stores such as Macy's, H&M, Filene's, and the legendary Filene's Basement. Additionally, smaller shops ranging from used CD retailers to discount athletic-shoe outlets attract a youthful mix. *Junction of Summer, Winter, & Washington sts • Map P4*

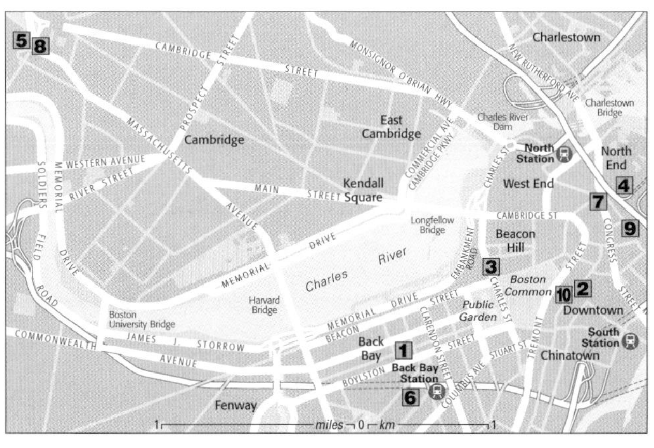

For shopping tips See p144

Left **Biking the Emerald Necklace** Right **People-watching on Boston Common**

Boston Pastimes

1 People-watching on Boston Common

Corralled by bustling, commercial Tremont Street, stately Beacon Street, and genteel Charles Street, Boston Common lies at the confluence of three disparate worlds. Whatever the season, a stroll through the common yields a veritable cross section of the city's residents. *See p14–15.*

Rollerblading

2 Pilgrimage to Revere Beach

The first hot day of summer sparks a massive northbound migration via the MBTA blue line to the popular Revere Beach *(see p71)*. Salsa music blares from passing cars on Ocean Avenue, soccer players stake out their pitches, and sun worshippers jostle for space at the shore break. *Revere Beach Blvd, Revere*

3 The "Is this the Year?" Debate

As soon as their ball club begins spring training, Red Sox fans rekindle the decades-old "Is this the year?" debate. Despite multiple appearances in the World Series, the Sox have not secured a world championship since 1918. Nevertheless, the Fenway Faithful keep their optimism alive until the end of the season. *See p113.*

4 Summer Saturdays on Memorial Drive

Closed to vehicular traffic on summer Saturdays, Cambridge's twisting, riverside Memorial Drive becomes a blur of rollerbladers, baby strollers, and joggers. *Rent a pair of rollerblades at Harvard Square's City Sports • 16 Dunster St, Cambridge • 617 868 9232*

5 Biking the Emerald Necklace

Taking in all 6 miles (9.5 km) of the Emerald Necklace *(see p15)* is best accomplished on a bicycle. The well-maintained trails lead riders from the wooded environs of Arnold Arboretum *(see p127)* to the Back Bay Fens *(see p113)* and onward to the Esplanade *(see p81)*. *Rent wheels from Boston Bike Tours & Rentals • Park Street Station, Boston Common • 617 308 5902*

6 Boating on the Charles

Dawn on the Charles River Basin sees local rowing crews taking advantage of the water's glass-smooth stillness. By late

Sailboats, Charles River

morning, a breeze kicks up, beckoning fleets of small sailboats. When the wind diminishes toward sunset, canoeists arrive to enjoy the water's renewed calm.

7 Skating on the Frog Pond

Few scenes capture quintessential Boston better than a snow-covered Boston Common *(see p14–15)* with figures twirling and sliding on the Frog Pond ice. Rent some skates and partake in the scene, then refuel in the cozy warming hut. ⊗ *Open mid-Nov–mid-Mar 10am–5pm Mon, 10am–9pm Tue–Thu & Sun, 10am–10pm Fri–Sat.*

8 Watching Quincy Market Street Performers

Even if you've had lunch and shopped until your shoe soles are worn out, a trip to Faneuil Hall Marketplace *(see p12–13)* is worthwhile if only to watch the street performances. Jugglers, magicians, and other acts are surrounded by crowds of onlookers, all rapt with amazement and amusement.

9 Tango by Moonlight

For five or six summer nights, the Tango Society brings a bit of Buenos Aires to the Weeks Foot Bridge *(see p63)*, inviting some 200 couples to summon the passion within and dance the tango from moonrise 'til midnight.
⊗ *Check www.bostontango.org*

10 Wedding Gown Shopping at Filene's Basement

Toward the middle of August and around Thanksgiving, Filene's Basement *(see p56)* transforms into a sea of designer wedding gowns, all discounted to unimaginable prices. When the doors open, frenzied brides-to-be race through the aisles clutching $200 dresses by the likes of Vera Wang.

Top 10 Beaches

1 Revere Beach
An old-fashioned boardwalk, lively crowds, and great Boston views. *See p71.*

2 Duxbury Beach
An uncrowded South Shore jewel with soft white sands. ⊗ *Canal St, Duxbury*

3 Crane's Beach
Five miles (8 km) of coastline with gentle waves and rolling dunes. *See p71.*

4 Singing Beach
Gorgeous blue waters, rocky outcrops, and a picture-perfect beach town. ⊗ *Beach St, Manchester-by-the-Sea*

5 Constitution Beach
Family friendly, with clean sand, picnic areas, lifeguards, and spectacular Boston views. *See p71.*

6 Carson Beach
Clean facilities, lifeguards, and kayak rentals. ⊗ *William J. Day Blvd, South Boston*

7 L Street Beach
Home of the "L Street Brownies," who swim year-round at this South Shore landmark. ⊗ *William J. Day Blvd, South Boston*

8 Malibu Beach
Hardly a match for its Left Coast namesake, but popular for swimming as well as tennis and basketball courts. ⊗ *Morrissey Blvd, Dorchester*

9 Pleasure Bay Beach
Enclosed by a man-made causeway; there are no waves, but clean sand, water, and facilities. ⊗ *Old Harbor Reservation, Day Blvd, South Boston*

10 Wollaston Beach
Boston Harbor's longest beach has clean sand and facilities attracting South Shore families. ⊗ *Quincy Shore Dr, Quincy*

Note: *For more information on beaches, contact the Metropolitan District Commission Community Affairs Office: 617 722 5530*

Left **Boston Duck Tours** Center **Children's Museum** Right **Franklin Park Zoo**

Top 10 Activities for Children

1 Boston Duck Tours

Board a refurbished, World-War II era, amphibious vehicle that plies the Charles River waters as smoothly as it navigates Back Bay streets. This historic tour encompasses all the peninsula and is conducted by courteous drivers and informative, entertaining guides who are wonderfully adept at keeping kids engaged. *Prudential Center • Map K6 • 617 723 3825 • Open Apr–Nov: 8:30am–dusk Mon–Sat • Adm*

2 Children's Museum

This venerable funhouse pioneered the interactive-exhibit concept that is now utilized in museums worldwide. Accolades aside, the Children's Museum is an absolute blast for kids and parents alike. It includes a climbing wall, a sprawling jungle gym, and cultural experiences like a walk-through, simulated Latin American supermarket. *300 Congress St • Map R5 • 617 426 8855 • Open 10am–5pm daily (to 9pm Fri) • Adm*

3 Swan Boats

If Boston were to have a mascot, it would most likely sport white feathers and a graceful, arching neck. The swan boats have been a Public Garden *(see p15)* fixture since the first fleet glided onto the garden's shimmering pond in 1877. *Public Garden • Map N4 • 617 522 1966 • Open mid-Apr–mid-Sep: usually 10am–5pm daily • Adm*

4 Museum of Science

Hands-on learning exhibits, like developing animated fish in the Virtual FishTank and racing marbles on sloping tracks, teach children about the physical world. The Omni Theater thrills with its fast-paced IMAX projections. And the planetarium places the cosmos within even the smallest child's reach. *Science Park • Map F2 • 617 723 2500 • Open 9am–5pm daily (to 9pm Fri; Jul–Aug: 9am–7pm daily) • Adm*

5 New England Aquarium

The aquarium goes to great lengths to keep kids engaged through a variety of interactive displays. Nothing illustrates this better than the Edge of the Sea exhibit, where children can touch some of the region's typical tidepool dwellers. *See p32–3.*

6 Fenway Park

For children with even the slightest interest in sports, a Red Sox game at legendary Fenway Park *(see p113)* is pure magic. Fans always feel part of the action at the country's most intimate professional baseball park. The peanut, hot dog, and soda vendors keep kids' enjoyment – and blood sugar levels – elevated. *4 Yawkey Way • Map D5 • 617 267 1700 • Check www.redsox.com for schedule*

Museum of Science

7 Prudential Skywalk

Located on the 50th floor of the Prudential Tower *(see p82)*, this observatory provides a rewarding Boston geography lesson. Should the jaw-dropping, 360-degree views not keep the youngsters enthralled, the audio/video tours of Boston's neighborhoods will. The swift, ear-popping elevator ride to the top also offers quite a rush. ⓢ *800 Boylston St • Map K6 • 617 859 0648 • Open 10am–10pm daily • Adm*

8 Frog Pond

The Frog Pond makes children feel like protagonists in a quaint picture book. As soon as temperatures dip below freezing, kids flock to the pond for ice skating and hot chocolate at the adjacent warming hut. Boston's oft oppressive summer days lure them back for splashing and frivolity beneath the central fountain. ⓢ *Boston Common • Map M4*

9 Street Entertainment

The best part of a visit to Faneuil Hall Marketplace is that you never know who – or what – you will see. "Benjamin Franklin" might administer a quick colonial history quiz to an unsuspecting child, a juggler might ask another to participate in a performance, or a street musician might stick the mic in a child's hand for a singsong. *See p12–13.*

Museum of Science

10 Franklin Park Zoo

Boston's urban zoo houses over 200 species of animals. Its Tropical Forest section boasts gorillas, leopards, all types of tropical birds, and many other exotic creatures. Butterfly Landing, open during the summer months, positively brims with the brilliantly colored insects. The Children's Zoo allows kids to get up close and personal with animals of the decidedly huggable variety. ⓢ *1 Franklin Park Rd, Dorchester • 617 541 5466 • Open 10am–5pm Mon–Fri, 10am–6pm Sat–Sun (Oct–Mar: 10am–4pm daily) • Adm*

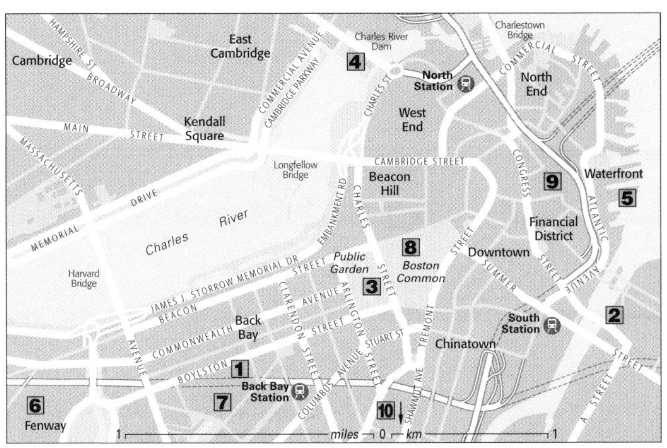

Left **Long Wharf** Right **No Name Restaurant, Fish Pier**

Top 10 Waterfront Areas

1 The Esplanade

Provided the Charles River Basin has not frozen over, collegiate rowing crews, canoeists, small sailboats, and the occasional coast guard patrol all share the waters off the Esplanade. Find a bench facing the water and take in the scene. *Map M3*

2 Castle Island Old Harbor Reservation

Connected to the mainland via an earthen causeway and crowned by the c.1851 Fort Independence, Castle Island is New England's oldest continually fortified site *(see p128)*. Aside from exploring the fort's bunkers and tunnels, visitors can take in fine panoramic views of Boston Harbor. *38 Taylor St, Dorchester • 617 727 5290*

3 Constitution Beach

Views of Downtown don't get much better than those from this recently revitalized beach and park area in East Boston. A clean beach, picnic areas, and lifeguards make this a favorite with families. *Bennington St, East Boston*

4 Fort Point Channel

Despite being situated inside the Big Dig *(see p37)* maelstrom, Fort Point remains one of Boston's most intriguing areas. Over the past 25 years, local artists have migrated to the neighborhood, lured by affordable studio space. Their warehouse workshops count the $300 million Federal Courthouse among their neighbors. *Map H5*

5 Fish Pier

By 1926 – 12 years after its construction – the Greco-Roman style Commonwealth Pier (aka Fish Pier) had become the world's busiest and largest fish market. The day's catch is still brought to the early-morning market here. Sample some of it in hearty chowders at the legendary No Name Restaurant *(see p42)*.

6 Long Wharf

The modern Marriott Hotel masks Long Wharf's near 300 years of indispensability to Boston's merchant industry. Given its deep frontage and proximity to waterfront warehouses, the biggest ships of their day could dock here. Today, ferry services and enormous cruise vessels depart from the wharf, creating a spirited dock scene. *Map R2*

The Esplanade

Note: *For more information on Boston's parks contact Boston Park and Recreation (617 635 4505)*

7 Rowes Wharf

Home to the imposing Boston Harbor Hotel *(see p146)*, Rowes Wharf is a popular docking spot for high-end harbor cruise outfits. Framed by the hotel's colossal courtyard-atrium, with its grand arches and copper dome, the wharf is a luxurious contrast to the city's grittier, saltier working docks. *Map R3*

Christopher Columbus Park

8 Christopher Columbus Park

Featuring an Italian marble sculpture of the seafaring Genoan, Christopher Columbus Park is among the North End's best-kept secrets. Vine-encrusted arches, manicured gardens, and sweeping harbor and skyline views make this a place to linger. *Map P2*

9 Puopolo Park

North End's Puopolo Park boasts supreme frontage on the harbor, looking out toward Charlestown. On warm days, the neighborhood's old guard enjoy a game of *bocce* (bowls). Nearby, kids play baseball or splash around in the outdoor pool. *Map H2*

10 Charles River Locks & Dam

The Charles River Dam controls water levels in the basin below and maintains separation of the river from the harbor. An ingenious series of locks permit boats to pass from one body of water to the other. Call for tour schedule. *Map F2 • 617 727 1188*

Top 10 Views

1 Prudential Skywalk

Jaw-dropping panoramic views from a 50th-floor observatory. *See p61.*

2 Longfellow Bridge

The entire Charles River Basin becomes your oyster on the "T" between Kendall and Charles/MGH stops. *Map M2*

3 Bunker Hill Monument

Climb to the capstone to see all of Charlestown, Cambridge, and Boston laid out before you. *See p31.*

4 Spirit of Boston Cruises

Ply the harbor waters and enjoy unrivaled city views. *World Trade Center • 617 748 1499*

5 Charlestown Bridge

Splendid harbor and Downtown vistas. *Map G2*

6 John J. Moakley Courthouse Park

This beautiful waterfront park has fine views of the towering Financial District.

7 Hyatt Regency Cambridge

Gaze across the Charles River from the hotel's revolving, top-floor restaurant. *575 Memorial Drive, Cambridge • Map C4 • 617 492 1234*

8 Weeks Foot Bridge

Prime spectator spot during the Head of the Charles Regatta *(see p55)*. *Map B2*

9 Dorchester Heights Monument

This colonial-style spire offers dizzying views of the city from its cupola.

10 Harborside Hyatt Hotel

The Hyatt's top-floor Harborside Grill boasts panoramic Boston views. *101 Harborside Drive, East Boston • 617 568 1234*

Following pages **Boston Harbor**

Left **Peddock's Island** Right **View of Deer Island from George's Island**

Boston Harbor Islands

1 George's Island

As the terminal for the harbor islands ferry and water shuttles to other islands, George's Island is the gateway to the Boston Harbor Islands National Park Area. This undeveloped archipelago of 30 islands consists of 1,200 acres (485 ha) spread over 50 sq miles (80 sq km) and is made up primarily of drumlins, or piles of glacial debris. The prime attraction on George's Island is the massive Fort Warren, a prison for Confederate soldiers during the Civil War. *Boston Islands Discovery Center, Fan Pier, 617 223 8666, www.bostonislands.com*

2 Grape & Bumpkin Islands

Both these islands are naturalist's delights – Bumpkin for its wildflowers, raspberries, and bayberries, Grape for its wild roses and bird life. On Bumpkin Island, hiking trails pass the ruins of a farmhouse and 19th-century children's hospital, which also housed German prisoners rescued from Boston Harbor in World War I.

3 Lovell's Island

Known for its extensive dunes, Lovell's also has a supervised swimming beach. Extensive hiking trails lead across dunes and through woodlands. The remains of Fort Standish, active during the Spanish American War and World War I, can also be explored.

4 Peddock's Island

Peddock's is one of Boston Harbor's largest and most diverse islands. Hiking trails circle a pond, salt marsh, and coastal forest and pass numerous buildings of interest including Fort Andrews, active in harbor defense from 1904 through to World War II. The island is known for its black crowned night herons and for the beach plums and wild roses which bloom profusely in the dunes.

5 Deer Island

Accessed by a causeway attaching the island to the mainland, 60 acres (24 ha) of the island were recently opened for recreation and walking – with dramatic views of the Boston skyline. Deer Island is also known for its state-of-the-art $3.8 billion sewage treatment plant. Distinguished by 12 gigantic egg-shaped digesters, it was key to cleaning up Boston Harbor. *Sewage treatment plant tour: 617 539 4248*

Fort Warren, George's Island

***Note:** Boston Harbor Cruises runs ferries to George's Island where there's a shuttle service to many of the islands (call 617 227 4321)*

6 Spectacle Island

Vastly enlarged by fill from the Big Dig *(see p37)*, Spectacle Island was opened to the public in 2003. It has some of the highest peaks of all the harbor islands as well as 5 miles (8 km) of trails, a marina, picnic areas, swimming beaches, and disabled access as well as the best Boston skyline view. A model for environmental sensitivity, the island's services run on photovoltaic cells and wind power.

7 Little Brewster Island

Boston Light, the first US lighthouse, was erected here in 1716 and it remains the last staffed offshore lighthouse in the country. Limited tours visit the small museum and lead visitors up the 76 spiral steps and two ladders to reach the top. *Island accessible by tour only: Jun–mid-Oct: Fri–Sun • Tour boats depart from Fan Pier & John F. Kennedy Library • Reservations essential: 617 328 3900 ext. 918 • Adm*

Boston Light, Little Brewster Island

8 Gallops Island

Once the site of a popular summer resort, Gallops also served as quarters for Civil War soldiers, including the Massachusetts 54th Regiment *(see p14)*. The island has an extensive sandy beach, a picnic area, hiking paths, and historic ruins of a former quarantine and immigration station. Grassy bluffs offer spectacular views of Boston Light.

9 Thompson Island

A learning center since the 1830s, Thompson is the site of an Outward Bound program serving more than 5,000 students annually. The island's diverse geography includes rocky and sandy shores, a large salt marsh, and a hardwood forest. Killdeer, herons, and shorebirds abound. *Open Jun–Labor Day: Sat • 617 328 3900 ext. 918 for guided tours • Ferries depart from Fan Pier at 11:30am, return at 5pm • Adm*

10 World's End

This 244-acre (99 ha) peninsula overlooking Hingham Bay is a geological sibling of the harbor islands, with its two glacial drumlins, rocky beaches, ledges, cliffs, and both salt and freshwater marshes. Frederick Law Olmsted laid out the grounds for a homestead development here in the late 19th century. The homes were never built, but paths, formal plantings, and hedgerows remain. World's End is accessed by road by driving through Hingham. *Operated by Trustees of Reservations: 1 781 740 6665 • Adm to non-members*

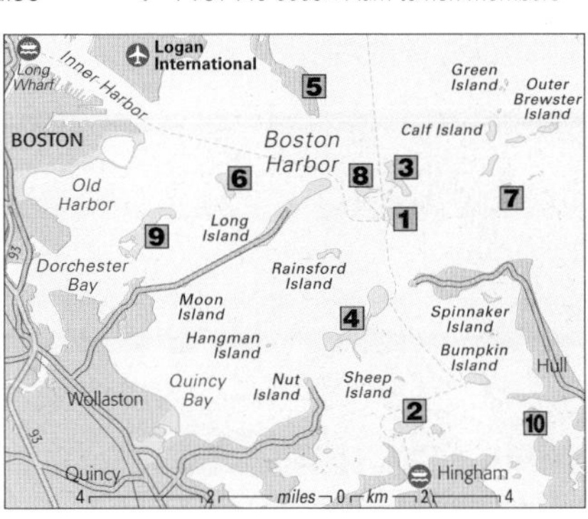

Note: *Islands are open 9am to sunset daily, closed in winter. Camping is permitted on Grape, Bumpkin, Lovell, & Peddock's by special permit*

Left **Old Sturbridge Village** Right **Elms Mansion, Newport**

Top 10 Day Trips: Historic New England

1 Lexington

Peaceful, leafy Lexington Green, surrounded by high-spired country churches, marks the first encounter of British soldiers with organized resistance by American revolutionaries. The rebels fortified their courage for the confrontation with a night of drinking at the adjacent Buckman Tavern (1 Bedford St). *Massachusetts • Route 2 • Visitor information: 1875 Massachusetts Ave; 1 781 862 1450*

2 Concord

Rebels put the Redcoats to rout at North Bridge, Concord's main revolutionary battle site. This historical town was also the epicenter of American literature in the mid-19th century. Visitors can tour the homes of writers Ralph Waldo Emerson (Cambridge Turnpike), Nathaniel Hawthorne (455 Lexington Rd), and Louisa May Alcott (399 Lexington Rd). Henry David Thoreau's woodland haunts at Walden Pond now feature hiking trails and a swimming beach. *Massachusetts • Route 2 • Visitor information: Heywood St; 1 978 369 3120*

Witch Museum, Salem

3 New Bedford

During the 19th century, local sailors and whalers plundered the oceans of the world, enriching the port of New Bedford. The National Historic District preserves many of the fine buildings of the whaling era, while the Whaling Museum (18 Johnny Cake Hill) gives riveting accounts of the enterprise. *Massachusetts • Routes I-95 & I-195 • Visitor information: 33 Williams St; 1 508 996 4095*

4 Salem

A witch may not have been killed in Salem since 1692, but witchcraft paraphernalia fills many stores, and several sites such as the Witch Museum (19 Washington Sq North) tell the tale of this dark episode. The city is more proud of its China Trade days (1780s–1880s), which are engagingly recounted on National Park walking tours. Visit the Peabody Essex Museum (East India Sq) to see the treasures sea captains brought home from distant ports. *Massachusetts • Route 1A • Visitor information: 2 New Liberty St; 1 978 740 1650*

5 Plymouth

The recreated historic village of Plimoth Plantation (137 Warren Ave) gives a full immersion in to

Note: Bonanza Bus Lines (617 723 7029) and MBTA commuter rail (617 222 3200) operate to many of these destinations from South Station

the lives of the first English settlers in Massachusetts. At the harbor, tour the *Mayflower II* (State Pier) and imagine the perilous crossing of the pilgrims in 1620. On Thanksgiving, the town celebrates its pilgrim heritage with a parade in period dress and also opens many historic buildings. ✎ *Massachusetts • Routes 3 & 44 • Visitor information: 170 Water St; 1 508 747 7533*

6 Lowell

Lowell was the cradle of the US's Industrial Revolution, where entrepreneurs dug power canals and built America's first textile mills on the Merrimack River. The sites within the National Historical Park (246 Market St) tell the parallel stories of a wrenching transformation from agricultural to industrial lifestyle, and the rise of the American labor movement. A 1920s weave room still thunders away at Boott Cotton Mills Museum (400 John St). ✎ *Massachusetts • Routes I-93, I-95, & 3 • Visitor information: 246 Market St; 1 978 970 5000*

7 Old Sturbridge Village

Interpreters in period costume go about their daily lives in a typical 1830s New England village. This large living history museum has more than 40 buildings on 200 acres (83 ha). Get a sense of the era by visiting the village, common, mill district, and the traditional family farm. ✎ *Massachusetts • Routes I-90, 20, & 84 • Visitor information: 380 Main St; 1 800 628 8379*

8 Portsmouth

Founded in 1623 as Strawbery Banke, the historic houses on Marcy Street document three centuries of city life from early settlement through 20th century immigration. Picturesque shops, pubs, and restaurants surround Market Square and line the waterfront, and the surrounding leafy streets boast fine examples of Federal architecture. ✎ *New Hampshire • Routes 1 or I-95 • Visitor information: 500 Market St; 1 603 436 1118*

9 Providence

Providence is a great walking city: stroll Benefit Street's "mile of history" to see an impressive group of Colonial and Federal houses; or visit Waterplace Park with its pretty walkways along the Providence River. Atwells Avenue on Federal Hill is Providence's Little Italy, bustling with restaurants and cafés. ✎ *Rhode Island • Routes 1 or I-95 • Visitor information: 1 West Exchange St; 1 401 274 1636*

10 Newport

With its yacht races and grand manses, Newport has been a playground for the rich since the late 1860s. Many of the elaborate so-called "cottages" built by 19th-century industrialists are open for tours, including Breakers (Ochre Point Av). For natural beauty, hike the 3.6-mile (5.5 km) Cliff Walk overlooking Narragansett Bay and Easton's Beach. ✎ *Rhode Island • Routes I-93, 24, & 114 • Visitor information: 23 America's Cup Av; 1 401 845 9123*

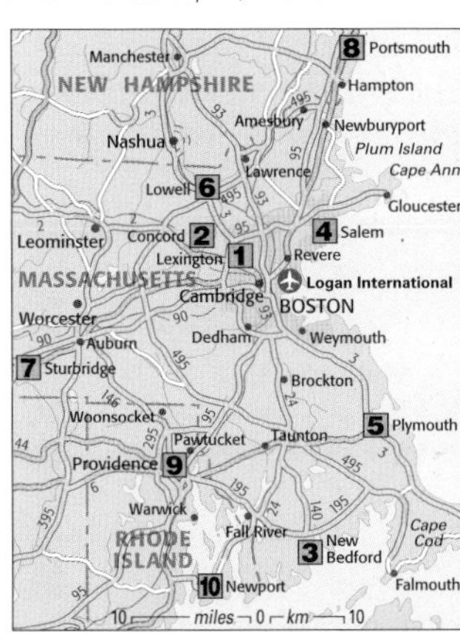

Note: *Costumed re-enactors dramatize the 1775 Battle of Lexington and Concord each year on Patriots Day (the third Monday in April)*

Left **Crane Beach, Ipswich** Right **Gloucester**

Top 10 Day Trips: The Seaside

1 Cape Ann

Thirty miles (48 km) north of Boston, the granite brow of Cape Ann juts defiantly into the Atlantic – a rugged landscape of precipitous cliffs and deeply cleft harbors. In Gloucester, the cape's main harbor, a waterfront plaque memorializes the 10,000 local fishermen who have perished at sea since 1623, and the Cape Ann Historical Association Museum (27 Pleasant St) displays some of the world's finest maritime paintings. The picturesque harborfront of adjacent Rockport is an artists' enclave and is lined with galleries and sweet shops. *Routes I-95 & 127 • Visitor information: 33 Commercial St, Gloucester; 1 978 283 1601*

2 Upper Cape Cod

The Upper Cape is tranquil and low-key. Watch the boats glide through Cape Cod Canal or take the Shining Sea bikeway from Falmouth village to Woods Hole. If it's beaches you're after, Sandwich's Sandy Neck has huge dunes and excellent bird-watching, but Falmouth's Surf Drive is best for swimmers and Old Silver Beach is tops for sunset views. *Routes 3, 6, & 28*

3 Mid Cape Cod

The Mid Cape tends to be congested, especially in the town of Hyannis. But the north shore can be peaceful, with amazing wildlife and stunning views, especially from Gray's Beach in Yarmouth. Warmer water and sandy strands line the south side of Mid Cape, with especially good swimming in Harwich and Dennisport. There's also excellent canoeing and kayaking on the Bass River. *Route 3, 6, & 28*

4 Outer Cape Cod

Here you'll find some of the area's best beaches. The 40-mile (64-km) National Seashore offers great surfing at Coast Guard and Nauset Light, and the beaches of Marconi, Head of the Meadow, and Race Point all have dramatic dunes and great ocean swimming. The artist colonies of Wellfleet and Truro are worth a visit as is Provincetown, a fishing village turned gay resort. *Routes 3 & 6*

5 Martha's Vineyard

Ferries to the 100 sq mile- (160 sq km-) island stop at Vineyard Haven. From here it's a short drive to old-fashioned Oak Bluffs with its gingerbread cottages and historic carousel. Venture south to Edgartown and the magnificent 19th-century homes of the rich whaling captains. The

Martha's Vineyard

Note: *For more information on Cape Cod contact the Chamber of Commerce at 1 508 862 0700 or go to www.capecodchamber.org*

nearby 3-mile (4.8-km) Katama Beach is also a magnet for sun worshipers. On the southwest of the island, Menemsha remains a picturesque fishing village and Gay Head's cliffs offers dramatic hiking. *Routes 3 & 28 to Woods Hole • ferry to Vineyard Haven: 1 508 477 8600 • Visitor information: Beach Rd, Vineyard Haven; 1 508 693 0085*

6 Nantucket Island

Nantucket's Whaling Museum tells the tale of the Quaker whalers who made Nantucket prosperous in the 19th century. The island has shed its Quaker past and now boasts trophy beach houses and million-dollar yachts. For sports, there's kayaking, casting for striped bass from Surfside Beach, or cycling to the former fishing village of Sconset with its rose-covered clifftop cottages. *Routes 3 & 6 to Hyannis • ferry to Nantucket: 1 508 477 8600 • Visitor information: 48 Main St, Nantucket; 1 508 228 1700*

7 Ipswich

Crane's Beach in Ipswich is one of New England's most scenic beaches, with more than 4 miles (6.5 km) of white sand, warm water, and outstanding bird-watching. Also on the Crane Estate, you can visit Castle Hill mansion and its lovely Italianate gardens. *Routes 95, 128, & 133, or 1A • Visitor information: 36 Main St; 1 978 356 8540*

8 Newburyport

In the 19th century, Newburyport was a prosperous seaport. The grand three-story mansions along the High Street present a virtual case study in Federal architecture, while boutiques and antiques shops line downtown Merrimac, Water, and State streets. The Parker River National Wildlife Refuge on the adjacent Plum Island is one of the US's top bird-watching sanctuaries. *Route I-95 & 1 • Visitor information: Merrimac St; 1 978 462 6680*

9 Revere Beach

Established in 1896, Revere Beach was the first public beach in the US. Thanks to a centennial restoration, it's also one of the best, with nearly 3 miles (4.5 km) of clean white sand and clear blue water. *Routes 1 & 1A • "T" station: Revere Beach/ Wonderland*

10 Hampton & Rye Beaches

The New Hampshire coast just south of Portsmouth has extensive sandy beaches. Wallis Sands State Park is ideal for swimming but the best of the rocky overlooks is Rye's Ragged Point picnic area. The honky-tonk social scene, however, is at Hampton Beach. Odiorne Point State Park in Rye has picnic areas and extensive walking trails. *Routes I-95, NH 101, & 1A • Visitor information: 1 Park Ave, Hampton; 1 603 926 8718*

Note: *Bay State Cruise Co. operates a high-speed ferry to Provincetown (mid-May–mid-Sep) from 200 Seaport Blvd, Boston, 617 748 1428*

AROUND TOWN

Left, **Sign, African Meeting House** Center **Reliefs, Federal-style mansion** Right **Louisburg Square**

Beacon Hill

WITH ITS ELEGANT, *200 year-old row houses, quaint grocers, pricey antique shops, and hidden gardens, Beacon Hill screams "old money" like no other area in Boston. That some of the city's most exorbitant apartment rentals can still be found here suggests it will remain an enclave of exclusivity for years to come. Yet throughout the 19th century and well into the 20th, this inimitably charming neighborhood was a veritable checkerboard of ethnicities and earning groups – segregated though they were. Little of Beacon Hill's diversity has survived its relatively recent gentrification, but visitors can still experience the neighborhood's myriad pasts inside its opulent mansions and humble schoolhouses, and along its enchanting cobblestone streets.*

TOP 10 Attractions

1. **Massachusetts State House**
2. **Museum of Afro-American History**
3. **Nichols House Museum**
4. **Louisburg Square**
5. **Harrison Gray Otis House**
6. **Appalachian Mountain Club Headquarters**
7. **Beacon Street**
8. **Boston Center for Jewish Heritage**
9. **George Middleton House**
10. **Parkman House**

Ivy-clad façade, Beacon Hill

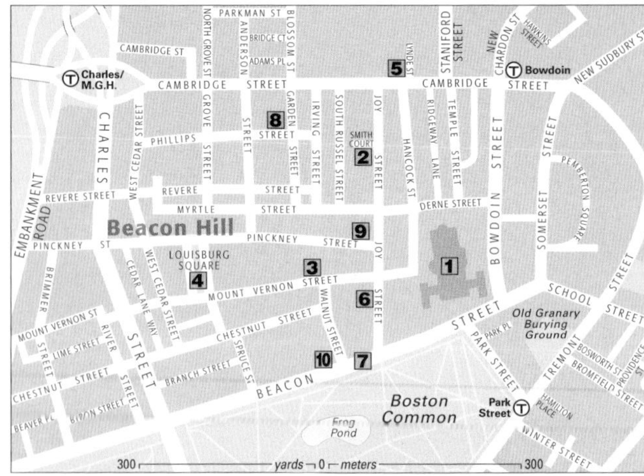

Note: *Massachusetts State House is situated on the Freedom Trail* **See p8**

1 Massachusetts State House

A 200-year-old codfish, a statue memorializing one of history's most sexually promiscuous individuals, and a 23-carat gold dome crowned with a pine cone – such are the curious eccentricities that distinguish Beacon Hill's most prestigious address *(see p11)*.
24 Beacon St • Map P3 • 617 722 2000 • Tours 10am–5pm Mon–Fri • Free

2 Museum of Afro-American History

Based in the African Meeting House (the oldest extant black church in the US) and the adjoining Abiel Smith School (the nation's first publicly funded grammar school for African-American children) – the MAAH offers a look into the daily life of free, pre-Civil War African-Americans. The meeting house was a political and religious center for Boston's African-American community and it was here that abolitionists such as Frederick Douglass and William Lloyd Garrison delivered anti-slavery addresses in the mid-19th century. The museum has successfully preserved their legacy and that of countless others through education workshops, exhibitions, and special events. *8 Smith Court • Map N2 • 617 725 0022 • Open Sep–May: 10am–4pm Mon–Sat; Jun–Aug: 10am–4pm daily • Free*

Drawing Room, Nichols House Museum

Senate Chamber, Massachusetts State House

3 Nichols House Museum

An 1804 Charles Bulfinch design, 55 Mount Vernon is one of the earliest examples of residential architecture on Beacon Hill. Rose Nichols, the house's principal occupant for 75 years, bequeathed her home to the city as a museum, which would provide a glimpse of late-19th and early 20th-century life on the Hill. A pioneering force for women in the arts and sciences, Nichols gained fame through her authoritative writings on landscape architecture and far-reaching philanthropic projects.
55 Mount Vernon St • Map N3 • 617 227 6993 • Open May–Oct: noon–4pm Tue–Sat; Nov–Dec & Feb–Apr: noon–4pm Thu–Sat • Adm

4 Louisburg Square

Cobblestone streets, a genteel little gated park, and a hefty dose of Boston Brahmin cachet make this tight block of townhouses the city's most exclusive patch of real estate. Modeled after the traditional residential squares of London in 1826, the square was named in remembrance of the 1745 Battle of Louisburg in modern-day Quebec. *Map N3*

Dining Room, Harrison Gray Otis House

5 Harrison Gray Otis House

One of the principal developers of Beacon Hill, Harrison Gray Otis *(see p38)* served in the Massachusetts legislature and gained a reputation for living la dolce vita in this 1796 Bulfinch-designed manse. Like a post-Revolutionary Gatsby, Otis went to great pains to ensure his parties were the social events of the year. After falling into disrepair, the property was acquired in 1916 by the historical preservation society and meticulously restored to its original grandeur. *141 Cambridge St • Map N2 • 617 227 3956 • Open 11am–4pm Wed–Sun • Adm*

6 Appalachian Mountain Club Headquarters

The Appalachian Trail, or the A.T. as it is known to hiking cognoscenti, is America's premier walking path. Snaking through 2,168 miles (3,492 km) of pristine eastern wilderness – including 90 miles (145 km) in Massachusetts – the trail is maintained by members of the club. With a scale model of the trail, informative plaques on the walls, maps, guidebooks, and a knowledgeable staff, this is an essential stop for those planning a hike. *5 Joy St • Map N3 • 617 523 0636 • Open 8:30am–5pm Mon–Fri • Free*

7 Beacon Street

Although it extends well beyond the Fenway, Beacon Street finds its true essence in the section between the Massachusetts State House *(see p11)* and Charles Street. Here it passes such highlights as the Bull and Finch Pub – of *Cheers* TV fame – and the Boston Athenaeum, one of the oldest independent libraries in the country. *Map N3*

8 Boston Center for Jewish Heritage

This synagogue testifies to the area's former vibrancy as Boston's first predominantly Jewish quarter. The congregation was founded in 1903 by immigrants from Vilna, Lithuania. While services are no longer held here, there are plans to rededicate the synagogue as a Jewish cultural center. *13–18 Philips St • Map N2 • 617 523 2324 • Tours Apr–Nov: 1–3pm Sun*

Boston Center for Jewish Heritage

9 George Middleton House

The oldest remaining private residence on Beacon Hill built by African-Americans is a highlight of the Black Heritage Trail. George Middleton, a white revolutionary war veteran, commissioned

Black Heritage Trail

By and large the Paul Reveres and John Adams' of this world have monopolized Bostonians' collective understanding of their city's history. As a refreshing counterpoint, the Black Heritage Trail posits that black Bostonians, through their long-marginalized histories, have played an indispensable role in the city's development. The trail illustrates this point at every turn, taking visitors past the homes, businesses, and schools of some of Boston's most influential black Americans. Tours leave from the Shaw Memorial at 10am, noon and 2pm (Memorial Day to Labor Day).

the house's construction shortly after the war. Legend has it that Middleton commanded an all-black company dubbed the "Bucks of America." ⓢ *6–7 Pinckney St • Map N3 • Closed to the public*

George Middleton House

10 Parkman House

George Parkman – once a prominent physician at Harvard Medical School – lived in this house during the mid-19th-century. In 1849, in one of the most sensationalized murder cases in US history, Parkman was killed by a faculty member over a financial dispute. Both the crime and its aftermath were grisly – in the ensuing trial dental records were entered as evidence for the first time. ⓢ *8 Walnut St • Map N3 • Closed to the public*

Beacon Hill by Day

Morning

Take the "T" to the Charles St/Massachusetts General Hospital stop and exit onto Charles Street. Enjoy a light breakfast at **Panificio Bakery** (144 Charles St) where the scones and muffins are other-worldly. Then continue along Charles Street and turn left onto Beacon Street for a glimpse of the **Bull and Finch Pub** (No. 84) – the bar that inspired the TV show *Cheers*. Continue up Beacon to the **Massachusetts State House** *(see p11)* for a free 45-minute tour; times vary but you can book. Afterward, cross the road to the Shaw Memorial, where a National Park ranger-led **Black Heritage Trail** tour departs at noon. The trail provides an excellent survey of the area's architectural styles as well as its black culture sites, and terminates at the **Museum of Afro-American History** *(see p75)*.

Afternoon

Walk back down the hill to Charles Street for a fortifying late lunch. Weather permitting, stock up on fresh fruit, a crusty baguette, and a sampling of imported cheeses at the charming **Deluca's Market** (11 Charles St) and have a picnic on the Common *(see pp14–15)*. Or for inexpensive, diner-style American fare (meatloaf and fruit pies), check out the **Paramount** (44 Charles St). After lunch, peruse the funky, modern home furnishings at **Koo de Kir** (34 Charles St) and spend the rest of the afternoon browsing Charles Street's antique shops *(see p78)*. Round the day off with a pint at **Seven's Ale House** *(see p79)*.

Left **Antiques at 80 Charles** Right **Room with a Vieux**

TOP 10 Antique Shops

1 Room with a Vieux
Owner Jeff Diamond scours France for unique furniture and light fixtures, which span the centuries. High-end Art Deco furniture pieces, bedboards, and Louis XV mirrors are strong points. *20 Charles St • Map M3 • Closed Sun*

2 Gallagher-Christopher
Exquisite, predominantly 18th- and 19th-century English furniture and lighting distinguish this shop. Browse Biedermeyer lamp tables, opaline vases, and fine accessories. *84 Chestnut St • Map M3 • Closed Sun*

3 Upstairs Downstairs
This cozy shop places a refreshing emphasis on affordability and function. Everything from mahogany four-poster beds to *belle époque* opera glasses are on display. *93 Charles St • Map M3*

4 20th Century Limited
Vintage designer costume jewelry and estate jewelry are the main attractions here. But don't overlook the handsome 1950s barware, vintage clothing accessories, and other collectibles. *73 Charles St • Map M3*

5 Boston Antiques Cooperative
Seven dealers run this bi-level space filled with dozens of 19th-century Japanese woodblocks and Impressionist landscape paintings. *119 Charles St • Map M3*

6 Antiques at 80 Charles
Should your predilection be antique jewelry, keep this address in mind. Ornate gold brooches, platinum earrings – plus excellent examples of Wedgwood ceramic work – populate the glass cases here. *80 Charles St • Map M3*

7 Elegant Findings
This intimate shop specializes in museum-quality, hand-painted 19th-century porcelain from all over Europe. You'll also find marble statuary, exquisite linens, and period furniture. *89 Charles St • Map M3 • Closed Tue & Wed*

8 Marika's Antiques
Packed to its dusty rafters with oil paintings, tarnished silverware, and mismatched china – nothing quite beats that thrill of discovery you'll find here. *130 Charles St • Map M3 • Closed Sun & Mon*

9 Antiques at 99 Charles
Formal pieces of 19th-century Continental furniture and accessories, such as drop-leaf dining tables, wrought iron wall sconces, and beautiful Tiffany-style lamps, are the draw at this elegant shop. *99 Charles St • Map M3*

10 Judith Dowling Asian Art
More of a gallery than an antique shop, Judith Dowling carries superlative Asian pieces, ranging from 17th-century Japanese Buddhist figurines to exquisite ceramics. *133 Charles St • Map M2 • Closed Sun & Mon (Jul–Aug: closed Sat–Mon)*

***Note:** Unless otherwise specified, antique shops are open Mon–Sat (10 or 11am to 5 or 6pm) and Sun (noon–6pm)*

Price Categories

For a three course meal for one with half a bottle of wine (or equivalent meal), taxes and extra charges.

$	under $30
$$	$30–$45
$$$	$45–$60
$$$$	$60–$75
$$$$$	over $75

Left **The Federalist at XV Beacon**

Top 10 Restaurants & Bars

1 The Federalist
Anchoring the ultra-modern XV Beacon hotel, the Federalist combines luxurious dishes (think braised lobster with seared foie gras) with a savvy wine list. *15 Beacon St • Map P3 • 617 670 2515 • $$$*

2 Torch
Don't let the chic interior fool you; Torch offers one of the most unpretentious French bistro-style dining experiences in town. *26 Charles St • Map M2 • 617 723 5939 • Closed lunch & Mon • $$$*

3 Lala Rokh
Authentic Persian cuisine is served in this casual spot. Citrus-based glazes and relishes give meats amazing piquant flavor. *97 Mount Vernon St • Map N3 • 617 720 5511 • Closed lunch Sat & Sun • $$*

4 Artù
Tuscan specialties like lamb sandwiches and roasted veggies come sizzling off the grill on to the table. *89 Charles St • Map M3 • 617 227 9023 • $$ • Closed lunch Sun & Mon*

5 Figs
A popular spot where local celeb-chef Todd English turns his deft hand to pizza with toppings like artichoke, caramelized leeks, goat's cheese, and basil oil. *42 Charles St • Map M3 • 617 742 3447 Closed lunch Mon–Fri • $$*

6 Beacon Hill Bistro
This kitchen (in the Beacon Hill Hotel) puts an American stamp on French bistro cuisine with delicious results. *25 Charles St • Map M3 • 617 723 1133 • Open for brunch Sat & Sun, closed lunch Sun • $$$*

7 King & I
No surprises here, just savory, well-priced Thai staples. *145 Charles St • Map M2 • 617 227 3320 • Closed lunch Sun • $*

8 Seven's Ale House
The epitome of a local Boston bar: dark wood, slightly surly staff, amiable patrons, a dartboard, and a rudimentary pub menu. *77 Charles St • Map M3*

9 75 Chestnut
This converted townhouse offers one of Beacon Hill's most refined, romantic dining experiences. The menu is upscale, bistro American. Desserts are stellar. *75 Chestnut St • Map M3 • 617 227 2175 • Open for brunch Sun, closed lunch • $$$*

10 Beacon Hill Pub
This pub attracts freshly-minted college grads with the promise of cheap suds and even cheaper conversation. *149 Charles St • Map M2*

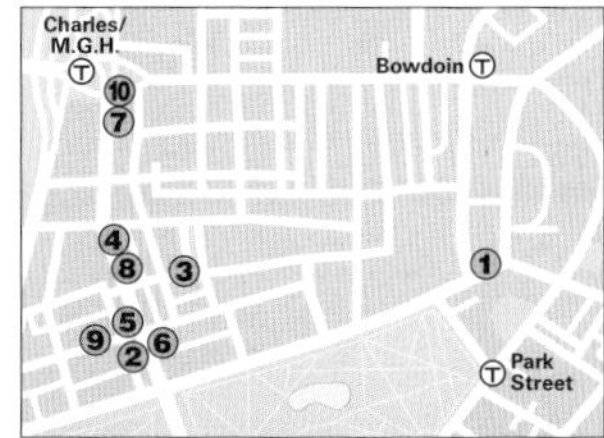

Note: *Reservations are recommended for most Beacon Hill restaurants*

Left **Institute of Contemporary Art** Center **Portico, Trinity Church** Right **Café, Newbury Street**

Back Bay

THE EASILY NAVIGATED GRID OF STREETS *in Back Bay bear little resemblance to the labyrinthine lanes around Downtown and the North End. In the early 1800s Back Bay was filled in to accommodate Boston's mushrooming population and by the mid-1800s, the area had become a vibrant, upscale neighborhood. Home to many of Boston's wealthiest families, the area was characterized by lavish houses, grand churches, and bustling commercial zones. Many of the original buildings stand intact, providing an exquisite 19th-century backdrop for today's pulsing nightlife, world-class shopping, and sumptuous dining.*

Prudential Center

TOP 10 Attractions

1. Newbury Street
2. Trinity Church
3. Boston Public Library
4. The Esplanade
5. Institute of Contemporary Art
6. Commonwealth Avenue
7. Prudential Center
8. Christian Science Center
9. Gibson House Museum
10. New England Life Murals

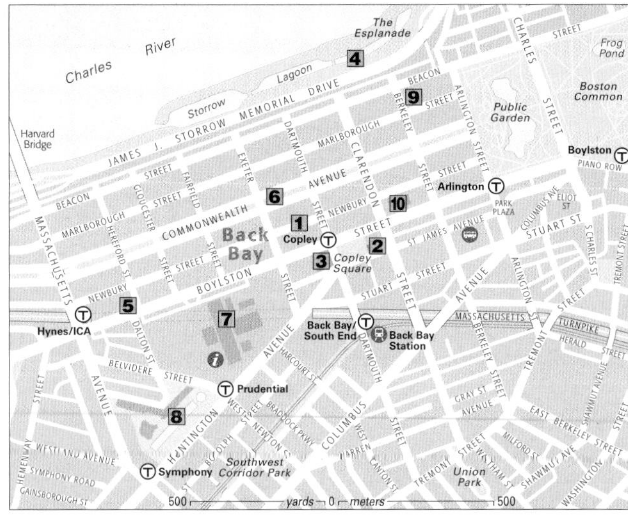

Note: *Cross streets in Back Bay run alphabetically, beginning with Arlington in the east and ending at Hereford Street in the west*

1 Newbury Street

Over the years, Back Bay's most famous street has proven to be amazingly adaptable. How else could fashion boutiques as *au courant* as Diesel and DKNY blend so seamlessly into their 140-year-old brownstone environs? This uncanny adaptability provides for the liveliest, most eclectic street scene in Boston: a babble of languages, skater punks walking alongside catwalk models, and delivery trucks and Ferraris jockeying for the same parking space – it's all here *(see pp20–21)*.

2 Trinity Church

When I. M. Pei's 60-story John Hancock Tower was completed in 1976, Bostonians feared Trinity Church would be overshadowed by its gleaming upstart neighbor. Yet H. H. Richardson's masterpiece, dedicated in 1877, remains just as vital to Copley Square, and as beautiful, as it appeared on its opening day *(see pp26–7)*.

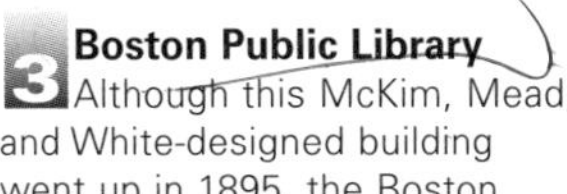

3 Boston Public Library

Although this McKim, Mead, and White-designed building went up in 1895, the Boston Public Library was actually founded in 1848 and is the oldest in the country. The interior's Greco-Roman style cues lavish use of marble, and John Singer Sargent's powerful "Judaism and Christianity" mural sequence clearly illustrates how highly public education was valued when the library was constructed. Guided tours offer insight into the building's architecture and history. *700 Boylston St • Map L5 • 617 536 5400 • Open 9am–9pm Mon–Thu, 9am–5pm Fri–Sat, 1–5pm Sun (Jun–Sep: closed Sun) • Tours: 2:30pm Mon, 6pm Tue & Thu, 11am Fri & Sat, 2pm Sun • Free*

Sargent mural, Boston Public Library

Bates Hall, Boston Public Library

The Esplanade

4 The Esplanade

The perfect setting for a leisurely bike ride, an invigorating jog, or a lazy, languid afternoon of soaking up the sun, the Esplanade is one of the city's most popular green spaces. Keep in mind that this gorgeous ribbon of green hugging the Charles' river banks is just one link in the Emerald Necklace *(see p15)*. July 4th *(see p54)* at the Esplanade's Hatch Shell concert venue brings the world-famous Boston Pops orchestra along with thousands of revelers to enjoy the incomparable mix of music, good cheer, and awe-inspiring fireworks. *Map M3*

For information on the origins of Back Bay **See pp20–21**
For information on Boston Common **See pp14–15**

5 Institute of Contemporary Art

Founded in 1936, the country's oldest non-collecting contemporary arts institution rewards its visitors with challenging, cutting-edge exhibitions. Over the years, the ICA has shown video installations, customized cars, and even blowtorches by internationally celebrated guest artists. Another ICA endeavor is its Vita Brevis program, which introduces works of contemporary art into public spaces around the city. *955 Boylston St • Map K6 • 617 266 5152 • Open noon–5pm Wed & Fri, noon–9pm Thu, 11am–5pm Sat–Sun • Check website for details of shows: www.icaboston.org • Adm*

Mapparium, Christian Science Center

6 Commonwealth Avenue

With its leafy pedestrian mall and *belle époque*-inspired architecture, Commonwealth Avenue aptly deserves its comparison to *les rues parisiennes*. A morning jog on the mall is a popular pastime, as is the occasional picnic or afternoon snooze on a bench. Highlights include Boston's first Baptist church (110 Clarendon; closed to non-worshipers) and the pedestrian mall's stately statues, including the William Lloyd Garrison bronze, sculpted by local artist Anne Whitney. *Map J5–L4*

Baptist Church window, Commonwealth Ave

7 Prudential Center

Although difficult to imagine, the Prudential Tower's 52 stories seem dwarfed by the huge swathe of street-level shops and restaurants that comprise the Prudential Center. With its indoor shopping mall, food court, supermarket, cluster of residential towers, and massive convention center, the Prudential Center is like a self-contained city within a city. For a jaw-dropping view of Boston, visit the Skywalk on the tower's 50th level *(see p61)*, or the Top of the Hub Lounge *(see p88)* two floors above. *800 Boylston St • Map K6 • 617 236 3100 • Open 10am–8pm Mon–Sat, 11am–6pm Sun*

8 Christian Science Center

You don't have to be a believer in the Church of Christ, Scientist – which posits that disease and sin can be overcome through faith in Jesus Christ – to be enamored with this sprawling complex. There's more to the center than the stunning Romanesque and Byzantine amalgam that is the Mother Church. Its map room, or mapparium, houses an immense stained-glass globe that visitors can walk through. Outside, a 670 ft- (204-m) long reflecting pool designed by I. M. Pei is lined with begonias, marigolds, and columbines. *175 Huntington Ave • Map K6 • 617 450 3790 • Tours 10am–4pm Mon–Sat, 11:30am–3pm Sun • Free*

***Note**: For those tight on time, the Prudential Center's glorified food hall, Marché Movenpick, makes perfect sense*

9 Gibson House Museum

One of the first private residences to be built in Back Bay (c.1859), Gibson House remains beautifully intact. The house has been preserved as a monument to the era, thanks largely to the efforts of its final resident (the grandson of the well-to-do merchant who built the house). So frozen in time does this house appear that you might feel like you're intruding on someone's inner sanctum, and an earlier age. Highlights of the tour include some elegant porcelain dinnerware, 18th-century heirloom jewelry, and exquisite black walnut woodwork throughout the house. *137 Beacon St • Map M4 • 617 267 6338 • Tours 1pm, 2pm, & 3pm Wed–Sun • Adm*

Library, Gibson House Museum

10 New England Life Murals

In the lobby of the New England Financial building, a series of eight murals depicts scenes from Boston's most formative moments. Mounted in 1942 by a Beaux Arts star pupil, Charles Hoffbauer, the series commemorates events such as the pilgrims' welcome by the Samoset Indians in 1621 and the 1797 launching of the USS *Constitution* *(see p30)*. *501 Boylston St • Map M5 • Open 9am–5pm Mon–Fri • Free*

Exploring Back Bay

Afternoon

Grab a patio table at the **Parish Café** *(see p45)* and enjoy an inventive sandwich while gazing out onto the **Public Garden**. Stroll one block over to Newbury Street and peruse the impressive contemporary art galleries concentrated between Arlington and Dartmouth streets. Cross back over to Boylston at Dartmouth and sit for a spell inside **Trinity Church** *(see pp26–7)* where La Farge's stained-glass windows top an inexhaustible list of highlights. And while you're in an aesthetics-appreciating mood, traverse St James Place to the **Copley Plaza Hotel** and lounge a moment in the ornate, Versailles-esque lobby. Next, cross Dartmouth to the **Boston Public Library** *(see p81)* and admire John Singer Sargent's gorgeous murals. Now it's time to warm up your credit card, so head back to Newbury Street for a dizzying shopping spree. Turn left onto Newbury for Boston-only boutiques such as **Allston Beat** *(see p85)* and **Trident Booksellers** *(see p85)*. Stop for a reinvigorating fruit smoothie or thick frappé at **Emack & Bolio's** (290 Newbury St). At Massachusetts Avenue, turn left, then left again onto Boylston and continue to the **Prudential Center** for name-brand shopping – think Saks Fifth Avenue, Neiman Marcus, and the like. Cap it all off with a bracing-cold cocktail and smooth jazz at the 52nd-floor **Top of the Hub Lounge** *(see p88)*, where you can soak in Boston's skyline – and with any luck, a dazzling sunset.

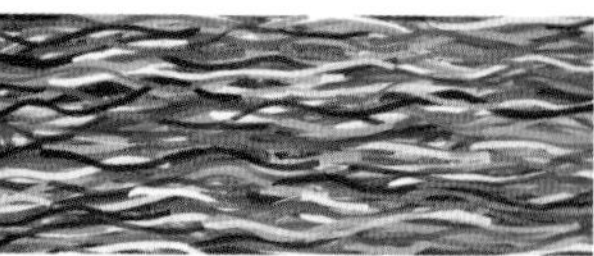

Left **Detail of work by John Walker, Nielsen** Right **Work by Sol Lewitt, Barbara Krakow Gallery**

Top 10 Art Galleries

1 Robert Klein
Everybody who's anybody in the world of photography vies for wall space at Robert Klein. Past coups include shows by Annie Liebovitz and Herb Ritts. *38 Newbury St • Map M5 • 617 267 7997 • Closed Sun*

2 Copley Society of Boston
With a commitment to exhibiting works by promising New England artists, this non-profit organization boasts a 120-year history of providing young artists with that crucial first break. *158 Newbury St • Map L5 • 617 536 5049 • Closed Sun–Mon*

3 Gallery NAGA
Representing some of New England's most regarded print-makers and painters, NAGA is possibly Newbury's best contemporary art gallery. *67 Newbury St • Map M5 • 617 267 9060 • Closed Sun–Mon*

4 Barbara Krakow Gallery
Since opening in 1964 with an exhibition of Ellsworth Kelly prints, Barbara Krakow's keen judgment of contemporary art has earned her many fans – and customers. *10 Newbury St • Map M5 • 617 262 4490 • Closed Sun–Mon*

5 Pepper Gallery
In welcome contrast to her peers, Audrey Pepper looks for a sense of playfulness in the pieces she exhibits – plenty of bold colors and amusing juxtapositions. *38 Newbury St • Map M5 • 617 236 4497 • Closed Sun–Mon*

6 The Artful Hand
With the American Crafts Movement of the late-19th century as its muse, The Artful Hand sells exquisite pieces of embroidery, woodwork, home accessories, and hand-painted glass. *100 Huntington Ave • Map L6 • 617 262 9601*

7 Judi Rotenberg Gallery
Intense colors and an emphasis on graphic design distinguish the works of artist-owner Rotenberg and her contemporaries. Most artists represented are New England-based. *130 Newbury St • Map L5 • 617 437 1518 • Closed Mon*

8 Dyansen
With sister galleries in Waikoloa (Hawaii), New York, and Beverly Hills, Dyansen shows contemporary art with a decidedly international flair. *132A Newbury St • Map L5 • 617 262 4800*

9 Nielsen
Favoring lush, contemporary paintings, and the occasional mixed-media sculpture, Nielsen is popular among Boston's art cognoscenti for the distinction of her artists. *179 Newbury St • Map L5 • 617 266 4835 • Closed Sun–Mon*

10 International Poster Gallery
Arguably the most fun – albeit the most populist – gallery on Newbury, the IPG stocks vintage first edition movie posters and print advertisements from the *belle époque*. *205 Newbury St • Map K5 • 617 375 0076*

***Note:** Unless otherwise specified galleries are open daily. Opening hours are generally from 10am–5:30pm*

Left **Allston Beat** Right **Trident Booksellers & Café**

TOP 10 Homegrown Newbury Shops

1 Jasmine Sola & Sola Men

For fashionistas on a budget, this local chain's flagship store stocks carefully selected, reasonably-priced women's wear, from the likes of BCBG and Central Park West, and sleek men's wear, too. *344 Newbury St • Map K6*

2 Trident Booksellers & Café

Trident is popular for its delicious, healthful sandwiches, strong coffee concoctions, and arguably the best informed book and magazine selections in the city. *338 Newbury St • Map K6*

3 The Closet Upstairs

Get outfitted in retro-chic without breaking the bank. The Closet overflows with vintage Levi's, cocktail dresses, funky shirts of all fabrics, and great Halloween costumes. *223 Newbury St • Map K5 • Closed Tue*

4 Appleton's

New England's rural charm infuses every piece of handiwork at this arts and crafts gift shop, from embroidered pillow cases to painted wooden jugs depicting lively scenes from the countryside. *134 Newbury St • Map L5*

5 Newbury Comics

Generally undercutting the chain stores on compact discs, Newbury Comics delivers value along with a stellar selection of rare import CDs, concert videos, and the latest comics. *332 Newbury St • Map J6*

6 Allston Beat

With everything for club hoppers, glam rockers, and hip-hop revivalists, Allston Beat is the place for clothing and accessories that positively ooze swagger. *348 Newbury St • Map J6*

7 Second Time Around

Before blowing your budget on that Chanel handbag, take a peek at Second Time Around, where used designer clothing and accessories get a second lease on life. Think head-to too Versace for a mere $100. *176 Newbury St • Map L5*

8 Condom World

Check your inhibitions at this subterranean boutique's door. While male anatomy-shaped ketchup dispensers deserve a laugh, some of the sex toys toward the back might sooner merit a wince. *332 Newbury St • Map J6*

9 Hope

With its mood crystals, gargoyle statuettes, and witchcraft journals, this rarest of boutiques may hold the ticket to a mythological netherworld, but you will still need cash or plastic to get there. *302 Newbury St • Map K5*

10 Deluca's Back Bay Market

This old world-style corner market stocks fabulous produce, chilled beer, ready-made sandwiches, and imported delights of all kinds. *239 Newbury St • Map K5*

***Note:** Unless otherwise specified shops are open daily*

Left **Zóe Home** Right **Teuscher Chocolates of Switzerland**

Top 10 Shops to Drain your Bank Account

1 Louis, Boston

Louis offers the city's most rarified shopping experience. The main attractions here are classically handsome Brioni suits, sharp Jil Sander leather pumps, and Apothecary cosmetics. *234 Berkeley St • Map M5 • Closed Sun*

2 Shreve, Crump & Low

The country's oldest retail jeweler has seen its diamonds grace the fingers of some of modern history's most famous – and fortunate – figures. Shreve's sterling silver is also highly coveted. *330 Boylston St • Map M5 • Closed Sun*

3 Alan Bilzerian

From a $4,000 John Galliano silk dress to a skimpy camouflage Christian Dior bikini, Alan Bilzerian is the place to go for high-end fashion that exudes personality. *34 Newbury St • Map M5 • Closed Sun*

4 Ermenegildo Zegna

For the successful businessman whose daydreams feature a vintage Ferrari and the Sardinian coast, Zegna fits like a glove. Classic Italian suits and ties that are unrivaled for style and quality. *39 Newbury St • Map M5*

5 Zóe Home

This bright boutique offers vibrant, playfully designed contemporary furniture that screams "unique." Choose from plush retro divans, utilitarian rolling desks, and whimsical decorative lighting. *279 Newbury St • Map K5*

6 Autrefois Antiques

Autrefois specializes in French and Italian furnishings from the 18th, 19th, and 20th centuries, like Louis XV gilded mirrors, Art Deco dining chairs, and wildly abstract iron sconces. *125 Newbury St • Map L5 • Closed Sun*

7 Lux, Bond & Green

While not quite as prestigious as its neighbor Shreve, Green still manages with Tag Heuer watches, Mikimoto pearls, and Garavelli diamonds at prices that remain this side of the stratosphere. *416 Boylston St • Map M5 • Closed Sun*

8 Priscilla of Boston

Boston's bridal gown queen has been helping to make weddings unforgettable for 50 years. Should you require a fitting, it is recommended that you call ahead. *801 Boylston St • Map K5 • 617 267 9070*

9 Akris

Footware by Jimmy Choo and Stuart Wietzman claim the back of the store, while cashmere suits, evening gowns, and luxurious coats rule the racks up front. *16 Newbury St • Map M5 • Closed Sun*

10 Teuscher Chocolates of Switzerland

Relishing a Teuscher truffle ranks among life's greatest pleasures. Perhaps no other chocolatier in the world gets the alchemy quite so right. *230 Newbury St • Map K5*

Note: *Unless otherwise specified shops are open daily*

Above **Davio's**

Price Categories		
For a three course	**$**	under $30
[illegible]	**$$**	$30–$45
a bottle of wine (or	**$$$**	$45–$60
equivalent meal), taxes,	**$$$$**	$60–$75
and extra charges.	**$$$$$**	over $75

TOP 10 Alfresco Scenes

1 Armani Café

Haute couture gets matched with equally haute cuisine at Armani Café. On the patio tables there's San Pelegrino and tuna tartare; on the patrons there's lots of black Giorgio. *⊗ 214 Newbury St • Map K5 • 617 437 0909 • $$*

2 Sonsie

With windows that open up onto the street, Sonsie sets the alfresco standard at this end of Newbury. The fashionable clientele enjoy light Italocentric cuisine upstairs, and devilish cocktails in the basement Red Room. *⊗ 327 Newbury St • Map J6 • 617 351 2500 • $$*

3 Stephanie's on Newbury

Enjoying one of the most generous portions of Newbury sidewalk, this American bistro packs the tables for the likes of duck and porcini risotto. *⊗ 190 Newbury St • Map L5 • 617 236 0990 • $$$*

4 Tapéo

Experience a sultry Barcelona night: Newbury's most romantic alfresco nighttime scene combines intensely flavorful tapas and an extensive Spanish wine list. *⊗ 266 Newbury St • Map K5 • 617 267 4799 • Closed lunch Mon–Fri • $$*

5 Ciao Bella

Ciao Bella is a favorite stop for star athletes, who come for the hearty portions of no-frills Italian cuisine and the sizzling alfresco scene. *⊗ 240 Newbury St • Map K5 • 617 536 2626 • $$*

6 Davio's

With a versatile menu of robust Italian specialties, design-your-own pizzas, and a spacious sidewalk café, Davio's is sure to please. *⊗ 269 Newbury St • Map K5 • 617 262 4810 • $$*

7 Joe's American Bar & Grill

Although the white tablecloths might suggest refined dining, Joe's fits squarely in the glorified-burger milieu. Its patio boasts prime people-watching and the staff are kid-friendly. *⊗ 270 Dartmouth St • Map L5 • 617 536 4200 • $$*

8 Parish Café

This split-level café with a patio has a lovely view onto the Public Garden *(see pp14–15)* and an inspired menu of delicious and wildly creative sandwiches *(see p45)*.

9 Other Side Café

The Other Side enjoys a loyal following of health-conscious hipsters who melt at the sight of its brie, apple, and pear sandwich. Its intimate outdoor patio is highly coveted real estate. *⊗ 407 Newbury St • Map J6 • $*

10 Charley's

Surrounded by lush greenery, Charley's patio feels remarkably secluded despite its prime Newbury Street frontage. Simple bar staples like burgers, chicken wings, and massive salads attract a raucous after-work crowd. *⊗ 284 Newbury St • Map K5 • $*

***Note:** Unless otherwise specified cafés are open daily for lunch and dinner. Reservations are recommended for those with phone numbers*

Left **Barcode** Right **Top of the Hub Lounge**

TOP 10 Nightclubs & Bars

1 Top of the Hub Lounge

Talk about a view: 52 stories above Back Bay, this bar dazzles with sweeping views, live jazz, and a wicked gin martini. *Prudential Tower, 800 Boylston St • Map K6 • Closes 1am Sun–Wed*

2 Daisy Buchanan's

Professional athletes, models, and local professionals are drawn to Daisy's for its friendly, casual vibe. *240 Newbury St • Map K5*

3 Barcode

The pan-Asian cuisine and French-colonial decor merit oohs and ahhs, but Barcode's real appeal lies in its sophisticated bar scene and upwardly mobile crowd. *955 Boylston St • Map J6*

4 Blue Cat Café

This sleek, modern lounge has quickly made a name for itself among cocktail aficionados for its addictive espresso martini. *94 Massachusetts Av • Map J6 • Closes 1am*

5 Whiskey's

You better have ID in hand before putting pint to mouth at this lively bar. It's full of hard-drinking collegiate types, who arrive around 6pm and stay until last call. *885 Boylston St • Map K6*

6 Rattlesnake Bar

Rattlesnake's roof deck hosts one of Boston's most boisterous after-work crowds. Dress is always casual, and people are always mingling. *384 Boylston St • Map M5*

7 The Pour House

Cheap, hearty pub grub and occasional drink specials lure college kids to this two-story bar and grill. It's loud, it's crowded, and you're bound to make a friend or two. *907 Boylston St • Map K6*

8 Bukowski Tavern

A beer drinker's paradise, Bukowski counts 100 varieties of suds. Its primary patrons are a professional crowd during the day and young hipsters at night. *50 Dalton St • Map K6*

9 Vox Populi

Slick bi-level Vox gets things right with a post-work dining scene. But after 8pm, the drink denizens pack in four-deep to the well-stocked bar *755 Boylston St • Map K5 • Closes 11.45pm Mon & Sun, 12.45am Tue–Sat*

10 Hard Rock Café

Boston's outpost of the hegemonic rock 'n' roll café has all the memorabilia you would expect, along with a hopping after-work bar scene. Thursdays bring local rock bands. *131 Clarendon St • Map M5*

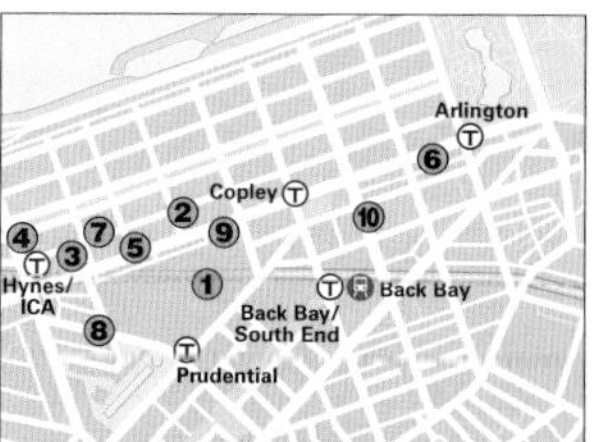

Note: *Unless otherwise specified, bars and nightclubs are open until 2am daily*

Price Categories

For a three course meal for one with half a bottle of wine (or equivalent meal), taxes, and extra charges.		
	$	under $30
	$$	$30–$45
	$$$	$45–$60
	$$$$	$60–$75
	$$$$$	over $75

Left **Gyuhama**

Top 10 Restaurants

1 L'Espalier

Ranked among America's best restaurants, L'Espalier impresses as much for its brownstone-mansion location as its exquisite French cuisine *(see p40)*.

2 Aujourd'hui

Highlights of the classic French menu at this refined eatery include feather-light soufflés and indulgent lobster. *Four Seasons, 200 Boylston St • Map N5 • 617 451 1392 • Closed lunch Sat • $$$$*

3 Oak Room

The grand, lavishly appointed Oak Room is known for its unfalteringly tender steaks. *Fairmont Copley Plaza Hotel, 138 St. James Ave • Map L5 • 617 267 5300 • Closed lunch • $$$*

4 Grill 23

Grill 23 harkens back to the days of exclusive, Prohibition-era supper clubs. Prime aged beef with an inventive spin is served in a sumptuously classic interior. *161 Berkeley St • Map M5 • 617 542 2255 • Closed lunch • $$$*

5 Azure

Executive chef Robert Fathman's four-star touch on New England seafood staples has made Azure one of Boston's hottest new restaurants. *Lenox Hotel, 65 Exeter St • Map L5 • 617 933 4800 • Closed lunch Mon–Sat • $$$*

6 Clio

Chef Ken Oringer presides over the grand Eliot Hotel's claim to culinary fame. Luxurious entrées complement the richly appointed dining room. *370A Commonwealth Ave • Map J5 • 617 536 7200 • Closed lunch & Mon • $$$*

7 Gyuhama

This mainstay Japanese restaurant slings some of the city's freshest sushi. *827 Boylston St • Map K5 • 617 437 0188 • $*

8 Brasserie Jo

Bustling Brasserie Jo captures the *savoir faire* of 1940s Paris. Hearty French classics like steak roquefort are immensely satisfying. *120 Huntington Ave • Map K6 • 617 425 3240 • $$$*

9 Pho Pasteur

This efficient kitchen churns out amazingly subtle French Vietnamese cuisine. *119 Newbury St • Map L5 • 617 262 8200 • $*

10 Ambrosia on Huntington

The angular dining rooms are an architectural *tour de force*, but it is the French-Asian cuisine that provides the real wow factor. *116 Huntington Ave • Map L6 • 617 247 2400 • $$$ • Closed lunch Sat & Sun*

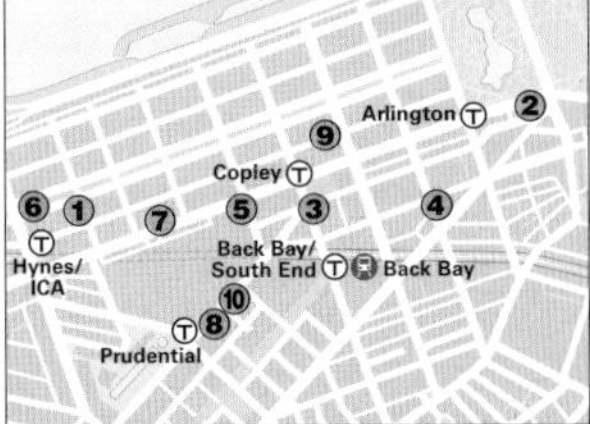

***Note:** Unless otherwise specified, restaurants are open for lunch and dinner daily. Reservations are generally required*

Left **Copp's Hill Burying Ground** Right **New England Aquarium**

North End & the Waterfront

THE NORTH END IS BOSTON'S ITALIAN VILLAGE, *where feast day blends into feast day all summer as the great-grandchildren of Southern Italian immigrants celebrate the music, food, and dolce vita of the old country. Every other storefront houses a restaurant, café, or bakery and the cheers of European football fans echo from the bars. These transplanted festivities continue year round, merely moving indoors when the season chills. Yet the North End predates its Italian inhabitants and the neighborhood is in fact the oldest in Boston. The perimeter of the area along the waterfront bristles with condo developments on the former shipping piers, which lead south to the bustle of Long, Central, and Rowes wharves. Boston was born by the sea and it is now reclaiming its waterfront as a vital center for business and pleasure.*

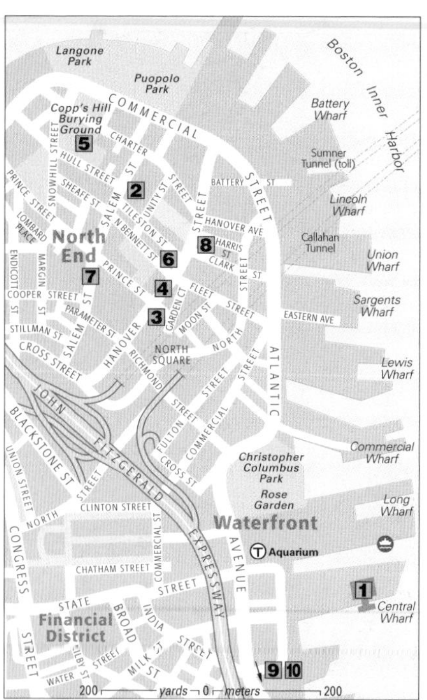

Old North Church

Top 10 Attractions

1. New England Aquarium
2. Old North Church
3. Paul Revere House
4. Hanover Street
5. Copp's Hill Burying Ground
6. Paul Revere Mall
7. Salem Street
8. St Stephen's Church
9. Children's Museum
10. Boston Tea Party Ship

***Note:** The Freedom Trail (see pp8–9) passes Paul Revere's House, Old North Church, and Copp's Hill Burying Ground*

1 New England Aquarium

Now the centerpiece of the downtown waterfront development, the aquarium's construction in the 1960s paved the way for the revitalization of Boston Harbor. Seals cavort in a tank in front of the sleek modern structure *(see p32–3)*. *Map R3*

2 Old North Church

An active Episcopal congregation still worships at Boston's oldest church, officially known as Christ Church (1723). The austere interior looks much as it did in its early days. It was here, in 1775, that sexton Robert Newman hung two lanterns in the belfry to warn horseback messenger Paul Revere of British troop movements *(see p10)*. *193 Salem St • Map Q1 • 617 523 6676 • Open 9am–6pm Mon–Fri, 9am–5pm Sat–Sun*

Old North Church clock

3 Paul Revere House

Home to Paul Revere for 30 years, this 17th-century clapboard house is the only surviving home of any of Boston's revolutionary heroes. A place of pilgrimage for history buffs, it provides an intriguing glimpse into the domestic life of Revere's family with displays of their furniture and possessions including silverwork made by Revere, who was highly regarded as a metalsmith. Well-trained staff perpetuate the tale of Revere's legendary midnight ride *(see p10)*. *19 North Sq • Map Q1 • 617 523 2338 • Open mid-Apr–Oct: 9:30am–5:15pm daily; Nov–mid Apr: 9:30am–4:15pm daily (closed Mon Jan–Mar) • Adm • limited DA*

Paul Revere House

Hanover Street

4 Hanover Street

Originally built in the 17th-century to connect the shipping wharves to Dock Square (now Faneuil Hall Marketplace; *see pp12–13)*, Hanover Street was widened in 1870 to accommodate the busy flow of commerce. Today, as the North End's principal artery with cafés and eateries aplenty, it is the place to come for a slice of the action. *Map Q2*

5 Copp's Hill Burying Ground

Trace the history of Boston on the thousands of tombstones here, from the mean-spirited Mather family, theocrats who ruled the early city, to the valiant patriots slain in the fight for freedom. In the Battle of Bunker Hill *(see p10)*, the British, who occupied the city in 1775, manned a battery from this site and fired on neighboring Charlestown. There are sweeping views of the harbor. *Entrance on Hull St • Map Q1 • Open 9am–5pm daily • No DA • 617 426 3115*

***Note:** Feast days of North End patron saints are celebrated with street parties and parades most weekends from mid-June through August*

Foraging for Formaggio

A recognized authority on Italian food, wine, and culture, Michele Topor has lived in the North End for more than three decades. Her tour of the neighborhood markets on Wednesday and Saturday (10am–2pm), and Friday (3pm) includes tastings, tips, and insights on local restaurants. Reservations required, contact L'Arte Di Cucinare: 617 523 6032, www.cucinare.com.

6 Paul Revere Mall

The North End's history as both revolutionary stronghold and Italian immigrant neighborhood comes together along this tree-lined mall, which old-timers persist in calling the Prado. Created in 1933, the pedestrian mall connects Hanover Street to the rear of Old North Church. Bronze plaques lining the walls capture snippets from the lives of former Bostonians, while an equestrian statue of Paul Revere surveys it all. Today, the mall is a social center, where mothers convene with baby carriages, kids play frisbee, and old men hunker over checkerboards. *Map Q1*

7 Salem Street

Running parallel to Hanover Street, Salem is as narrow and intimate as Hanover is broad and public. Lined with a growing number of restaurants, this is also where North Enders shop for the necessities of daily life – from rabbit and veal to pillowy loaves of bread, which come fresh from local ovens around the clock. The Italian flavor of the neighborhood, though fading in recent years as gentrification inflates the cost of housing, remains its strongest on Salem Street's narrow sidewalks. *Map Q1*

St Stephen's Church

Children's Museum

8 St Stephen's Church

Renowned architect Charles Bulfinch completely redesigned the church's original 1714 structure in 1802–4. This church is the only surviving example of his religious architecture. The complex Neo-Classical exterior contrasts with the open, airy, and relatively unadorned interior. In 1862, the Roman Catholic archdiocese took over the church to accomodate the area's growing number of Irish immigrants. Rose Fitzgerald, daughter of Boston mayor John "Honey Fitz" Fitzgerald and mother of President J. F. Kennedy *(see p39)*, is another name linked to the church. She was baptized here in 1890, and her funeral took place here in 1995. *401 Hanover St • Map R1 • 617 523 1230 • Open 8am–5pm Mon–Sat, 8am–noon Sun • Free*

Boston Tea Party Ship

9 Children's Museum

Educators at this groundbreaking interactive museum for kids pioneered some of the features now found in similar facilities around the world, including giant soap bubbles and complex rampways for marbles *(see p60)*.

10 Boston Tea Party Ship

The historic occasion (known as the Boston Tea Party) when patriots, dressed as native Americans, threw a consignment of English tea overboard to protest against the Stamp Tax of 1773, proved to be a precipitating event of the American Revolution *(see p10)*. The Boston Tea Party ship is a replica of the brig *Beaver*, one of the vessels deprived of its cargo that fateful December night. Aboard the ship, costumed storytellers recount events in rousing detail while visitors sip tea (or dump it over the rail). Over the centuries Boston has expanded into the harbor and the tea party site now lies firmly inland at 470 Atlantic Avenue, where a plaque marks the event. *Congress St Bridge • Map R5 • 617 338 1773 • Open Mar–Nov 9am–5pm daily (to 6pm in summer) • Temporarily closed until mid 2004 • Adm*

From Narrow Byways to the Sea

Morning

Walk through the underpass to Hanover Street from the Haymarket "T". Follow Richmond Street to North Square and the **Paul Revere House** *(see p91)* for a glimpse of the domestic life of the revolutionary hero. Return to Hanover for an espresso and some prime people-watching at lively **Caffè Vittoria** *(see p44)*. Continue up Hanover and turn left through Paul Revere Mall to **Old North Church** *(see p91)*. The bust of George Washington inside is reputedly the world's most accurate rendering of his distinctive face – compare the resemblance to a dollar bill. Then stroll up Hull Street past **Copp's Hill Burying Ground** *(see p91)* for a great vantage point of USS *Constitution (see p30)* before continuing to the waterfront. Grab a bench in **Puopolo Park** to watch a match of *bocce*, an Italian lawn bowling game. Walk south along Commercial Street and stop for an al fresco waterside lunch at **Joe's American Bar & Grill** (100 Atlantic Ave).

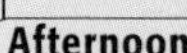

Afternoon

Resume your waterfront stroll, stopping off to enjoy the roses in the **Rose Kennedy Rose Garden** before whiling away an hour or so in the **New England Aquarium** *(see p32–3)* where highlights include the swirling Giant Ocean Tank. Then relax with a sundowner and watch the harbor activities from the patio of the **Boston Harbor Hotel** (70 Rowes Wharf) before heading to **Sel de la Terre** *(see p95)* for a Provençal dinner.

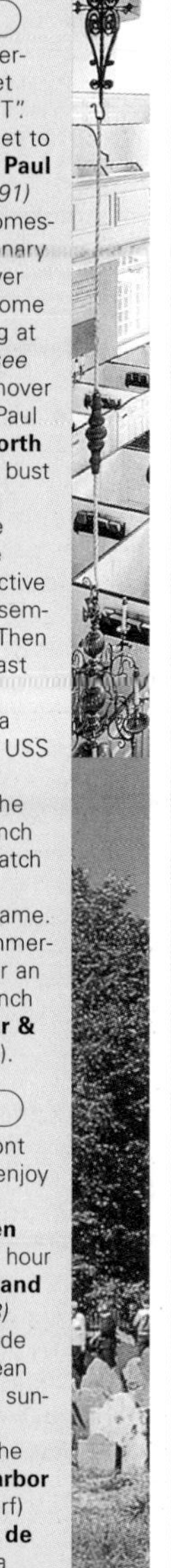

Note: *Numerous water tours and excursions leave from Long Wharf including trips to the Boston Harbor Islands* **See pp66–7**

Left **Monica's Salumeria** Right **Polcari's Coffee Co.**

Top 10 Italian Bakeries & Grocers

1 Mike's Pastry
Large glass cases display a huge selection of cookies and *cannoli* (crunchy pastry filled with a sweet ricotta cream). Purchase a box to go, or grab a table and order a drink and a delectable pastry. *300 Hanover St • Map Q1*

2 Salumeria Italiana
This neighborhood fixture is a premier stop for esoteric Italian canned goods and rich olive oils, as well as spicy sausages and cheeses from many Italian regions. *151 Richmond St • Map Q2 • Closed Sun • No DA*

3 Modern Pastry
House specialties here include rich ricotta pie and nougat made on the premises, as well as chocolate truffles from Italy and delicate Florentines. Modern makes a thinner *cannoli* shell than Mike's. *257 Hanover St • Map Q2*

4 Polcari's Coffee Co.
The premier bulk grocer in the North End, this charming store has sold Italian roasted coffee since 1932. It's still the best place to find spices, flours, grains, and legumes. *105 Salem St • Map Q1 • Closed Sun • No DA*

5 Bova's Bakery
Fresh bread emerges from the ovens at all hours. When the bars and coffee shops close, night owls head to Bova's for hot sandwiches and cookies. *134 Salem St • Map Q1 • No DA*

6 V. Cirace Wine & Spirits
The North End's most upscale seller of Italian wines and liqueurs stocks both fine wines to lay down and cheerfully youthful ones to enjoy right away. *173 North St • Map Q2 • Closed Sun • No DA*

7 Monica's Salumeria
Linked to a nearby restaurant, this *salumeria* has the usual cheeses and sausages, but its specialties are prepared foods such as cold salads for picnics and pasta dishes for reheating. *130 Salem St • Map Q1 • No DA*

8 Martignetti Liquors
One of the city's most comprehensive wine and liquor stores, Martignetti imports wines from many small producers in Italy, Spain, and Portugal. The store is particularly known for its broad selection of Nebbiolo-based wines of the Piemonte. *64 Cross St • Map Q2 • Closed Sun*

9 Calore Fruit
This small and basic shop, located below street level, stocks vegetables and exotic fruits. *99 Salem St • Map Q1 • Closed Sun • No DA*

10 Trio's Ravioli Shoppe
Trio family pasta is manufactured at a suburban factory for supermarket distribution, but this small store makes fresh pasta by hand for discerning customers. Also delicious pizza slices to go. *222 Hanover St • Map Q2 • Closed Sun • No DA*

***Note:** Unless otherwise specified, all bakeries and grocers are open daily*

Left **Maurizio's**

Price Categories

For a three course meal for one with half a bottle of wine (or equivalent meal), taxes, and extra charges.		
	$	under $30
	$$	$30–$45
	$$$	$45–$60
	$$$$	$60–$75
	$$$$$	over $75

Top 10 Restaurants & Bars

1 Maurizio's
A cozy, buzzy spot where chef Maurizio Lodo draws on his Sardinian heritage to create dishes that often include brilliant preparations of fish. *364 Hanover St • Map Q1 • 617 367 1123 • Closed Mon & lunch Sun–Thu • No DA • $$*

2 Taranta
An artistic blend of Sardinian and Catalan cuisine spells intense flavors (pork with vinegar peppers and broccoli). *210 Hanover St • Map Q2 • 617 720 0052 • Closed lunch Sun • $ • No DA*

3 Daily Catch
Fans of garlic and calamari dishes line up on the sidewalk for the tiny tables at one of the areas friendliest restaurants. *323 Hanover St • Map Q1 • No DA • $*

4 Pomodoro
Pomodoro's eponymous red sauce is arguably the tastiest in the North End. Roasted vegetables and veal dishes are excellent, and portions are large. *319 Hanover St • Map Q1 • No DA • $*

5 Pizzeria Regina
The original Regina's thin crust, old-fashioned pizza is far better than the pale imitations served at its other branches. *11½ Thatcher St • Map Q1 • No DA • $*

6 Bricco
This lively, stylish trattoría is a very popular spot for socializing over Venetian-style sardines or rabbit casserole. *241 Hanover St • Map Q2 • 617 248 6800 • $$*

7 Davide
Decorated like an Italian restaurant from a 1950s mobster movie, Davide specializes in southern Italian dishes such as crab and salt cod cakes with roasted pepper and basil sauce. *326 Commercial St • Map R1 • 617 227 3115 • Closed lunch • No DA • $$$*

8 Legal Sea Foods
The ironic location across from the aquarium doesn't detract from the first-class dishes of impeccably fresh fish. *255 State St • Map R2 • 617 227 3115 • $$*

9 Sel de la Terre
A restaurant for all meals – from morning muffins to great sandwiches and fries at lunch to sophisticated Provençal dinners. *255 State St • Map R2 • 617 720 1300 • $–$$$*

10 Prezza
One of the longest wine lists in town guarantees just the right glass to accompany hearty Tuscan fare as well as sinfully rich desserts. *24 Fleet St • Map R1 • 617 227 1577 • Closed lunch • $$*

***Note:** Many restaurants in this area do not accept reservations (phone numbers have been given for those that do)*

Left **Post Office Square** Right **Interior, Quincy Market**

Downtown & the Financial District

THE HEART OF BOSTON *is sandwiched between Boston Common and the harbor. Unlike many US cities, Boston has held tenaciously to its past and there are reminders of nearly four centuries of history embedded in the center of this modern metropolis. The 18th-century grace of historic buildings like the Old State House still shines within a canyon of skyscrapers. Even the heroes of Boston's early years remain here – city founder John Winthrop, patriot Paul Revere, and revolutionary Samuel Adams are buried just steps from sidewalks abuzz with shoppers. Rolled in to this amorphous area is Faneuil Hall Marketplace* (see pp12–13)*, the oldest of Boston's commercial districts, and the Financial District, which stands as testament to Boston's continuing worldwide economic clout.*

Left **Filene's Department Store, Downtown Crossing** Right **Financial District skyscrapers**

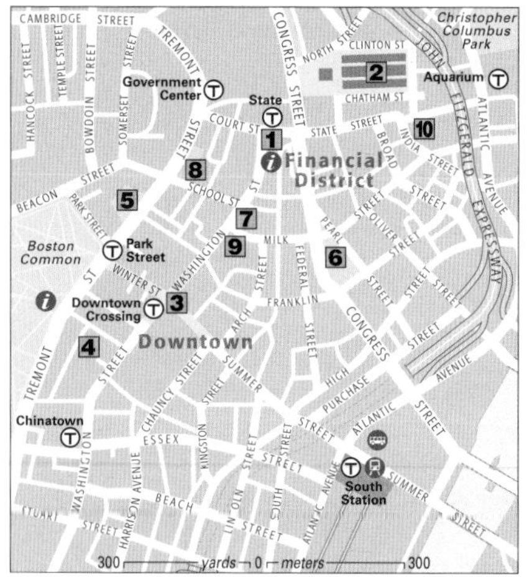

Top 10 Attractions

1. Old State House
2. Faneuil Hall Marketplace
3. Downtown Crossing
4. Ladder District
5. Old Granary Burying Ground
6. Post Office Square
7. Old South Meeting House
8. King's Chapel
9. Dreams of Freedom Museum
10. Custom House

1 Old State House

Built in 1713 as the seat of colonial government, the Old State House was designed to look down State Street to the shipping hub of Long Wharf. In 1770, the Boston Massacre *(see p36)* occurred just outside its doors. And on July 4, 1776, the Declaration of Independence was first read to Bostonians from its balcony *(see p9)*. Today, it's home to the Boston Historical Society & Museum. *Washington & State Sts • Map Q3 • 617 720 3290 • Open 9am–5pm daily • Adm*

2 Faneuil Hall Marketplace

Many a fiery speech urging revolution echoed in Faneuil Hall in the late 18th century; in the 1820s it was the city's food distribution that was revolutionized in adjacent Quincy Market. Today the buildings and surrounding plazas form a festival marketplace – the successful model for dozens of markets worldwide *(see pp12–13)*.

3 Downtown Crossing

This pedestrian shopping area is flanked by Filene's and Macy's department stores but is given its real life by the pushcart vendors and downtown office workers who fill the streets. *Junction of Summer, Winter, & Washington Sts • Map P4*

4 Ladder District

The network of short streets connecting Washington and Tremont streets has, in recent years, assumed a new identity as the Ladder District. Once derelict and abandoned after dark, the area now throbs with clubs, bars, and restaurants. Anchoring the new district, the Millennium Tower houses the ultra chic Ritz Carlton Boston Common *(see p146)* and the top-of-the-line Loews Cineplex (175 Tremont St). A few stalwarts, such as the landmark used-book seller, Brattle Book Shop, are holding out against the moneyed big boys. *Map P4*

Vendor, Downtown Crossing

Central staircase, Old State House

5 Old Granary Burying Ground

Dating from 1660, the Granary contains the graves of many of Boston's most illustrious figures, including John Hancock, Samuel Adams, and Paul Revere *(see p38)* who joined his revolutionary comrades here in 1818. Other notables include the hugely influential architect Charles Bulfinch, Benjamin Franklin's parents, and Crispus Attucks – an escaped slave who was allegedly the first casualty of the so-dubbed Boston Massacre *(see p10)*. The neatly aligned gravestones bear little relation to actual graves. *Tremont St at Park St • Map P3 • 617 635 7383 • Open 8am–5pm daily • Free*

Murals, **Verizon building, Post Office Square**

6 Post Office Square

On a sunny day, every bench and patch of grass in this green oasis is filled with office workers. Surrounding the park are several of the area's most architecturally distinctive buildings, including the Art Deco post office building (Congress St), the Renaissance revival former Federal Reserve building (now Le Méridien hotel *see p146*), and the Art Moderne Verizon building (185 Franklin St). The lobby of the latter houses a small telephone museum and has labor murals celebrating the telephone industry workers. *Map Q3*

7 Old South Meeting House

Old South's rafters have rung with many impassioned speeches exhorting the overthrow of the king, the abolition of slavery, women's right to vote, an end to apartheid, and many other causes. Nearly abandoned when its congregation moved to Back Bay in 1876, it was saved in one of Boston's first acts of historic preservation. *310 Washington St • Map Q3 • 617 482 6439 • Open Apr–Oct: 9.30am–5pm daily; Nov–Mar: 10am–4pm daily • Adm*

Old South Meeting House

Interior, King's Chapel

8 King's Chapel

The first Anglican Church in Puritan Boston was established in 1686 to serve the British Army officers. When the majority of Anglicans fled Boston along with retreating British forces in the evacuation of 1776, the chapel became the first Unitarian Church in the New World. The church is known for its ambitious program of classical concerts. *58 Tremont St • Map P3 • 617 227 2155 • Open 10am–4pm Mon & Thu–Sat, services on Sun (mid-Nov–May only open Sat and for Sun services, and 12.15 Tue for recitals)*

9 Dreams of Freedom Museum

Sandwiched between sites associated with the American Revolution, this museum embellishes Boston's history by focusing on the immigrants who followed their "dreams of freedom" to the US. The museum was established in

***Note:** The Financial District is a good place for quick, inexpensive weekday lunches. Try Cosi at 53 State St and 133 Federal St*

2000 by an organization that provides resettlement services to immigrants and refugees. The permanent exhibition focuses on a handful of modestly famous immigrants to try to convey experiences common to newcomers. Temporary exhibitions highlight related subjects, such as American stereotypes of specific immigrant groups. *1 Milk St • Map P3 • 617 338 6022 • www.dreamsoffreedom.org • Open Apr–Dec: 10am–6pm daily, Jan–Mar: 10am–5pm Tue–Sun • Adm*

10 Custom House

When the Custom House was built in 1840, Boston was one of America's largest overseas shipping ports, and customs fees were the mainstay of the Federal budget. The Neo-Classical structure once sat on the waterfront, but now stands two blocks inland. The 16-story Custom House tower, added in 1913, was Boston's first skyscraper. Since the 1990s, peregrine falcons have nested in the clock tower under the watchful eyes of wildlife biologists. The lobby displays a few artifacts from the Peabody Essex Museum in Salem, and tours of the tower give sweeping harbor views. *3 McKinley Sq • Map Q3 • 617 310 6300 • Tours 10am & 4pm Sun–Fri, 4pm Sat • Adm*

Custom House Tower

A Shopping Spree

Morning

The "T" will deposit you at Downtown Crossing's underground entrance to **Filene's Basement** *(see p56)*, where you can join Bostonians in a hunt for bargain clothing and accessories. At street level, peruse the windows of **Filene's** and **Macy's** department stores for other temptations. Then take the scenic route to Quincy Market down Franklin Street past the soaring Financial District skyscrapers. Turn left at Post Office Square and stop for an early lunch at the old-fashioned ice cream and sandwich shop, **Brigham's** (50 Congress St). At Water Street, detour left to the **Boston Globe Store** (1 School St) for a selection of Boston-oriented books and souvenirs.

Afternoon

Stop to rest outside **Quincy Market** *(see p12)* before you begin your spree in earnest. Myriad name-brand shops such as Abercrombie & Fitch await. For local flavor try the **Bill Rodgers Running Center** (Quincy Market Pl), operated by the champion Boston Marathon runner, and **Whippoorwill Crafts** (126 South Market), which carries work by American craftspeople. All shopped out? Have an early dinner and make new friends at the communal tables of **Durgin-Park** (North Market, 617 227 2038). Order the gigantic prime rib and the Indian pudding (a cornmeal-molasses dish) for dessert. After dinner, laugh it up at the **Comedy Connection** (2nd floor, Quincy Market, 617 248 9700), where comics perform every night.

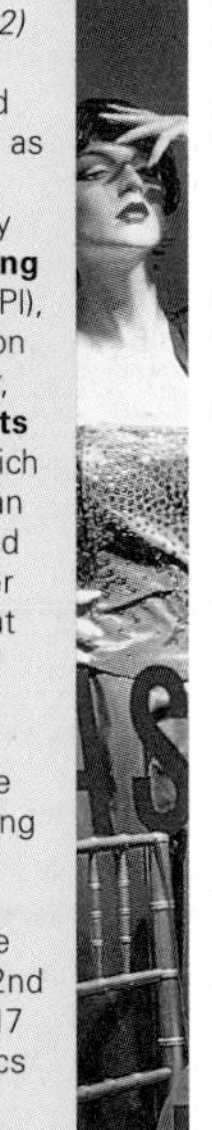

Following Pages **Custom House**

Left **Kingfish Hall** Center **A pint of Guinness** Right **Black Rose**

TOP 10 Bars & Clubs

1 Good Life Downtown
This retro lounge lizard bar-restaurant jumps after work and on weekend nights with downtown execs. Cosmopolitan cocktails are top notch *(see p46)*.

2 The Littlest Bar
The name is no joke. Three's company but four's a crowd. There are just two taps, and one of them is Guinness. Like the beer, the crowd tends to be Irish – well, Boston Irish *(see p47)*.

3 Times Irish Pub & Bar
You can usually get a table at this large pub. Settle in for a night of live music and taste some of the 20 beers on tap.
112 Broad St • Map R3

4 Limbo
How low can you go? The snazzy, gleaming Limbo bar is the Ladder District's trendiest and most frenetic scene. There's an upstairs dining section, too.
49 Temple Pl • Map P4

5 Silvertone Bar & Grill
This surprisingly unpretentious, contemporary jazz bar and casual restaurant makes an excellent place to sip good value wine, kick back, and engage in intelligent conversation with your neighbors.
69 Bromfield St • Map P3 • Closed Sun

6 The Rack
This well-mannered pool hall boasts a pair of full-service bars, 22 tables, and live music nightly. It is often frequented by pro athletes. No grungy dress.
24 Clinton St • Map Q2

7 Kingfish Hall
The first floor of this trendy fish restaurant hosts a dynamic bar scene replete with preening singles. Appropriately, one of the house cocktails is a "flirtini".
188 South Market • Map Q3

8 Parker's Bar
It's posh, it's civilized, and it's expensive. Relax in a brocade chair, sip a single malt, and light up a cigar without the high-octane haze found elsewhere downtown. *Omni Parker House Hotel, 60 School St • Map P3*

9 The International
Middle management guys loosen their ties and sip cocktails to mainstream rock upstairs. Downstairs, the polo-shirt crowd shoots pool and swigs Heineken.
184 High St • Map R3 • Closed Sun

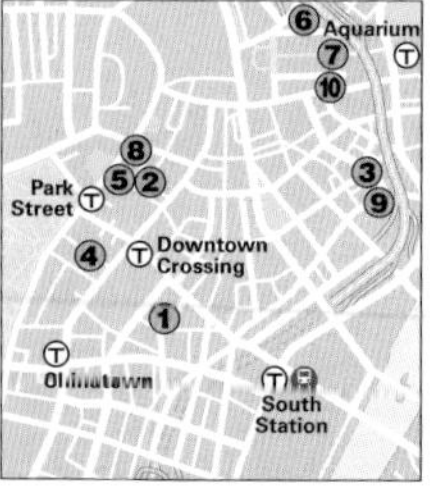

10 Black Rose
This pub has all the good points of a bar in Dublin's Temple Bar – Guinness, Harp, darts – along with the shortcomings (loud music and too many tourists).
160 State St • Map Q3

Note: *Unless otherwise specified, all clubs and bars are open daily; most close around 2am*

Price Categories

For a three [illegible] meal for one with half a bottle of wine (or equivalent meal), taxes and extra charges.

$	under $30
$$	$30–$45
$$$	$45–$60
$$$$	$60–$75
$$$$$	over $75

Left **The Vault**

Top 10 Restaurants for Luxury Dining

1 Locke-Ober

Chef-owner Lydia Shire champions rich and luscious foods. Boston Brahmins frequent Locke-Ober for the re-imagined American fare and original 1890s decor *(see p40)*.

2 Radius

Chef and co-owner Michael Schlow is a stickler for detail and he creates some of the most explosively sensual New American dishes in town *(see p41)*.

3 blu

Light, fresh, delicately nuanced, and artistically presented international cuisine is complemented by soaring post-modern architecture. *4 Avery St • Map P4 • 617 375 8550 • $$$$*

4 Julien

Crisp formality characterizes this sumptuous, traditional French restaurant. Think roasted rack of lamb crusted with Niçoise olives. Excellent wine list also. *250 Franklin St • Map Q4 • 617 451 1900 • Closed Sun, lunch Mon • $$$$$*

5 Mantra

Chef Thomas John wins national accolades for his Indian flavors and French technique. Fine food makes up for gimmicky decor. *52 Temple Pl • Map P4 • 617 542 8111 • Closed lunch Sat • $$$$$*

6 No 9 Park

Hobnob with Beacon Hill high flyers in this bold bistro overlooking Boston Common, where Mediterranean flavors meet an imaginative wine list. *9 Park St • Map P3 • 617 742 9991 • $$$$*

7 Maison Robert

This fine, French, family-run restaurant features classic fare in the dining room, lighter bistro meals in the café, and patio dining in summer. *45 School St • Map P3 • 617 227 3370 • $$$$*

8 The Vault

Chefs come and go, but The Vault maintains a high standard of New American cuisine. Lots of wines by the glass keep the bar scene lively. *105 Water St • Map Q3 • 617 292 9966 • No DA • $$$$*

9 Bay Tower Room

From the 33rd floor the best view in Boston is matched by impeccable service and a litany of luxury menu items, including caviar. *60 State St • Map Q3 • 617 723 1666 • Closed lunch • $$$$*

10 Spire

French Mediterranean dishes get a heavy dose of California produce and cooking trends. Stylish and chic but only for the big spender. *90 Tremont St • Map P3 • 617 772 0202 • $$$$$*

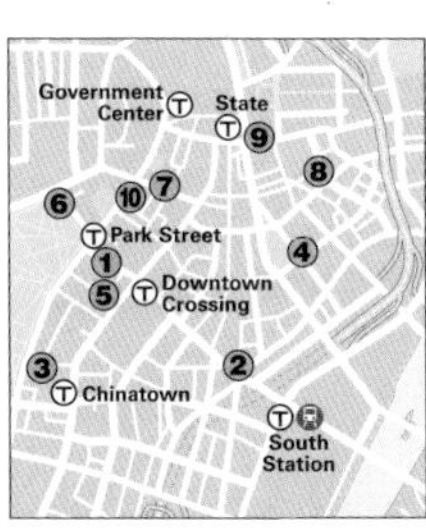

***Note:** Unless otherwise specified, restaurants are open lunch Mon–Fri, dinner Mon–Sat*

Left **Beach Street, Chinatown** Right **Victorian townhouses, South End**

Chinatown, the Theater District, & South End

BOSTON'S COMPACT CHINATOWN is the third most populous Chinese neighborhood in the US, concentrating a wealth of Asian experience in a small patch of real estate. Theater-goers find the proximity of Chinatown to the Theater District a boon for pre- and post-show dining. The Theater District itself is among the liveliest in the US, and its architecturally distinctive playhouses are nearly always active, often with local productions. Adjoining the Theater District to the south is South End, once an immigrant tenement area and now Boston's most diverse neighborhood by race, cultural background, and sexual orientation. The country's largest historical district of Victorian townhouses, South End has been undergoing gentrification since the 1980s and today is home to a burgeoning and energetic club, café, and restaurant scene.

Top 10 Attractions

1. Wang Center
2. Boston Center for the Arts
3. Tremont Street
4. Beach Street & Chinatown
5. Piano Row
6. South Station
7. Holy Cross Cathedral
8. Villa Victoria
9. Union Park Square
10. Southwest Corridor Park

Sign, Theater District

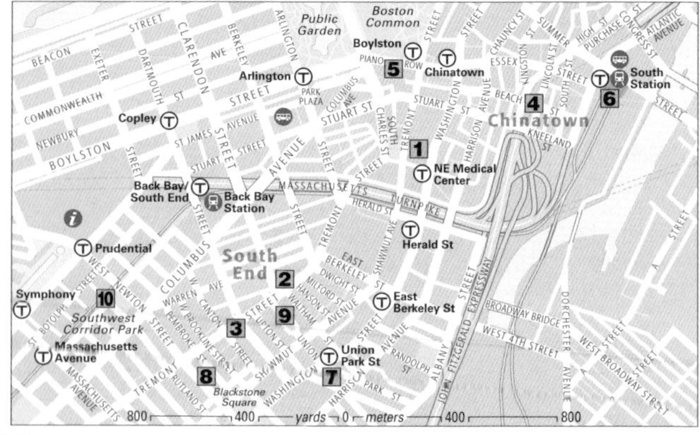

For bargain tickets and theater deals See p142

1 Wang Center

With a theater modeled on the Paris Opera House and a foyer inspired by the Palace of Versailles, the opulent Wang Center (opened 1925) is a grand venue for touring musicals, block buster concerts, and the prestigious Boston Ballet *(see p52)*.

2 Boston Center for the Arts

The massive Cyclorama building is the centerpiece of the BCA, a performing and visual arts complex dedicated to nurturing new talent. The center provides studio space to more than 50 artists, and its Mills Gallery mounts rotating visual arts exhibitions. The BCA's three theaters host some of the city's most avant-garde productions of dance, theater, and performance art *(see p52)*.

3 Tremont Street

The section of Tremont Street between East Berkeley and Massachusetts Avenue is the social and commercial heart of the South End. Many of the handsome brick and brownstone townhouses have been restored to circa-1890 perfection, some with a boutique or café added at street level; others remain boarded up and awaiting renovation. The liveliest corner of the South End is the intersection of Tremont with Clarendon and Union Park streets, where the Boston Center for the Arts and a plethora of restaurants and cafés create a compact entertainment and dining district. *Map N5–M6*

Grand Lobby, Wang Center

4 Beach Street & Chinatown

As the periphery of ethnic Chinatown becomes increasingly homogenized, Beach Street remains the purely Chinese heart of the neighborhood, home to the traditional apothecaries and other merchants who serve a primarily immigrant population. An ornate Dragon Gate at the base of Beach Street creates a ceremonial entrance to Chinatown. The wall behind the adjacent small park is painted with a dreamy mural of a Chinese sampan boat. *Map P5*

Contemporary city mural, Chinatown

For information on culinary tours of Chinatown **See p137**

Colonial Theatre, Piano Row

5 Piano Row

In the late 19th century, the HQs of leading piano makers Steinert, Vose, Starck, Mason and Hamlin, and Wurlitzer were located on the section of Boylston Street facing Boston Common, giving the block (now a historic district) its nickname as Piano Row. Nearly a century later, those Beaux Arts buildings still echo with music. The Colonial Theatre, its ornate interior fully restored to the sumptuous 1900 original, is an active venue for drama and musicals, while Boylston Place is a small-scale club and nightlife center. *Map N4*

Detail, Colonial Theatre

6 South Station

A brick temple to mass transportation, the Neo-Classical Revival South Station was erected in 1898 at the height of rail travel in the US, and was once the country's busiest train station. Following extensive restoration in 1989, it now serves as an Amtrak terminal for trains from the south and west of the city, as well as a "T" stop and a social and commercial center with a lively food court and occasional lunchtime concerts. *Map Q5*

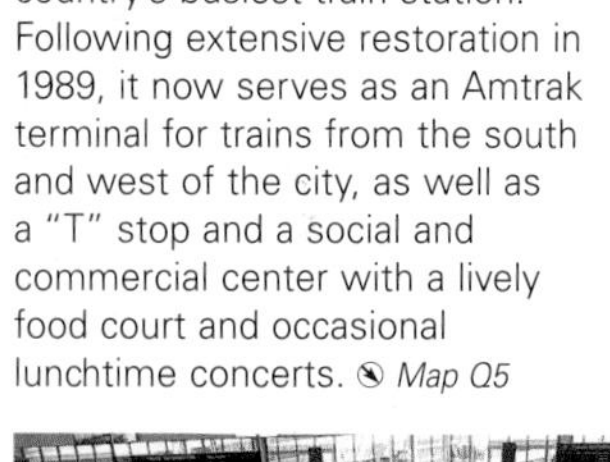

7 Holy Cross Cathedral

Holy Cross, the largest Roman Catholic church in Massachusetts, acts as the seat of the archbishop of Boston. The cathedral was constructed in 1875 (on the site of the municipal gallows) to serve the largely Irish-American workers who lived in the adjoining shantytown. Today the congregation is principally of Hispanic origin. Of note are the magnificent stained glass windows, which include rare colored glass imported from Munich in the 19th century, and the powerful Hook & Hastings organ, which seems to make every piece of Roxbury puddingstone in the building reverberate.
1400 Washington St • Map F6 • 617 542 5682 • Open 9:30am–4pm daily

8 Villa Victoria

Villa Victoria is a virtually self-contained, primarily Hispanic neighborhood that grew out of a unique collaboration among Puerto Rican community activists, flexible city planners, and visionary architects. With its low-rise buildings, narrow streets, and mom-and-pop stores, Villa Victoria replicates the feel of Puerto Rican community life. At its center, the Jorge Hernandez Cultural Center sponsors

South Station

Note: South End's Festival Betances (third weekend in July) is a celebration of Puerto Rican culture. Call 617 927 1730 for information

Stained glass, Jorge Hernandez Cultural Center, Villa Victoria

classes and exhibitions, and becomes a dance and social club in the evenings – one of the hottest places in Boston for Latin dance. *Area bounded by Shawmut Ave, Tremont St, W Newton St, & W Brookline St • Map F6* *Jorge Hernandez Cultural Center: 85 W Newton St • 617 867 9191*

9 Union Park Square

Constructed between 1857 and 1859, this small park surrounded by English-style brick row houses was built to contrast with the French-inspired grid layout of nearby Back Bay. Graced with lovely trees and fountains and verdant with a thick mat of grass, the square was one of the first areas in the South End to be gentrified. *Map F6*

10 Southwest Corridor Park

The first section of the five-mile (8-km) Southwest Corridor Park divides South End and Back Bay along the "T" orange line corridor. In the residential South End portion, a path strings together numerous small parks. Between Massachusetts Avenue and West Roxbury, the park broadens to include recreational amenities. *Map E6*

Exploring Chinatown & South End

Morning

Walk down Essex Street, ducking into Oxford Place to see the mural, *Travelers in an Autumn Landscape*, based on the famous scroll painting by the same name at the Museum of Fine Arts. Follow Essex to Edinboro Street, where you can commission your own traditional Chinese chop carving at **Oriental Arts and Crafts** *(see p108)*. The distinctive and colorful **Dragon Gate** to Chinatown stands at the corner of Edinboro Street and Beach Street, along with picturesque pagoda-style phone booths. Continue to Kneeland Street to peruse the contemporary couture of **Kim's Fashion Design** *(see p108)*. Then stop for a bowl of *pho* at **Hù Tiéu Nam-Vang** *(see p110)*.

Afternoon

Walk down Tremont Street to the South End, or hop on the "T" two stops to Back Bay Station. Go west on Columbus Avenue to see the elaborate bronze sculptures that tell the story of escaped slave Harriet Tubman, who led many others to freedom on the Underground Railroad, a series of hiding places in non-slave states. Back at Tremont Street, take a coffee and pastry break at **Garden of Eden** *(see p45)*. Visit the **Boston Center for the Arts** *(see p105)* to get a snapshot of local contemporary art at the Mills Gallery. Then, if you have extra time, take a spin around **Union Park Square**. Make sure you have dinner reservations to enjoy a sumptuous, romantic meal in the artfully decorated **Icarus** *(see p111)*.

***Note:** More than 200 South End artists' studios open to the public in September. Call the Boston Center for the Arts (617 426 5000)*

Left **Jack's Joke Shop** Center **Oriental Arts & Crafts** Right **Aunt Sadie's**

TOP 10 Shops

1 Jack's Joke Shop
"It's April Fool's every day," says the sign at Jack's, which has sold the likes of whoopee cushions, fake spills, Groucho Marx glasses, and hand buzzers since 1922. *226 Tremont St • Map N5 • Closed Sun*

2 J. M. W. Gallery
People come from miles around to this antiques dealer specializing in furniture in the Arts & Crafts and Mission styles as well as exquisite New England art pottery from the early decades of the 20th century. *144 Lincoln St • Map P5 • Closed Sun & Mon*

3 Vinh Kan Ginseng Co
There's a vast selection of teas from across Asia and half an aisle of ginseng products (both Asian and American). Get your herbalist's prescription from the Chinese apothecary here. *675 Washington St • Map P4*

4 Kim's Fashion Design
Designer Kim Pham has been creating timeless ready-to-wear and custom-tailored Asian fashion for more than two decades. Embroidered silks are a specialty. Also the place to get scarves and bags. *12 Kneeland St • Map P5*

5 Silky Way
This all-purpose martial arts store carries robes, belts, books, magazines, videos, plus a few swords and other weapons. *38 Kneeland St • Map P5 • Closed Sun & Mon*

6 Aunt Sadie's
Whimsical housewares fill this shop known for its hand-dipped and scented candles. Aromas include root beer, popcorn, and "home" (which smells like apple pie). *18 Union Park St • Map F6*

7 Hank Lee's Magic Factory
The hand can be quicker than the eye, especially with the aid of various patented tricks and props available at Hank's. Magician staff demonstrate the wares. *112 South St • Map Q5 • Closed Sun*

8 Mei Tung Oriental Food Super Market
This is home to an exhaustive selection of fresh, frozen, canned, and dried foods essential to cuisines from Singapore to Seoul. *109 Lincoln St • Map Q5*

9 Oriental Arts & Crafts
This tiny basement shop sells and frames contemporary prints from China among other things, and will carve your name in a stone seal for $10 per character. *11 Edinboro St • Map P5*

10 Syrian Grocery Importing Company
Harking back to the South End's days as a Middle Eastern immigrant neighborhood, this grocery sells southern and eastern Mediterranean essentials, from preserved lemons to rare Moroccan argan oil. *270 Shawmut Ave • Map G5 • Closed Mon*

***Note:** Unless otherwise specified shops are open daily*

Left **Delux Café** Center **Wally's Café** Right **Pravda 116**

TOP 10 Nightclubs & Bars

1 Pravda 116
A sleek and sophisticated bar in the front fades into a Euro-trance dance floor in the back. Very popular with the international set *(see p48)*.

2 Roxy
This massive two-story dance hall sometimes morphs into a live-performance concert venue for touring acts. High-energy Latin on Thursday, pop rock on Friday, techno on Saturday *(see p49)*.

3 Wally's Café
Exhale before you squeeze in the door at Wally's. This thin, chock-full sliver of a room is one of the best jazz bars in Boston, and has been since 1944. *427 Massachusetts Ave • Map E6*

4 Buzz @ Europa
The hottest DJ dance club in town designates Saturday nights for twentysomething boyz. Cool off between sets at the mahogany bar or in the martini lounge *(see p50)*.

5 Delux Café
Cheap drinks and an Elvis shrine lend an edge to the trendy scene here. It's good clean fun for hipster grandchildren of the beatniks *(see p46)*. *100 Chandler St • Map M6 • Closed Sun*

6 Aria
The lush life: sugar daddies and their trophies get on down amid red velvet and goth art. Admission on a busy night may depend on how hot you look. *246 Tremont St • Map N5 • Closed Sun & Mon*

7 Venu
Music varies each night of the week, but it's always the same Prada-Armani-Versace clad crowd. The Art Deco bar makes for a beautiful look. *100 Warrenton St • Map N5 • Closed Sun & Mon*

8 Jacque's
This two-level pioneer drag queen bar features female impersonators on weekdays and edgy rock bands on weekends. Set aside your preconceptions and relax *(see p50)*.

9 Encore Lounge
Live entertainment – jazz, blues, show tunes – creates a nice backdrop for this swank hotel bar. *275 Tremont St • Map N5*

10 The Big Easy
A rowdy good time is to be had at this New Orleans by way of Boston dance club, with cheap drinks and a brazen crowd. Live cover bands alternate with a DJ on weekends. *1 Boylston Pl • Map N5 • Closed Sun–Thu*

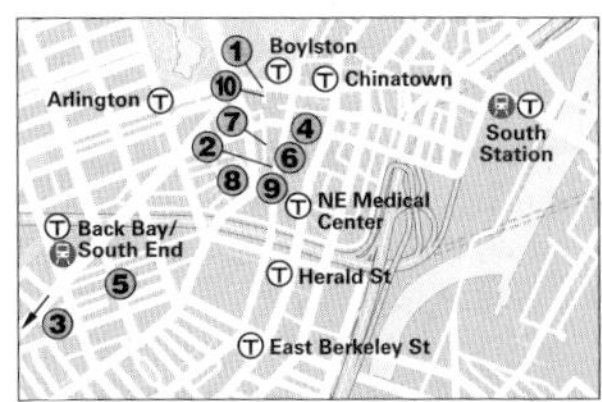

Note: *Most bars stop serving at around 1am from Sun–Thu, around 2am on weekends*

Left **Restaurant sign, Chinatown** Right **Pho Republique**

TOP 10 Asian Restaurants

1 Jumbo Seafood
Outstanding Guandong-style seafood and perfect treatment of whole fish Hunan-style. Most dishes with hot pickles and mustards are exceptional *(see p43).*

2 Chau Chow City
Contemporary Hong Kong seafood reigns on the first two levels of this multi-story dining emporium. Some of Boston's best dim sum is served on the top floor. *83 Essex St • Map P4 • 617 [illegible] • No DA • $*

3 Ginza
This slice of Tokyo in Boston comes alive after midnight, as bar-goers pile in for the outstanding *maki* rolls and Japanese hot pots. *16 Hudson St • Map P6 • 617 338 2261 • No DA • $$*

4 Penang
Nominally "pan-Asian," Penang has a chiefly Malay menu, ranging from inexpensive noodle staples to more contemporary concoctions. *685 Washington St • Map N5 • 617 451 6372 • $*

5 Jae's
Jae's light, fresh dishes drawn from Korea, Japan, China, and Southeast Asia attract the young and beautiful who want to stay that way. *520 Columbus Ave • Map M5 • 617 421 9405 • $$*

6 New Shanghai
Many Boston chefs flock to New Shanghai to taste chef C. K. Sau's clever use of New England ingredients in Shanghai cuisine. Dim sum served on Sundays (but no cart service). *21 Hudson St • Map P6 • 617 338 6688 • No DA • $$*

7 King Fung Garden
Mongolian hot pots are the big draw in this modest restaurant with a decor straight out of 1960s Taipei. *74 Kneeland St • Map P5 • 617 357 5262 • No credit cards • No DA • $*

8 Pho Republique
Hipsters come in droves for the French-Vietnamese food – duck crepes, braised spareribs – the atmosphere, and the mango martinis. *1415 Washington St • Map F6 • 617 262 0005 • Closed lunch • $$*

9 Buddha's Delight
Vegan food in the tradition of Chinese and Vietnamese temple cuisine wins over even the most devoted of carnivores. *3 Beach St • Map P5 • 617 451 2395 • No DA • $*

10 Hù Tiéu Nam-Vang
House specialties are beef and noodle soups with side bowls of chopped basil and mung bean sprouts. *7 Beach St • Map P5 • 617 422 0501 • No credit cards • No DA • $*

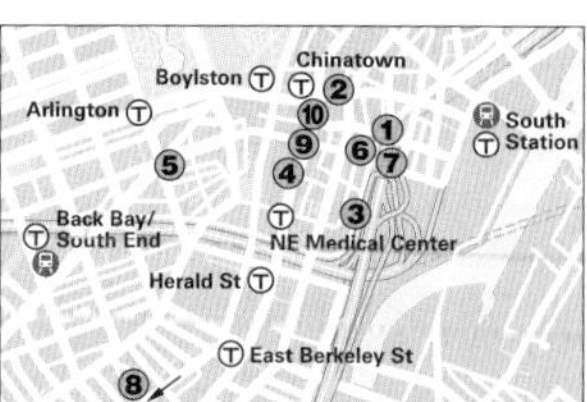

Price Categories

For a three-course meal for one with half a bottle of wine (or equivalent meal), taxes, and extra charges.

$	under $30
$$	$30–$45
$$$	$45–$60
$$$$	$60–$75
$$$$$	over $75

Left **Aquitaine**

Top 10 Restaurants

1 Hamersley's Bistro
French provincial dishes are both simple and sophisticated, with Gordon Hamersley's signature lemon-infused chicken as the model *(see p40).*

2 Bob the Chef's
American soul food (cornbread, collard greens, ribs, and barbecue) served with a healthy side of live jazz draws a stylish crowd. *604 Columbus Ave • Map E6 • 617 536 6204 • Closed Mon • $*

3 Claremont Café
Some locals must fast on Mondays, since they eat all their other meals – even breakfast – at this family-run local bistro. The emphasis is on Latin American and Mediterranean flavors. *535 Columbus Ave • Map E6 • 617 247 9001 • Closed Mon & dinner Sun • $$*

4 Tremont 647
Chef Andy Husbands' New American cooking favors big portions, bold flavors, and lots of smoke with the meat. The bar is a magnet for local trendsetters. *647 Tremont St • Map F6 • 617 266 4600 • Closed lunch Mon–Sat • $$$*

5 Les Zygomates
French bistro fare, 30 wines by the glass, and live jazz *(see p46).*

6 Bomboa
Mediterranean cooking by way of Brazil results in lively, spicy fare such as crispy red snapper marinated in vanilla and oregano. *35 Stanhope St • Map M5 • 617 236 6363 • Closed lunch • $$$*

7 Troquet
A stylish restaurant where wines get top billing, with suggested small plates of French bistro fare to accompany each flight of drinks. *140 Boylston St • Map N5 • 617 695 9463 • Closed lunch & Mon • $$$*

8 Masa
Refined New American dishes with southwestern accents are complemented by killer margaritas, colorful decor, and good wines. *439 Tremont St • Map N6 • 617 338 8884 • Closed lunch • $$$*

9 Icarus
South End's most romantic restaurant serves sophisticated, inventive New American cuisine. *3 Appleton St • Map N6 • 617 426 1790 • Closed lunch • No DA • $$$*

10 Aquitaine
A Parisian-style bistro popular for its snazzy wine bar and its French market cooking. Black truffle vinaigrette makes Aquitaine's steak-frites Boston's best. *569 Tremont St • Map F5 • 617 424 8577 • Closed lunch Mon–Sat • $$$*

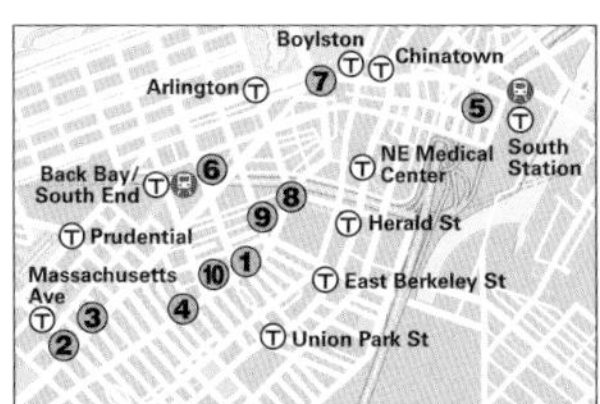

Note: *Unless otherwise specified all restaurants are open daily for lunch and dinner*

Left **Photographic Resource Center, Boston University** Center **Heron, Back Bay Fens** Right **Jordan Hall**

Kenmore & the Fenway

ON DAYS WHEN THE RED SOX *are playing a home baseball game at Fenway Park, Kenmore Square is packed with fans. By night, Kenmore becomes the jump-off point for a night of dancing, drinking, and socializing at the myriad clubs on Lansdowne Street. Yet for all of Kenmore's genial rowdiness, it is also the gateway into the sedate parkland of the Back Bay Fens and the stately late-19th- and early-20th-century buildings along The Fenway. The Fenway neighborhood extends all the way southeast to Huntington Avenue, aka the "Avenue of the Arts," which links key cultural centers such as Symphony Hall, Huntington Theatre, Museum of Fine Arts, Massachusetts College of Art, and the not-to-be-missed Isabella Stewart Gardner Museum along a tree-lined boulevard.*

Symphony Hall

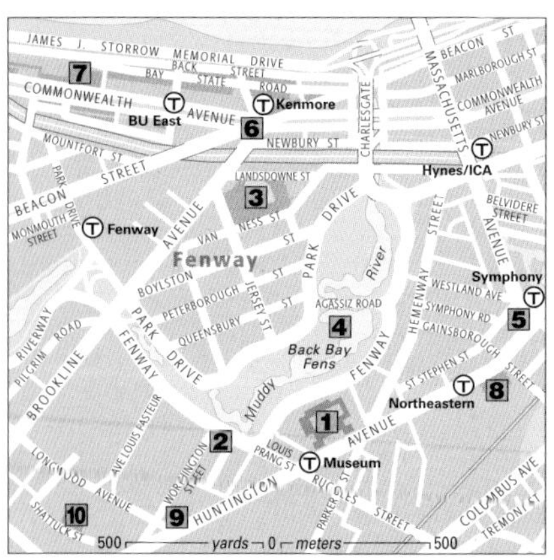

Top 10 Attractions

1. Museum of Fine Arts
2. Isabella Stewart Gardner Museum
3. Fenway Park
4. Back Bay Fens
5. Symphony Hall
6. Kenmore Square
7. Boston University
8. Jordan Hall
9. Massachusetts College of Art Galleries
10. Warren Anatomical Museum

***Note:** Take the E branch of the green line for the museums along Huntington Avenue*

Back Bay Fens

1 Museum of Fine Arts

One of the most comprehensive fine arts museums in the country, the MFA is especially renowned for its collections of French Impressionism and of ancient Egyptian and Nubian art and artifacts. Its Asian art holdings are said to be the largest in the US *(see pp22–5)*.

2 Isabella Stewart Gardner Museum

This Fenway museum, in a faux Venetian palace, represents the exquisite personal tastes of its founder, Isabella Stewart Gardner, who was one of the country's premier art collectors at the end of the 19th century *(see pp28–9)*.

3 Fenway Park

Built in 1912, the home field of the Boston Red Sox is the oldest surviving park in major league baseball, and aficionados insist that it's also the finest. An odd-shaped parcel of land gives the intimate park quirky features, such as the high, green-painted wall in left field, affectionately known as "the Green Monster." Although previous owners threatened to abandon Fenway, the current ones hope to enlarge the park to accommodate the many loyal Sox fans. Behind-the-scenes tours of the park include areas normally closed to the public, like the dugouts and private boxes. *4 Yawkey Way • Map D5 • 617 267 8661 for tickets, 617 236 6666 for tours • Tours during season (Apr–Sep): game days 9am, 10am, 11am, noon; 1pm; non-game days additional tour at 2pm • Adm*

Fenway Park

4 Back Bay Fens

This lush ribbon of grassland, marshes, and stream banks follows Muddy River and forms one link in the Emerald Necklace of parks *(see p15)*. The enclosed James P. Kelleher Rose Garden in the center of the Fens provides a perfect spot for quiet contemplation. A path runs from Kenmore Square to the museums and galleries on Huntington Avenue, which makes a pleasant short cut through the Fens. *Bounded by Park Dr & The Fenway • Map D5–D6*

5 Symphony Hall

The restrained Italian Renaissance exterior of this 1900 concert hall barely hints at the acoustic perfection of the interior hall as designed by Harvard physics professor Walter Clement Sabine. Home of the Boston Symphony Orchestra, the hall's 2,361 seats are usually sold out for their extensive season of classical concerts, as well as for the lighter orchestral fare of the Boston Pops *(see p52)*.

For more on Boston's performance arts venues **See pp52–3**

Kenmore Square

6 Kenmore Square

Largely dominated by Boston University, Kenmore Square is now being transformed from a student ghetto into an extension of upmarket Back Bay, losing some of its funky character but gaining élan in the process. As the public transportation gateway to Fenway Park, the square swarms with baseball fans and sidewalk vendors, rather than students, on game days. The most prominent landmark of the square is the CITGO sign, its 5,878 glass tubes pulsing with red, white, and blue neon from dusk until midnight. *Time* magazine designated this sign an "objet d'heart" because it was so beloved by Bostonians that they prevented its dismantling in 1983. *Map D5*

7 Boston University

Founded as a Methodist Seminary in 1839, BU was chartered as a university in 1869. Today it enrolls approximately 28,000 students from all 50 states and some 125 countries. The scattered colleges and schools were consolidated at the Charles River Campus in 1966. Both sides of Commonwealth Avenue are lined with distinctive university buildings and sculptures. The Special Collections department of the Mugar Memorial Library is big on the memorabilia of show biz figures, displayed on a rotating basis. Artifacts include Gene Kelly's Oscar and a number of Bette Davis's film scripts. The department also exhibits selections from its holdings of rare manuscripts and books. The Photographic Resource Center, a focus for Boston's considerable photographic community, frequently mounts challenging exhibitions of local and international photographers. *Special Collections of the Mugar Memorial Library: 771 Commonwealth Ave • Map C4 • 617 353 3696 • Exhibit rooms open 9am–4:30pm Mon–Fri • Free* *Photographic Resource Center: 602 Commonwealth Ave • Map C5 • 617 353 0700 • Open noon–5pm Tue–Sun (to 8pm Thu) • Adm*

Mugar Memorial Library, Boston University

8 Jordan Hall

The New England Conservatory of Music's 1,013-seat concert hall opened in 1903 and underwent an $8.2 million restoration in 1995. Musicians frequently praise its acoustics, heralding Jordan "the Stradivarius of concert halls." Hundreds of free classical concerts are performed at this National Historic Landmark hall every year *(see p52)*.

Huntington Gallery, Massachusetts College of Art

9 Massachusetts College of Art Galleries

The Huntington and Bakalar galleries in the South Building of the Massachusetts College of Art mount some of Boston's most dynamic exhibitions of contemporary visual art. It is the only independent state-supported art college in the US and exhibitions tend to emphasize avant-garde experimentation as well as social commentary and documentary. *621 Huntington Ave • Map D6 • 617 879 7337 • Open 10am–6pm Mon–Fri, 11am–5pm Sat • Free*

10 Warren Anatomical Museum

Established in 1847 from the private holdings of Dr. John Collins Warren, this museum contains the former anatomical teaching collections of the Harvard Medical School, including clinical examples of rare deformities and diseases. Among the displays are several delicate skeletons of stillborn conjoined twins. *10 Shattuck St • Map C6 • 617 432 6196 • Open 9am–5pm Mon–Fri • Free*

A Day of the Arts

Afternoon

Take the green line "T" (B train) to Boston University Central and make your way to the Special Collections at the **Mugar Memorial Library**, part of Boston University, for a glimpse of Fred Astaire's dancing shoes and other show business ephemera. Then head west toward **Kenmore Square** to explore the stores, including the encyclopedic Boston University Bookstore (660 Beacon St), directly under the CITGO sign. Stroll along Brookline Avenue to **Fenway Park** for a tour of the stadium *(see p113)* and then take Yawkey Way to the **Back Bay Fens** *(see p113)*, where you can rest beneath the wings of the angel on the Veteran's Memorial. Then continue to the **Museum of Fine Arts** *(see p22–5)* to view the outstanding art collections – from ancient Egyptian artifacts to contemporary installations. Afterwards, follow The Fenway three blocks left to continue your immersion in art at the gorgeous **Isabella Stewart Gardner Museum** *(see pp28–9)*. Then walk down to the corner of Westland and Massachusetts avenues for a spicy Asian meal at **Tigerlily** *(see p117)*.

Evening

You can pack in a full evening of entertainment by taking in a recital at **Jordan Hall** *(see p52)*. When the final applause has died down, catch a cab to Lansdowne Street, where the evening will be just beginning. Dance the night away at any of the many nightclubs, including **Avalon** *(see p116)*.

Left & Center **Boston Billiard Club** Right **Axis**

TOP 10 Nightclubs & Bars

1 Avalon

Superstar DJs rank Avalon as one of the top US dance clubs, and the animated weekend throngs reveal why. Avalon also stages live concerts from hard rock to the hippest of hip-hop *(see p48).*

2 Axis

Avalon's little sibling picks up a more collegiate crowd for its pulsating dance sessions: Friday nights have an underground feel with DJs plucked from around the globe. *13 Lansdowne St • Map D5 • Closed Sun, Tue & Wed*

3 The Modern

This glam martini bar offers a more poised alternative on Lansdowne Street for local urbanites. The swank Latin night on Fridays draws a hip crowd. *36 Lansdowne St • Map D5 • Closed Sun & Mon*

4 Cask 'n' Flagon

At Fenway's premier sports bar, fans hoist a cold one and debate the merits of the Sox manager's latest tactics. *62 Brookline Ave • Map D5 • Closed Sun*

5 Boston Beer Works

This cavernous brew pub specializes in lighter American ales and serves giant plates of ribs and chicken that can easily feed two ravenous Red Sox fans. *61 Brookline Ave • Map D5*

6 Bill's Bar

Despite nightly live music (you name it, they program it) and hardcore dance DJs on Saturdays, Bill's regulars view it as a place to drink first and dance later. *5½ Lansdowne St • Map D5*

7 7 Embassy

Narrow lounge downstairs has neo-Deco luxury look, but the prime (young and wealthy) clientele cluster on the dance floor upstairs. *36 Lansdowne St • Map D5 • Closed Sun–Mon & Wed*

8 Boston Billiard Club

Top brand liquors and an extensive martini menu set BBC apart from less swanky pool halls. Clientele ranges from fraternity boys to young lawyers. *126 Brookline Ave • Map D5*

9 Sophia's

Sophia's gets its sleek crowd moving to salsa, merengue, and rumba on three dance floors. On warm nights, the sangria-fueled action spills out onto the roof deck. *1270 Boylston St • Map D5 • Closed Sun–Tue*

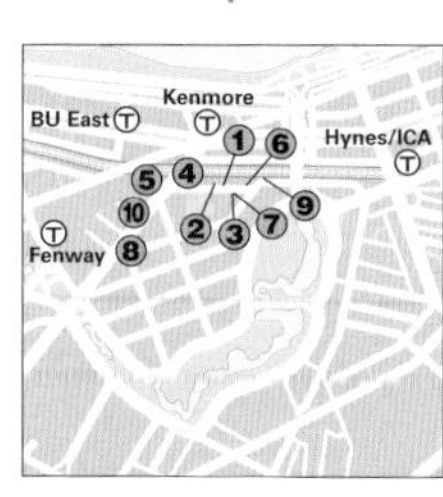

10 B. B. Wolf

Featuring light American ales brewed nearby at Boston Beer works, B. B. Wolf draws a quieter crowd than the bars located near Fenway Park. *109 Brookline Ave • Map D5*

Note: *Unless otherwise specified nightclubs and bars are open nightly*

Price Categories

For a three course meal for one with half a bottle of wine (or equivalent meal), taxes and extra charges.

$	under $30
$$	$30–$45
$$$	$45–$60
$$$$	$60–$75
$$$$$	over $75

Left **Linwood Grill**

Top 10 Restaurants

1 Buteco
One-of-a-kind, homey Buteco dishes up the rich African-tinged Brazilian cuisine of Bahia, including *feijoada*, a hearty black-bean and meat stew. *130 Jersey St • Map D6 • 617 247 9508 • $*

2 Elephant Walk
Chef Nadsa de Monteiro has shown Bostonians just how sophisticated Cambodian food can be. Served in an airy bamboo-trimmed room. *900 Beacon St • Map C5 • 617 247 1500 • Closed lunch Sat & Sun • $$*

3 Tigerlily
This pan-Asian spot is at its best with such Malaysian dishes as jumbo shrimps battered with coconut. Reasonable prices make it a student favorite. *8 Westland Ave • Map E5 • 617 267 8881 • $*

4 Linwood Grill
Don't let the faux Dixie decor fool you: Linwood makes a mean Carolina-style pulled pork barbecue. *69 Kilmarnock St • Map D6 • 617 247 8099 • Closed lunch Sat • $$*

5 Audubon Circle Restaurant
Trendy sandwiches and heavenly burgers make this genteel spot a step above the rest. *838 Beacon St • Map C5 • 617 421 1910 • Closed lunch Sat & Sun • $*

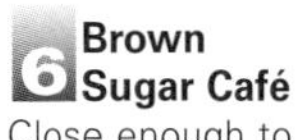

6 Brown Sugar Café
Close enough to Fenway Park to grab a tasty pre- or post-game meal, Brown Sugar sets the Boston standard for subtly seasoned Thai food. *129 Jersey St • Map D6 • 617 266 2928 • $*

7 El Pelon Taquería
There's no beer to wash it down with, but El Pelon produces authentic Mexican and Tex-Mex specialties. *92 Peterborough St • Map D5 • 617 262 9090 • $*

8 Betty's Wok & Noodle
The diner decor is half the fun. The other half is picking a rice or noodle base, a protein, and a sauce from the menu to make your own combos. *250 Huntington Ave • Map E6 • 617 424 1950 • $$*

9 Fraser Garden Court Terrace
This attractive dining room at the Museum of Fine Arts *(see pp22–5)* focuses on light and healthy cuisine like crisp salads and pastas tossed with fresh vegetables. *465 Huntington Ave • Map D6 • 617 369 3935 • Closed dinner Sat–Wed, lunch Mon & Tue • $$*

10 Naha Café
Although tiny Naha has fine tempura and noodle dishes, fans of Japanese food come here for the sushi: it's fresh, delicious, and affordable. *90 Peterborough St • Map D5 • 617 536 6688 • Closed Sun & lunch Sat • $*

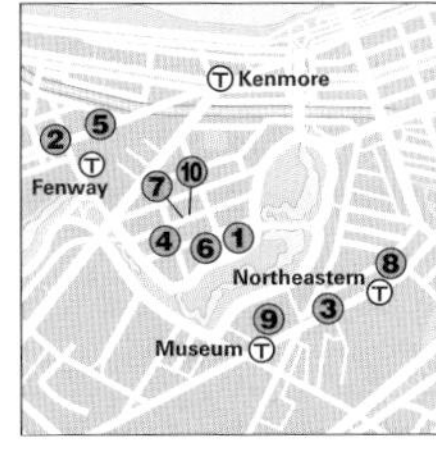

Note: Unless otherwise specified restaurants are open for lunch and dinner daily

Left **Mural, Inman Square** Center **Musician, Harvard Square** Right **Museum of Science**

Cambridge & Somerville

HARVARD MAY HOLD CAMBRIDGE'S *undeniable claim to worldwide fame, but that is not to diminish the city's vibrant neighborhoods, superb restaurants, unique shops, and colorful bars lying just beyond the school's gates. Harvard Square, with its international newsstands, name-brand shopping, and numerous coffee houses, is a heady mix of urban bohemia and Main Street USA. And despite its 350-plus years, Cambridge is one of the most youthful cities in the country, welcoming tens of thousands of college students to Harvard, the Massachusetts Institute of Technology (MIT), and a handful of other schools every fall. To the northwest, the heavily residential city of Somerville is distinguished by its tightly knit European-style squares, where tourists seldom tread and local character abounds.*

Harvard Square

Top 10 Attractions

1. Harvard University
2. Harvard Art Museums
3. Peabody & Natural History Museums
4. Charles River Banks
5. Museum of Science
6. Davis Square
7. Inman Square
8. Longfellow House
9. Cambridge Multicultural Arts Center
10. Massachusetts Institute of Technology (MIT)

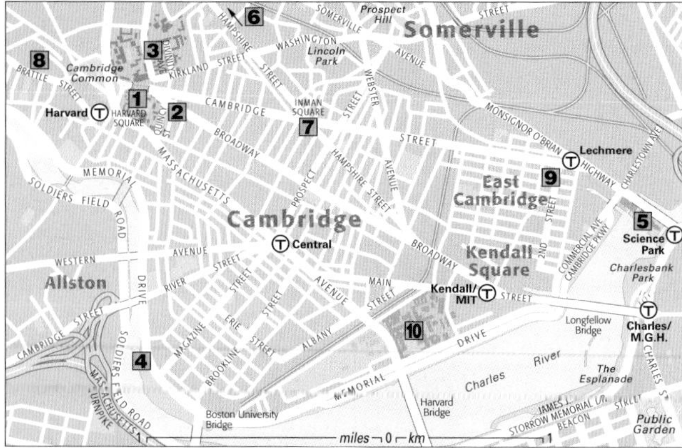

Note: *Cambridge is served by the "T" red line; Somerville is best accessed by bus*

1 Harvard University

While its stellar reputation might suggest visions of ivory towers in the sky, Harvard is a surprisingly accessible, welcoming place. Too often, visitors limit themselves to what is visible from the Yard: Massachusetts Hall, the Widener Library, maybe University Hall. But with top-notch museums, the eclectic Harvard Square, and daring performing arts spaces such as the Loeb Drama Center and Memorial Hall's Sanders Theater *(see p52)* lying just beyond the university, Harvard provides every incentive to linger a while *(see p16–19)*.

2 Harvard Art Museums

Harvard's three art museums, the Fogg, Busch-Reisinger, and Sackler, may be radically different but they share the privilege of exhibiting one of the world's finest collegiate art collections. While the Fogg boasts the city's most extensive Picasso collection, the Busch-Reisinger downstairs leans toward the Bauhaus and German expressionist movements. And just down the block, the Sackler frequently rotates its impressive holdings of Egyptian and later Indian art *(see p16–19)*. *Map B1* *Fogg & Busch-Reisinger, 32 Quincy St • 617 495 9400* *Sackler Museum, 485 Broadway • 617 495 9400 • All open 10–5pm Mon–Sat, 1–5pm Sun • Adm*

Charles River Banks

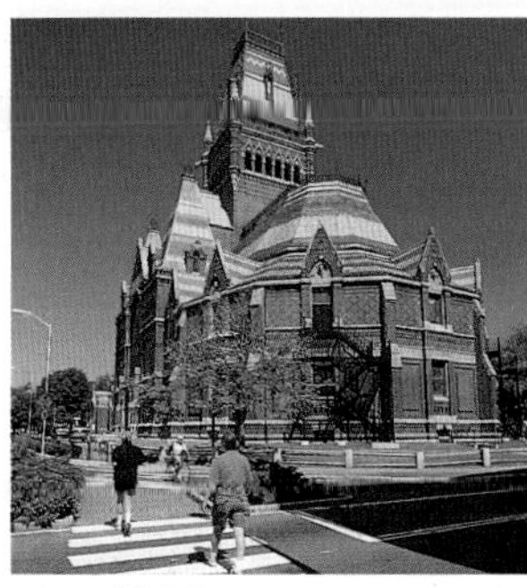

Memorial Hall, Harvard University

3 Peabody & Natural History Museums

Its ongoing commitment to research aside, the Peabody excels at illustrating how interactions between distinct cultures have in turn affected peoples' lives and livelihoods. Its North American Indian exhibit displays artifacts that reflect the aftermath of encounters between white Europeans and Native Americans. Meanwhile, the university's Natural History museum delves even deeper in time, exhibiting eons-old natural wonders *(see p16–19)*.
Peabody Museum: 11 Divinity Ave • Map B1 • 617 496 1027 • Open 9am–5pm daily • Adm *Natural History Museum: 26 Oxford St • Map B1 • 617 495 3045 • Open 9am–5pm daily • Adm*

4 Charles River Banks

Whether you're cheering the rowers of the Head of the Charles Regatta *(see p55)* or watching the "T" cross Longfellow Bridge through a barrage of snowflakes, the banks of the Charles River offer a fantastic vantage point for taking in Boston's celebrated scenes. In summer, the adjacent Memorial Drive becomes a sea of strollers, joggers, and rollerbladers *(see p123)*. *Map B2–F3*

Note: *Combined entrance tickets for the Fogg, Busch-Reisinger, and Sackler museums are available*

Local Stages

The performing arts form an integral part of the character of Cambridge and Somerville. The ornate Somerville Theater *(see p53)* draws nationally recognized musical acts, while the Loeb Drama Center *(see p53)* stages The American Repertory Theatre's daring, top-notch productions. And Harvard student-produced pieces grace the Hasty Pudding Theatre's stage (12 Holyoke St, Cambridge, 617 495 5205).

5 Museum of Science

Exploring the cosmos in the Hayden Planetarium, hitting the high notes on a musical staircase, experiencing larger-than-life IMAX films in the Mugar Omni Theater – the Museum of Science knows how to make learning enjoyable. In addition to these attractions, the museum frequently hosts blockbuster touring exhibits like *Alice the Tyrannosaurus Rex*. And on Friday nights, staff lead free star gazing sessions on the museum roof. *Science Park • Map N1 • 617 723 2500 • Open 9am–5pm Mon–Thu, Sat & Sun (to 7pm Jul–Sep) 9am–9pm Fri • Adm*

6 Davis Square

With its cooler-than-thou coffee shops, lively bar scene, affordable restaurants, and the renowned Somerville Theater *(see p53)*, Davis Square, Somerville stands as the metro area's most desirable neighborhood for many young Bostonians. And with prestigious Tufts University just a 10-minute walk away, the square's youthful spirit is in a constant state of replenishment.

7 Inman Square

Oft-overlooked Inman Square is possibly Cambridge's best-kept secret. Boasting such renowned restaurants and cafés as the East Coast Grill and 1369, an ace jazz club (Ryles; *see p49*), plus the inspired lunacy of the Improv-Boston comedy theater, Inman handsomely rewards those willing to take the road less traveled to experience a real-deal Cambridge 'hood. *Map D1*

8 Longfellow House

Poet Henry Wadsworth Longfellow can be credited with helping to shape Boston's – and America's – collective identity. His poetic documentation of Paul Revere's midnight ride *(see p38)* immortalized both him and his subject. In 1837, Longfellow took up residence in this house in the country's academic heart, a few blocks from Harvard Yard. He was not the house's first illustrious resident. General George Washington headquartered and planned the 1776 siege of Boston in these rooms. The building is preserved with furnishings of both Longfellow's and Washington's heydays, and houses the poet's personal archives. *105 Brattle St • Map A1 • 617 876 4491 • Open 10am–4:30pm Wed–Sun • Adm*

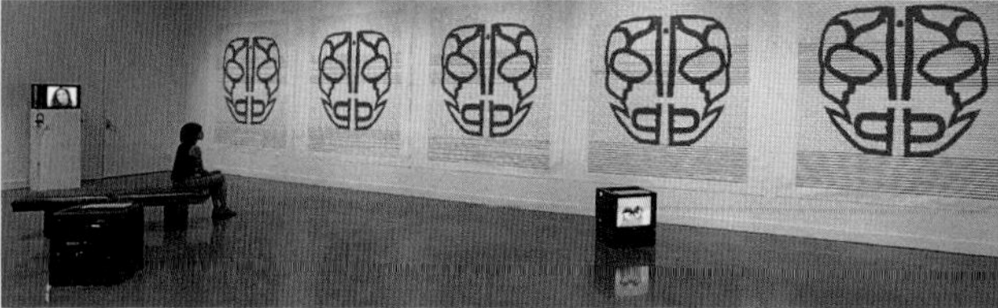

Amorales vs Amorales **by Carlos Amorales, at MIT's List Visual Arts Center**

Museum of Science

9 Cambridge Multicultural Arts Center

Housed in a beautiful 19th-century courthouse, the CMAC presents performance and visual art exhibitions which promote cross-cultural exchange. A unique feature is the encouragement of dialogue between audience and artist after performances and openings.
41 2nd St • Map F2 • 617 577 1400 • Open 9:30am–5:30pm Mon–Fri • Free

10 Massachusetts Institute of Technology (MIT)

Not to be outdone by its irrepressible Ivy League neighbor, MIT has been the country's leading technical university since its founding in 1861. This school of improbable theorems and calculator-toting world shapers offers many places of interest. Its List Visual Arts Center exhibits work that comments on technology or employs it in fresh, surprising ways. Also of note is the MIT Museum, which engages visitors with interactive exhibits on artificial intelligence, holography, and the world's first computers. *77 Massachusetts Ave • Map D3 • 617 253 1000 • List Visual Arts Center: 20 Ames St, Cambridge • 617 253 4680 • Open noon–6pm Tue–Sun (to 8pm Fri) • Free • MIT Museum: 265 Massachusetts Ave • 617 253 4444 • Open 10am–5pm Tue–Fri, noon–5pm Sat–Sun • Adm*

The Cambridge Curriculum

Morning

Call the Museum of Science early to learn what features are playing at the Omni Theater and book tickets over the phone for an afternoon show. Then begin your morning with a stack of pancakes at Davis Square's legendary **Rosebud Diner**. Next, ride the "T" inbound to Harvard and head straight to **Out of Town News** (0 Harvard Sq) to peruse their mind-boggling selection of international magazines and newspapers. Take time in Harvard Yard *(see p16)* to stop at the **John Harvard Statue** *(see p16)*, in front of Charles Bulfinch's University Hall, to scrutinize its "three lies." Then return to Massachusetts Avenue and walk east to Quincy Street for a dose of superlative artwork at the **Fogg** and **Busch-Reisinger Museums** *(see p17)*.

Afternoon

Head back on Massachusetts Avenue toward the square to **Bartley's Burger Cottage** (1246 Massachusetts Ave) for a lunch of freshly prepared specialty burgers and irresistible sweet potato fries. You can fully digest on the 20 minute "T" ride to Science Park. Head to the **Museum of Science's** Omni Theater and claim your tickets. After an exhilarating, in-your-face feature, retrace your steps toward Cambridge on the "T" as far as Kendall Square. At Kendall, walk west to **Toscanini's** *(see p45)* for a scoop of ice cream so rich that it could be mistaken for a priceless work of art.

***Note:** MIT is a scenic 20-minute walk from Downtown Boston across Longfellow Bridge*

Left **Curious George Goes to WordsWorth** Right **Garment District**

Top 10 Offbeat Shops

1 Garment District
For guys and gals after vintage duds, behold your personal nirvana. More than 40,000 pieces of vintage and contemporary clothing await at this colossus of fashionable kitsch. *200 Broadway, Cambridge*

2 Revolution Books
Che Guevara and Mao Tse Tung are alive and well here. You can read up on Communism and purchase left-leaning T-shirts, posters, buttons, and stickers. *1156 Massachusetts Ave, Cambridge • Map B2 • Closed Mon*

3 Abodeon
Abodeon stocks home furnishings of the decidedly retro variety. Items include 1940s rolling chaise longes, vintage cocktail services, and even the occasional Wurlitzer jukebox. *1731 Massachusetts Ave, Cambridge*

4 Curious George Goes to WordsWorth
An outpost of Brattle Street's WordsWorth Books, this playfully decorated children's bookstore pays homage to the timeless travails of its mischievous namesake. *1 JFK St, Cambridge • Map B1*

5 Hubba Hubba
If only Cambridge's Puritanical founders could have seen it: fetishist accessories, spiked belts, sexy leather corsets, and not-so-innocent toys line the shelves of this risqué Central Square boutique. *534 Massachusetts Ave, Cambridge • Map C3–D3 • Closed Sun*

6 Million Year Picnic
New England's oldest comic bookstore keeps its faithful customers happy with an extensive back-issue selection, rare imports, and all the latest indie comics. *99 Mt Auburn St, Cambridge • Map B2*

7 Disc Diggers
This Davis Square gem fulfills the needs of even the most discriminating music shopper without taxing the wallet. Browse thousands of new and used indie, cult-classic, and mainstream discs. *401 Highland Ave, Somerville*

8 Marathon Sports
Whether you're a casual jogger or a Boston Marathon hopeful, this runners-only store will get you outfitted. *1654 Massachusetts Ave, Cambridge • Map B1*

9 Blades Board & Skate
Everything for the blader, rider, and skater: Shorty's decks, K2 snowboards, and Salomon and Rollerblade inline skates. *38 JFK St, Cambridge • Map B1*

10 Porter Exchange Mall
Take a trip to Tokyotown in this renovated 1928 Deco building, boasting a Japanese-style noodle hall and gift shops with all forms of Far Eastern ephemera. *1815 Massachusetts Ave, Cambridge*

Note: *Shops are open daily unless otherwise specified*

Left **1369 Coffee House** Right **The Pit**

TOP 10 Places to Mix with the Locals

1 Memorial Drive
Memorial Drive is a magnet for joggers and rollerbladers. On summer Saturdays, the road closes to vehicular traffic and becomes the city's best people-watching spot. *Map B4–F3*

2 The Pit
On and around this sunken brick platform, street musicians, protesters, punk rockers, and uncategorizables create a scene worthy of a *Life* magazine spread. *bounded by JFK St & Massachusetts Ave, Cambridge • Map B1*

3 The Neighborhood
Sunday brunch at the Neighborhood brings throngs intent on securing seating beneath the outdoor grape arbors. Equally coveted are the house's Portuguese breakfast bread platters. *25 Bow St, Somerville • Map D1 • 617 628 2151 • $*

4 1369 Coffee House
Set in the somewhat detached Inman Square, this branch of 1369 has poetry readings, mellow music, and courteous staff, which give it a neighborly atmosphere. *1369 Cambridge St, Cambridge • Map D1 • 617 576 1369 • $*

5 Brattle Theater
A Harvard Square institution, the Brattle screens cinema greats daily. Rainy afternoon? Take in a 2-for-1 Fellini double feature for a meager $7. *40 Brattle St, Cambridge • 617 876 6837 • Map B1*

6 Mama Gaia's Café
In keeping with Cambridge's left-of-center cultural ethos, Mama Gaia's brews exclusively fair trade coffees and hosts environment and social justice-oriented community forums. *401 Massachusetts Ave, Cambridge • Map D3 • 617 441 3999 • $*

7 Café Pamplona
Pamplona's strong coffee and light Spanish snacks keep the new-breed bohemians sated. The café opens and closes at the owner's whim. *12 Bow St, Cambridge • Map B2 • 617 547 2763 • $*

8 Club Passim
The subterranean epicenter of New England's thriving folk music scene regularly welcomes nationally renowned artists. It boasts an inventive vegetarian kitchen, Veggie Planet. *47 Palmer St, Cambridge • Map B1 • 617 492 7679*

9 Richard Trum Playground
Summer in Somerville is epitomized by one thing: baseball at the playground. On most weeknights, you can watch youngsters take their swings. *Broadway, Somerville*

10 Carberry's Bakery & Coffee House
A popular Davis Square destination for its impeccably fresh baked goods, creative sandwiches, and view onto bustling Elm Street. *187 Elm St, Somerville • 617 666 2233*

Note: *All cafés are open daily*

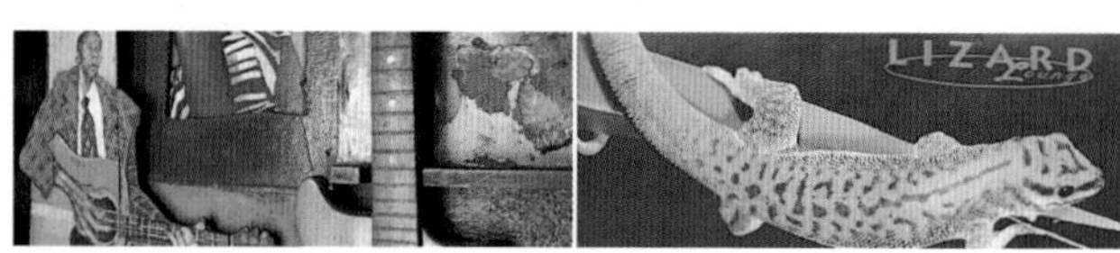

Left **House of Blues** Right **Lizard Lounge**

TOP 10 Nightclubs & Bars

1 The Middle East
A live music club to rival any in New York or Los Angeles, the Middle East rocks its hipster patrons from three stages and nourishes them – appropriately enough – with delicious kebabs and curries *(see p48)*.

2 House of Blues
Unlike its nationwide sister clubs, which overwhelmingly lean toward rock and pop, the original HOB books blues acts almost exclusively. Its Gospel Brunch is a popular Sunday Cambridge ritual *(see p48)*.

3 Regattabar
Befitting its location in the sleek Charles Hotel, Regattabar offers a refined yet casual setting for watching today's giants of jazz. Book early, since shows sell out quickly *(see p47)*.

4 Johnny D's
Dance to live zydeco, East Coast swing, and salsa all in one night. Davis Square's – and arguably all of Boston's – home for eclectic live music keeps the beat going seven nights a week. Dinner served Tue–Sat *(see p49)*.

5 B-Side Lounge
Nestled deep in MIT *(see p121)* territory, the B-Side serves up classic cocktails to a kitsch-loving, amiable young crowd. The kitchen's glorious Southern cookin' shouldn't be overlooked either. *92 Hampshire St, Cambridge • Map E3*

6 Phoenix Landing
By day, enjoy pints of Guinness and excellent pub grub at the mahogany bar. By night, cut loose to an ever-changing roster of hip-hop, jungle, and notable dub DJs. *512 Massachusetts Ave, Cambridge • Map D3*

7 Rhythm & Spice
Spicy Caribbean cuisine, potent rum-based cocktails, and live reggae music make this one of Cambridge's more spirited institutions. An ideal escape on frosty winter nights. *315 Massachusetts Ave, Cambridge • Map D3*

8 Lizard Lounge
Just outside Harvard Square, the Lizard Lounge attracts a young, alternative-rock and folk-loving crowd with the promise of good live music and a small cover charge. *1667 Massachusetts Ave, Cambridge • Map B1*

9 T. T. the Bear's Place
T. T.'s is a rock club in the tradition of New York's C.B.G.B.: small, dingy, and incredibly loud. Expect to sweat, expect to leave with ringing ears, and above all, expect to rock out. *10 Brookline St, Cambridge • Map C3*

10 Cantab Lounge
Rhythm & Blues man "Little" Joe Cook has held court at this low-key, unassuming Central Square bar for years. Catch his energetic live show on Friday and Saturday nights *(see p49)*.

See also Ryles and Good Life Cambridge **See pp49 & 48**

Price Categories

For a three course meal for one with half a bottle of wine (or equivalent meal), taxes, and extra charges.

$	under $30
$$	$30–$45
$$$	$45–$60
$$$$	$60–$75
$$$$$	over $75

Left **Dalí**

TOP 10 Restaurants

1 Oleana
Chef Ana Sortun's mastery of exotic spices is clearly evident in Oleana's sumptuous Middle Eastern cuisine, served in a casually elegant dining room. *134 Hampshire St, Cambridge • Map D2 • 617 661 0505 • Closed lunch daily • $$*

2 Redbones
Redbones' kitchen slings some of the best barbecue north of the Carolinas, and the atmosphere could not be more emphatically, casually Southern if it tried. *55 Chester St, Somerville • 617 628 2200 • $*

3 EVOO
While EVOO's cuisine defies categorization, it is unequivocally and uniformly delicious. Think along the lines of cornmeal-fried oysters, arugula (rocket) and plum salad, and mocha-mousse chocolate cake. *118 Beacon St, Somerville • Map C1 • 617 661 3866 • Closed lunch & Sun • $$*

4 Rialto
A perennial favorite among the restaurant press, Rialto's list of accolades could stretch across the Charles. The kitchen performs deft twists on Mediterranean and French country cuisine *(see p40)*.

5 Atasca
The bold flavors of Portugal are yours for the tasting at the warmly appointed, cozy Atasca. Flavorful sautées and rustic grilled dishes are just some of its many charms. *50 Hampshire St, Cambridge • Map D2 • 617 621 6991 • $$*

6 Chez Henri
Cuba might seem an unlikely place for a French restaurant to draw inspiration, but therein lies Chez Henri's irresistible appeal. *1 Shepard St, Cambridge • Map B1 • No reservations • Closed lunch • $$*

7 Dalí
Sangría flows, tapas are devoured, and desserts with names like "kisses of love" seal unforgettable evenings at Dalí. *415 Washington St, Somerville • Map C1 • No reservations • Closed lunch • $$*

8 East Coast Grill
Chef Chris Schlesinger cranks up the heat at his Pacific Rim-influenced Inman Square fish house. Sample dishes such as dry-rubbed *mahi mahi* and rare *ahi* tuna with *wasabi* – or should you be up to the challenge – Fries from Hell *(see p42)*.

9 Diva
Sleekly appointed Diva seduces before the first plates of carefully prepared Indian cuisine even arrive. *246 Elm St, Somerville • Map D2 • 617 629 4963 • $*

10 Henrietta's Table
Serving generous portions of classic American fare, the Charles Hotel's capacious bistro amply rewards hearty appetites. *1 Bennett St, Cambridge • Map B2 • 617 661 5005 • $$*

***Note:** Unless otherwise specified, reservations are recommended for all the above restaurants. See also Salts* p40

Left **Gorilla at Franklin Park Zoo** Right **Franklin Park**

Boston South

SOUTH OF FORT POINT CHANNEL, *Boston's neighborhoods of Jamaica Plain, Roxbury, Dorchester, and South Boston are a mixture of densely residential streets and leafy parklands that form part of Frederick Law Olmsted's Emerald Necklace* (see p15). *The lively street scenes of Boston's African-American, Latin American, and Irish-American communities make the city's southerly neighborhoods a dynamic ethnic contrast to the more homogenized city core. Virtually ignored by tourists, Boston South is full of quirky shops, local bars, hot nightclubs, and great off-beat places to enjoy ethnic food. This area is a little harder to reach but it is worth the effort to experience a more edgy, diverse Boston that many call home.*

Jamaica Pond

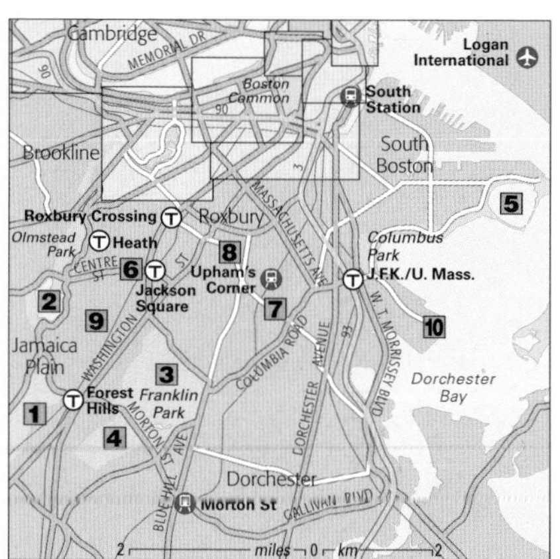

Top 10 Attractions

1. Arnold Arboretum
2. Jamaica Pond
3. Franklin Park
4. Forest Hills Cemetery
5. Pleasure Bay
6. Centre Street
7. Upham's Corner
8. Dudley Square
9. Samuel Adams Brewery
10. John F. Kennedy Library & Museum

Note: *For the parks and cemetery take the "T" down to Green Street or Forest Hills (orange line)* **See back flap**

1 Arnold Arboretum

One of the US's foremost collections of temperate-zone trees and shrubs covers the peaceful 265-acre (107 ha) arboretum. Grouped in scientific fashion, they are a favorite subject for landscape painters, and a popular resource for botanists and gardeners. The world's most extensive lilac collection blooms from early May through late June, and thousands of Bostonians turn out for Lilac Sunday, the third Sunday in May, to enjoy the peak of the *Syringa* blooms. The main flowering period of mountain laurel, azaleas, and other rhododendrons begins around Memorial Day (end of May). *125 Arborway, Jamaica Plain • 617 524 1718*

2 Jamaica Pond

This 70-acre (28-ha) pond and its surrounding leafy park was landscaped by Frederick Law Olmsted to accentuate its natural glacial features and it offers an enchanting piece of countryside within the city. Locals take avidly to the 1.5-mile (2.4-km) bankside path or fish in the 90 ft- (28-m) deep glacial kettle pond (fishing is permitted with a Massachusetts license, call 617 626 1590).

Forest Hills Cemetery

Arnold Arboretum

The boathouse rents small sail boats and rowboats for a minimal fee during the summer months. *Jamaica Pond Boathouse, Jamaica Way • 617 522 6258 • Open 9am–dusk daily*

3 Franklin Park

Frederick Law Olmsted considered Franklin Park the masterpiece of his Emerald Necklace *(see p15)*, but his vision of urban wilds has since been modified to more modern uses. The park boasts the second oldest municipal golf course in the US and the child-friendly Franklin Park Zoo *(see p61)*, which contrasts contemporary ecological exhibits with charming zoo architecture, such as a 1912 Oriental bird house. *Franklin Park Rd, Dorchester • 617 265 4084*

4 Forest Hills Cemetery

More than 100,000 graves dot the rolling landscape in this Victorian-era "garden cemetery", one of the first of its kind. Maps available at the entrance identify graves of notable figures, including poet e e cummings and playwright Eugene O'Neill. Striking memorials include the bas-relief *Death Stays the Hand of the Artist* by Daniel Chester French, near the main entrance. *95 Forest Hills Ave, Jamaica Plain • 617 524 0128*

Note: *Parks and cemeteries are generally open from dawn to dusk*

Pleasure Bay

5 Pleasure Bay

South Boston's Pleasure Bay park encloses a pond-like cove of Boston harbor with a causeway boardwalk, where locals turn out for their daily constitutionals. Castle Island, now attached to the mainland, has guarded the mouth of Boston harbor since the first fortress, Fort Independence, was erected in 1779. A grisly murder here in 1817 inspired Edgar Allen Poe to write his short story *The Cask of Amontillado*. Anglers gather on the adjacent Steel Pier and drop bait into the midst of striped bass and bluefish runs.

6 Centre Street

Jamaica Plain is home to many artists, musicians, and writers as well as a substantial contingent of Boston's gay and lesbian community. Centre Street is the area's main artery and hub. There is a distinctly Latin American flavor at the Jackson Square end, where Caribbean music shops and Cuban, Dominican, and Mexican eateries abound. At the 600 block, Centre Street morphs into an urban counter-cultural village, with design boutiques, funky second-hand stores, and small cafés and restaurants.

7 Upham's Corner

The area known as Upham's Corner in Dorchester was founded in 1630, and its venerable Old Dorchester Burial Ground contains ethereal carved stones from this Puritan era. Today, Upham's Corner is decidedly more Caribbean than Puritan, with small shops specializing in food, clothing, and music of the islands. The Strand Theatre, a 1918 luxury movie palace and vaudeville hall, functions as an arts center and venue for live concerts and religious revival meetings. *Strand Theatre, 543 Columbia Rd, Dorchester • 617 282 8000*

8 Dudley Square

Roxbury's Dudley Square is the heart of African-American Boston as well as the busiest hub in Boston's public transport network. The Beaux-Arts station is modeled on the great train stations of Europe. Among the square's many shops and galleries is the Hamill Gallery of African Art, as much a small museum as a gallery. A few blocks from the square, the modest Georgian-style Dillaway-Thomas House reveals

John F Kennedy Library & Museum

Note: *Take the "T" to Dudley Square for Roxbury (silver line), or to Jackson Square for Jamaica Plain (orange line)* **See back flap**

Roxbury's early history, including the period when it served as HQ for the Continental Army's General John Thomas during the Siege of Boston. *Hamill Gallery of African Art, 2164 Washington St, Roxbury • 617 442 8204 • Open noon–6pm Wed–Sat* *Dillaway-Thomas House, 183 Roxbury St, Roxbury • 617 445 3399 • Open for tours 10am–4pm Wed–Sat • Free*

Barrels, Samuel Adams Brewery

9 Samuel Adams Brewery

With its supply of good local water and German immigrants Jamaica Plain has long been Boston's brewing center. The Boston Beer Company, creator of Samuel Adams lagers, maintains this small brewery and a tongue-in-cheek beer museum. *30 Germania St, Jamaica Plain • 617 368 5080 • Tours 2pm Thu, 2pm & 5:30pm Fri, noon, 1pm & 2pm Sat (May–Aug 2pm Wed also) • Free*

10 John F. Kennedy Library & Museum

This nine-story white pyramidal building designed by I. M. Pei in 1977 stands like a billowing sail on Columbia Point, as inspiring as the president it memorializes. Inside, the 1,000 days of the Kennedy presidency are recreated in more than 25 exhibits. Kennedy was the first president to grasp the power of broadcast, and video exhibits include campaign debates and coverage of Kennedy's assassination and funeral. *Columbia Point, Dorchester • 617 929 4500 • Open 9am–5pm daily • Adm*

Street Heat & Pond Cool in Jamaica Plain

Afternoon

The orange line "T" will deliver you to the Latin end of Jamaica Plain's **Centre Street** at Jackson Square, where life is more Santo Domingo than downtown Boston. Head west from the station and get in the rhythm by perusing more than 10,000 titles of Caribbean and Latin music at **Franklin CD** (314 Centre St). On the opposite side of the thoroughfare – musically and geographically – check out the gospel, blues, and R&B at **Skippy White's** (315 Centre St). A promenade along Centre Street is a lesson in Latin fashion and food. Pass **El Miami** *(see p131)* and other Cubano sandwich joints, before the street doglegs left. Next stop: **Rhythm & Muse** (470 Centre St) for a brush with Jamaica Plain's hippest muses. Look over the racks for local writers, ranging from the Nobel prize winners to the self-publishing poets. At **J P Licks** (659 Centre St), order a cone of super-premium ice cream and head up Burroughs Street to **Jamaica Pond** *(see p127)*. Take a stroll, rest in the shade of a big maple tree, or rent a rowboat.

Evening

Having worked up a hunger, return to Centre Street for a dinner of enchiladas in spicy molé sauce at **Tacos el Charro** *(see p131)*. Afterwards, walk farther down Centre Street to **Milky Way Lounge & Lanes** *(see p130)* and join the cool cats for a bottle of chilled beer, live music, and a game of bowling.

***Note:** For the John F. Kennedy Library and the east of the area catch the "T" to JFK/U Mass (red line)* **See back flap**

Left **Doyle's Café** Right **Amrhein's**

TOP 10 Bars & Clubs

1 Doyle's Café

The apex of Irish-American political culture, Doyle's has been serving beer since 1882, and corned beef and cabbage on Thursdays for as long as anyone can remember. Busy nightly. *3484 Washington St, Jamaica Plain*

2 Milky Way Lounge & Lanes

Latinos and Jamaica Plain hipsters rub shoulders at the Milky Way for the dancing, the latest local live bands, the cosmopolitans, and bowling under the dim blue Christmas lights. *403 Centre St, Jamaica Plain*

3 Playwright Bar

A spiffy Dublin-style pub with good food, excellent pints, and large windows that let in the sunlight and the breeze. *658 East Broadway, South Boston*

4 Woody's L Street Tavern

This classic Southie dive immortalized in the film *Good Will Hunting* has gained a certain fame from the movie but retains its insular South Boston crustiness and ultra-conservative political viewpoint. *195 L St, South Boston*

5 Boston Beer Garden

On weekends this watering hole is packed both inside and outside in the garden – it's a typical beer-drinking, South Boston singles scene. Modern pub food hits a fairly high mark. *734 East Broadway, South Boston*

6 Amrhein's

The vintage bar at Amrhein's – a South Boston fixture since 1890 – is reason enough to visit the 'hood. Locals debate the issue of the day over a drink or two. *80 West Broadway, South Boston*

7 Lucky's Lounge

A Fort Point Channel underground bar that swaggers with rat pack retro ambience, right down to the lounge acts and the Frank Sinatra tribute nights. *355 Congress St, South Boston*

8 Brendan Behan Pub

This classic "new" Irish pub, frequented by cheerful neighborhood types with vaguely poetic pretensions, is properly outfitted with Guinness and Murphy's on tap and live music most nights. *378 Centre St, Jamaica Plain*

9 Slade's Bar & Grill

Generous drinks, good jazz, and sometimes even free eats ensure Slade's hops on the weekends. Don't let the seedy exterior put you off – this is one of Roxbury's liveliest social scenes. *958 Tremont St, Roxbury*

10 Biarritz Lounge

The outstanding jukebox plays steadily during the week, a DJ spins R&B, reggae, and hip-hop on the weekend, and live jazz and blues start every Sunday at 7pm. Biarritz vies for a place as Roxbury's hippest night spot. *177 Dudley St, Roxbury*

***Note:** On the Sunday after Labor Day, ethnic music and food rule the Jamaica Plain World Fair (btw. Hyde and Jackson squares)*

Price Categories

For a three course [illegible] a bottle of wine (or equivalent meal), taxes and extra charges.

$	under $30
[illegible]	[illegible]
$$$	$45–$60
$$$$	$60–$75
$$$$$	over $75

Left. **Jimbo's Fish Shanty**

Top 10 Restaurants & Eateries

1 Jake's Boss BBQ

Kenton "Jake" Jacobs is the acknowledged master of barbecue in Boston, and makes a mean Memphis dry rub. No alcohol. *3492 Washington St, Jamaica Plain • 617 983 3701 • Closed Mon • $*

2 Perdix

This tiny neighborhood bistro is the kind of place visitors dream of finding – an out-of-the-way eatery where the chef-owner enjoys cooking wonderful New American fare. *597 Centre St, Jamaica Plain • 617 524 5995 • Closed lunch Mon–Sat, dinner Sun • $$$*

3 224 Boston Street

This chef-driven northern Italian trattoria is the longest lasting and most successful restaurant in the 'hood. Feast on grilled Tuscan meats and pasta dishes at half the price of North End's restaurants. *224 Boston St, Dorchester • 617 265 1217 • Closed lunch • $$*

4 Abubacar Seafood

This ultra-casual Jamaican Halel deli-restaurant serves seafood, but is best known for its outstanding curried chicken and curried goat. *2360 Washington St, Roxbury • 617 427 0003 • $*

5 El Miami Restaurant

The self-proclaimed "King of the Cuban sandwiches." Check out the photos of the Latino pro baseball players who often eat here when in town. *381 Centre St, Jamaica Plain • 617 522 4644 • $*

6 J. P. Seafood Café

Loyal customers come from afar for this restaurant's Korean and Japanese specialties. *730 Centre St, Jamaica Plain • 617 983 5177 • Closed Mon & lunch Sun • $$*

7 Barking Crab

Place your order and grab a table outside at Boston's only fish shack. In winter, sit inside their cozy dining room *(see p42)*.

8 Tacos el Charro

This is the best place in town for real northern Mexican food, plus it has the most complete line of Mexican beers in town. The owner plays in a *mariachi* band at weekends. *349 Centre St, Jamaica Plain • 617 983 9275 • Closed lunch Mon–Thu • $*

9 Bukhara Indian Bistro

Northern Indian dishes predominate at Bukhara. There is a particularly wide selection of lamb dishes and rich *biryanis,* and Tandoor-roasted meats are a specialty. Gets extremely busy at lunch time. *701 Centre St, Jamaica Plain • 617 522 2195 • $$*

10 Jimbo's Fish Shanty

The waterfront deck makes Jimbo's the perfect casual alternative to the more formal Jimmy's Harborside *(see p42)* next door. Most of the fish comes from one pier away, so it couldn't be fresher. Stick to the simpler preparations. *247 Northern Ave, South Boston • 617 542 5600 • $$*

***Note:** The seafood restaurant No Name on Fish Pier is also in this area* **See p42**

the
River
92.5

STREETSMART

Left **New England fall foliage** Center **US money** Right **Student card**

Top 10 Planning Your Trip

1 When to Go

Boston's main tourist season is from May to October. The largest number of visitors come during the summer vacation, and in late September and early October when people flock to see the famous New England fall foliage. Hotel rooms are scarce during these periods. The second half of October offers a combination of good weather with lower accommodation rates.

2 Weather

From December to February daytime temperatures generally remain just above freezing and snow is possible. March to May is characterized by warm, sunny days alternating with showery ones. June to August is warm to hot with high humidity. September and October are mostly dry with crisp nights. November is cool and damp, with sporadic cold but sunny days. For detailed forecasts log on to www.thebostonchannel.com/weather.

3 Passports & Visas

Canadian citizens need only show photo ID and proof of residence. Citizens of European Union countries (including the UK), Australia, New Zealand, and Japan need a valid passport and can stay up to 90 days without a visa. Citizens of other countries must have a passport and visa, which can be obtained from a US consulate or embassy – apply well before you travel. For the latest information check on-line: www.state.gov.

4 Money

MasterCard, Visa, and American Express are accepted almost universally, and ATMs (cash machines) are located throughout the city and at Logan airport (on the departures level). It's always best to have a few dollars on arrival to pay for transportation into the city.

5 Insurance

Insurance for medical and dental care is strongly recommended, as US medical fees are costly. It is also invaluable in case of an emergency. You may have to pay for services and be reimbursed later. It's advisable to take out comprehensive insurance, which covers lost baggage, trip cancellation fees, etc.

6 Drivers License

A drivers license valid in your home country is also valid for driving in Boston and the surrounding states. Additional photo ID may be necessary to rent a vehicle.

7 What to Pack

The weather is unpredictable and can change quickly so dress in layers with a sweater or light jacket for cool summer evenings. Be sure to bring a folding umbrella, sunglasses, and comfortable walking shoes. Pack smart casual outfits for restaurants and evening entertainment.

8 Current & Phone Adapters

US electricity is 110–120 volts, 60 cycles, and uses a polarized two-prong plug. Non-US appliances will need an adapter and a voltage converter available at airport shops and some department and electrical stores. Most laptops and travel appliances are dual voltage and many hotels have dedicated dual-voltage sockets for electric shavers.

9 Student & Senior ID

Public transit, movie theaters, most major attractions, and some hotels offer discounted rates for people 65 and older. Most museums and attractions also offer discounted admission charges for students with relevant photo ID.

10 Time Zone

Like the rest of the US east coast, Boston is in the Eastern time zone, which is GMT minus five hours. Daylight saving time begins at 2am on the first Sunday in April, and reverts to standard time at 2am on the last Sunday of October.

Left **Amtrak train** Right **Trolleys, Logan International Airport**

TOP 10 Arriving in Boston

1 Logan International Airport
Logan International Airport lies on an island across the inner harbor 2 miles (3.2 km) northeast of downtown. It's served by almost all major North American airlines (except Southwest) and by most international airlines. ✆ *Information: 617 561 1800*

2 Connections from Logan Airport
Taxis are available at all terminals but harbor tunnels can make Downtown journeys slow and expensive ($15–$25). The cheapest way ($1) into town is on the MBTA subway (approx. 15 minutes). Free buses connect air terminals to the subway. The most scenic approach is the Water Shuttle ($10 weekdays, $5 weekends; runs approx every 15 minutes), which crosses the harbor to Rowes Wharf from Hyatt Harborside, just a short bus ride from the airport. ✆ *MBTA Water Shuttle: 1-800-23-LOGAN*

3 Alternate Airports
Some international charter flights and several domestic carriers use the less crowded Worcester Airport, Massachusetts, 49 miles (78.5 km) from Boston, and TF Green Airport, Rhode Island, 59 miles (94.5 km) from Boston. Bonanza Bus Lines provides a service to/from both airports and South Station. ✆ *Worcester: 508 799 1741* ✆ *TF Green Airport: 401 737 8222*

4 Customs Allowances
$100 worth of gifts, 200 cigarettes or 50 (non-Cuban) cigars, and one liter of liquor may be brought into the US without paying duty. Meat, seeds, growing plants, and fresh fruit are not allowed.

5 Immigration
Landing cards and customs declaration forms are usually distributed on the plane.

6 By Train
Amtrak trains arrive at South Station (Atlantic and Summer sts) via Back Bay station (145 Dartmouth St). There are frequent trains to New York via coastal Connecticut and Rhode Island and a "Downeaster" service to Portland, Maine. ✆ *Amtrak: 617 345 7460 or 1 800 872 7245*

7 By Bus
Buses are the least expensive way to travel in the US. Greyhound and Peter Pan Trailways provide a nationwide service; Bonanza operates solely within New England. All carriers share the South Station Bus Terminal (700 Atlantic Av). ✆ *Bonanza: 617 723 7029* ✆ *Greyhound Bus Lines: 617 526 1800 or 1 800 231 2222* ✆ *Peter Pan Trailways: 1 800 343 9999*

8 By Ship
Cruise ships dock at Black Falcon Terminal, South Boston, which is a $10 taxi ride to Downtown. The bus service is infrequent (No. 6 from Marine Industrial Park).

9 By Car
Most major northeast highways converge on Boston, with I-95 (also known as Route 128) circumventing the city center. 1-90, the Massachusetts Turnpike, comes in from the west. I-93 cuts through the city north to south. The Big Dig project is repositioning I-93 as an underground highway; expect major traffic delays through 2004. The new purple-lit Zakim suspension bridge, connecting underground and surface highways, provides a dramatic northern gateway to Boston.

10 Car Rental
Most car rental companies have desks at Logan airport. Drivers must be aged between 25 and 75 with a valid driver's license. All agencies require a credit card or cash deposit. Collision damage waiver and liability insurance are recommended. ✆ *Alamo: 1 800 327 9633* ✆ *Avis: 1 800 831 2847* ✆ *Budget: 1 800 527 7000* ✆ *Dollar: 1 800 800 4000* ✆ *Enterprise: 1 800 736 8222* ✆ *Hertz: 1 800 654 3131* ✆ *Thrifty: 1 800 847 4389*

Left **Harbor Islands ferry** Center **Visitor's Passport** Left **Bicycling on the Esplanade**

Top 10 Getting Around

1 Subways/Trolleys

The MBTA subway and trolley system (known collectively as the "T"), gets you close to almost anywhere in the city. Most of the lines are underground in the city center, and go partially above ground in the suburbs *(see back flap for "T" map)*. Fares are $1 almost everywhere. ✆ *MBTA: 617 222 3200; www.mbta.com*

2 Buses

The MBTA bus system enlarges the transit network to cover more than 1,000 miles (1,620 km). Buses run less frequently than the "T". There are also nightowl buses running parallel to some subway routes from midnight to 2.30am ($1 per ride).Two useful bus routes are Charlestown to Haymarket (No. 93) and Harvard Square to Dudley Square via Massachusetts Avenue (No. 1). Make sure you have the exact change (75 cents) or a combo "T" pass when traveling by bus. Bus maps are available on the MBTA website or at the main office at Downtown Crossing.

3 "T" Pass

Visitor's Passports for unlimited travel on the MBTA system for one, three, or five days ($6/$11/$22) can be purchased at Downtown Crossing and airport "T" station, or at Visitors' Bureau information kiosks *(see p138)*.

4 Water Taxis & Ferries

City Water Taxis operates throughout Boston's inner harbor. Boston Harbor Cruises offers a ferry service to Provincetown from Long Wharf. The Bay State Cruise Company connects the World Trade Center with Provincetown, and the inexpensive MBTA ferry links Long Wharf to Charlestown Navy Yard *(see pp30–31)*. ✆ *City Water Taxi: 617 422 0392* ✆ *Boston Harbor Cruises: 617 227 4321* ✆ *Bay State Cruise Company: 617 748 1428*

5 Walking

Unlike many American cities, Downtown Boston is compact and easy to negotiate on foot.

6 Bicycling

Boston has many dedicated bike paths including those along the Charles River and on some major streets. Note, cycling on highways is illegal and riding on sidewalks is discouraged and, in some places, illegal. Boston Bike Tours rents bikes on Boston Common *(see pp14–15)*. ✆ *Boston Bike Tours: 617 308 5902*

7 Finding Your Way

Use public transportation to reach neighborhood centers and explore on foot from there. If you're going farther out get the *Arrow Metro Street Atlas*.

8 Taxis

Taxis can be hailed on the street in the Downtown area or found at taxi stands throughout the city. Cambridge taxis can only collect in Cambridge, and Boston taxis in Boston (except at the airport). You can also call a taxi company to arrange a pick up. Rates are calculated by both mileage and time. ✆ *Boston Cab Dispatch: 617 262 2227* ✆ *Yellow Cab Cambridge: 617 547 3000*

9 Driving

Visitors should familiarize themselves with basic US driving rules and signage. Information is available at most vehicle-rental agencies. "Rotary" traffic intersections (roundabouts) confuse even local drivers. In theory, vehicles on the rotary have right of way.

10 Parking

Bostonians own twice as many cars as there are spaces, so parking spaces are limited. Metered parking costs 25 cents per 15-minute period from 8am to 6pm. Garage and open lot parking starts around $5 per hour, $21 per day. Boston Common (Charles St) and Haymarket (Congress and Sudbury sts) garages are two of the most central.

Note: *See the subway map on the back flap*

Left **Ticket office, Whale Watches** Center **Trolley tour** Right **Gondola tour**

Top 10 Guided Tours & Excursions

1 Trolley Tours

Several city tours depart from the Visitor Information Center on Boston Common *(see p138)*, including Old Town Trolley Tours, which offers narrated sightseeing in old-fashioned trolley buses, as well as theme tours (beer, ghosts, chocolate, etc). These trolley tours permit re-boarding all day, making them easy transit to major sites. *Old Town Trolley Tours: 617 269 7010 • www.trolleytours.com*

2 Water Tours

Boston Harbor Cruises depart from Long Wharf and offer a variety of tours. "Boston by Sea" is a scripted dramatic history of the harbor aboard a cruise boat from Rowes Wharf, sponsored by the Boston History Collaborative. Tours of the Charles River depart from the Esplanade on traditional small cruise boats or by gondola. *Boston Harbor Cruises: 617 227 4321 • www.bostonharborcruises.com* *Boston History Collaborative: 617 350 0358* *Charles River Boat Company: 617 621 3001* *Gondola di Venezia: 617 876 2800 or 1 866 283 6423 • www.bostongondolas.com*

3 Boston Duck Tours

Boston Duck Tours, especially popular with families *(see p60)*, use open-air amphibious vehicles that tour the streets and navigate the Charles River. *617 723 3825 • www.ducktours.com*

4 Boston by Foot

Enthusiastic volunteers share their love of the city on guided walks. Tour options include Heart of the Freedom Trail, Victorian Back Bay, South End, Beacon Hill, North End, and Boston Underground. *617 367 2345 • www.bostonbyfoot.com*

5 Park Service Ranger Tours

Boston National Historic Park rangers run daily tours of the Freedom Trail *(see pp8–11)*, Black Heritage Trail *(see p77)*, and Charlestown Navy Yard *(see pp30–31)*. Rangers at Fairsted, Frederick Law Olmsted's National Historic site, run tours of the home and offices as well as portions of the Emerald Necklace *(see p15)*. *National Park Service: 617 242 5642* *Olmsted National Historic Site: 617 566 1689, ext. 207*

6 Charles River Park Tours

Metropolitan District Commission Charles River rangers lead walking tours along the river and give occasional tours of the Charles River Locks and Dam *(see p63)*. *MDC Rangers: 617 727 9650, ext. 119*

7 Architectural Walking Tours

Pedestrian advocacy group WalkBoston sponsors tours and walking events. *Walk Boston: 617 451 1570 • www.walkboston.org*

8 Whale Watches

The New England Aquarium operates whale watches with trained marine biologists. Ships carrying approximately 200–400 passengers make the 3.5–5 hour roundtrip to the Stellwagen Bank whale feeding grounds. Tours run from late May to October. *New England Aquarium: 617 973 5200 • www.neaq.org*

9 Culinary Tours

Tours through Chinatown and the North End focus on cuisine. Mein Dish tours Chinatown on weekends visiting food markets, an herbalist, and other shops and ending with a dim sum lunch. L'Arte Di Cucinare runs culinary tours of the North End *(see p92)*. *Mein Dish: www.meindish.com • L'Arte Di Cucinare: 617 523 6032*

10 Bicycle Tours

Narrated bicycle tours start on Boston Common and include the Freedom Trail *(see pp8–11)*, Harvard Square, the Emerald Necklace *(see p15)*, and South Boston *(see p126–131)*. Two-hour tours run Monday through Saturday, with four-hour tours on Sunday. *Boston Bike Tours: 617 308 5902 • www.bostonbiketours.com*

Note: *Horse and carriage rides operate from Quincy Market behind South Market building (late May–mid Oct; $30 for two people)*

Left **Information kiosk, Boston Common** Right **Magazine stand**

Top 10 Useful Information

1 Information Kiosks

The Boston Convention and Visitors' Bureau (BCVB) operates two information centers with multilingual counselors and free information. One is on the northeastern edge of Boston Common *(see pp14–15)*, the other on the main floor of the Prudential Center. There's also an information kiosk at Harvard Square. *BCVB: 1 888 733 2678*

2 Websites

For extensive information on Boston, including promotional rates at hotels and a detailed calendar of events, check the BCVB website *(www.bostonusa.com)*. The Cambridge Office of Tourism maintains a smaller site *(www.cambridge-usa.org)*. For foodies, Boston Chefs Collaborative site *(www.boston chefs.com)* displays current menus of many Boston restaurants.

3 Events Listings

The *Boston Globe's (www.boston.com/globe/calendar)* calendar section is the leading source of information about upcoming events. Similar listings appear in the *Boston Phoenix (www.bostonphoenix.com)*, which focuses on the club and bar scene. Boston Citysearch *(www.boston.citysearch.com)* posts entertainment listings and restaurant reviews.

4 Radio & TV

Boston's competitive media market includes all the US network broadcasters: CBS (channel 4), ABC (channel 5), NBC (channel 7), Fox (channel 25), and UPN (channel 56). All five stations have strong local news and weather programs. New England Cable News provides non-stop regional news coverage. Channel 2 is a leading program producer for the national public broadcasting system (PBS). Radio station WBUR (90.9 FM) originates the humorous "Car Talk" which muses on life and love while dispensing auto repair advice. Other popular Boston stations include WFNX (101.7 FM) for rock music and WCRB (102.5 FM) for classical.

5 Opening Hours

Most stores and attractions are open daily, although many museums close on Mondays. Banks close on weekends; post offices close on Sundays. Hours and days of opening may become abbreviated during winter periods – check with venues.

6 Tipping

Plan to tip for most services: 15–20 per cent to waitstaff; $1 per bag for porters; $2 to valet parking attendants; 50 cents–$1 per drink to bartenders, and 10 per cent plus the change up to the next dollar for taxi drivers.

7 Smoking

Smoking is prohibited in most public indoor spaces. Check for no-smoking signs before lighting up. Massachusetts has the highest tobacco prices in the US and requires photo ID proving age of 18 or older to purchase cigarettes.

8 Drinking

You must be 21 or over to buy alcohol and the law requires bartenders or store clerks to check photo ID if in doubt. Stores cannot sell alcohol on Sunday – except between Thanksgiving and January 1.

9 Consulates

Consulates based in Boston provide limited services to visiting nationals. *Canadian: 3 Copley Pl • 617 262 3760* *Great Britain: 600 Atlantic Ave • 617 248 9555* *Ireland: 535 Boylston St • 617 267 9330*

10 Public Holidays

New Year's Day (Jan 1); Martin Luther King Jr Day (3rd Mon in Jan); Presidents' Day (3rd Mon in Feb); Evacuation Day (Mar 17); Patriots' Day (3rd Mon in Apr); Memorial Day (Last Mon in May); Independence Day (July 4); Labor Day (1st Mon in Sep); Columbus Day (2nd Mon in Oct); Veterans' Day (Nov 11); Thanksgiving (4th Thu in Nov); Christmas Day (Dec 25).

***Note:** For lost property call Boston Police Department Lost Property Office 8am–4pm at 617 343 5267*

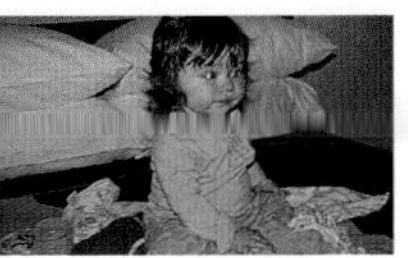

Left **Disabled sign** Center **Local taxi** Right **Traveling with children**

Top 10 Boston for Special Needs

1 Sources of Information

VSA Arts publishes *Access Expressed!*, a $5 guide to accessibility at arts venues, public buildings, and some hotels and restaurants. The basic database can also be searched online *(www.accessexpressed.net)*. VSA Arts' principal website *(www.vsamass.org)* lists a calendar of accessible arts events. The New England Index website *(www.disabilityinfo.org)* gives hundreds of sources of aid for the disabled. *VSA Arts: 617 350 7713 • TTD: 617 350 6836*

2 Wheelchair Access

All facilities built or renovated since 1987 are legally required to provide wheelchair accessible entrances and restrooms. Most attractions are wheelchair accessible. Anticipate problems in historic buildings and older B&Bs and restaurants by calling ahead.

3 Aids for the Hearing Impaired

The following venues offer listening aids for the hearing impaired. Wheelock Family Theatre and Huntington Theatre also offer performances signed in ASL (American sign language). *Emerson Majestic Theater: 617 824 8000* *Jordan Hall: 617 585 1122* *Wheelock Family Theater: 617 734 4760 • TTD 617 731 4426* *Huntington Theatre Company: 617 266 0800*

4 Aids for the Visually Impaired

Guide dogs are permitted in all establishments. Most busy road intersections have audio signals to indicate safe crossing times. The Wheelock and the Huntington theaters *(see above)* offer audio descriptions of some performances. The New England Aquarium *(see pp32–3)*, Museum of Science *(see p60)*, and Museum of Fine Arts *(see pp22–5)* have tactile displays for the visually impaired.

5 Taxis

The following taxi companies will send wheelchair accessible vehicles on request. *Boston Cab: 617 536 5010* *Checker Cab – Cambridge: 617 497 9000* *Town Taxi: 617 536 5000*

6 Public Transit

Most buses, subways, commuter rail lines, and ferries are at least partially accessible for wheelchair users. *MBTA Office for Transportation Access (OTA): 617 222 5976 • TTY 617 222 5415*

7 Restrooms

Visitors' centers, museums, and galleries have public restrooms with disabled and baby-changing facilities. There are a few high-tech public toilet kiosks along parts of the Freedom Trail *(see pp8–11)*.

8 Children's Needs

Some hotels permit children under a certain age to stay in their parents' room for free, and some offer family rates. The concierges at most larger downtown hotels can arrange babysitting. Short-term babysitting can also be arranged through Parents-in-a-Pinch. For child-oriented services and entertainment, pick up a free copy of the *Parents Paper* at libraries and grocery stores. *Parents in a Pinch: 617 739 5437 • www.parentsinapinch.com*

9 Legal Assistance

US citizens in need of legal assistance should contact the Legal Advisory & Resource Center of the Boston Bar Association; non-US citizens should telephone their consulate for legal assistance (check Blue Pages), or their embassy in Washington, D.C. *Legal Advisory & Resource Center: 617 742 9179*

10 Special Tours

The alternative Leisure Company arranges excursions for persons with special needs, including physical disabilities. Outdoor Exploration organizes active sports outings for the physically and developmentally challenged. *Alternative Leisure Company: 1 781 275 0023 • www.alctrips.com* *Outdoor Exploration: 1 781 395 4999 • www.outdoorexp.org*

Left **Post office** Center **Boston phone card** Right **Public telephones**

Top 10 Banking & Communications

1 Banking Hours

Most banks are open Monday to Friday from 9am to 2pm or later, and on Saturdays from 9am to noon or 1pm. Banks close on Sundays and holidays.

2 Currency Exchange

Currency exchange is available at main branches of large banks, which are generally open weekdays from 9am to 5pm (passport required). Travelex has booths at Terminals B, C, and E at Logan Airport.

3 Travelers' Checks

Dollar-denominated travelers' checks issued by American Express or Thomas Cook are widely accepted; personal checks from foreign banks are not. American Express offices will cash checks for their cardholders. *American Express Travel Service: 1 State St • 170 Federal St • 432 Stuart St • 39 JFK St, Cambridge*

4 ATMs

ATMs (cash machines) are usually found near bank entrances. Widely accepted bank cards include Cirrus, Plus, NYCE, and VISA and MasterCard credit cards. Most ATMs levy a withdrawal fee for cards not affiliated to that bank. It's often cheaper to withdraw money using a debit card.

5 Credit Cards

American Express, VISA, MasterCard, Diner's Club, and Discover are widely accepted. Credit cards are safer than carrying cash and may offer benefits such as insurance and favorable exchange rates. They are essential to reserve a hotel room or book a rental car.

6 Internet Access

Many hotels and B&Bs offer Internet access for guests with their own computers. High-speed access usually requires an Ethernet card, dial-up connections, and an RJ-11 plug. Internet cafés are uncommon in Boston, but public libraries, like the Boston Public Library (700 Boylston St), offer limited free access.

7 Telephones

Most accept coins as well as phone cards. Prepaid phone cards (available at gas stations, convenience stores, and newsstands) are the least expensive way to call long distance. Local calls cost 25 to 35 cents for three minutes from pay phones but are free from private land lines. Directory inquiries is free from public phones. Note, you always need to dial the 617 within Boston. Dial a 1 for other US codes. To dial abroad, key 011 followed by the country code and the city code (omitting any initial 0). If you want to hire a cell phone, try ACPR Cellular Phone Rental. *ACPR: 1 800 888 9001*

8 Sending Mail

Most Boston-area post offices are open from 8am to 6pm Monday to Friday, and Saturday from 8am to noon. The main General Post Office stays open around the clock. Letters and parcels weighing less than 16 oz (512 g) can be put in any blue mailbox. *General Post Office: 25 Dorchester Ave • Map Q5 • 617 654 5302 • For branch locations: 1 800 725 2161*

9 Express & Courier Delivery

The US Postal Service Express Mail next-day delivery service starts at $13.65 for up to 8 oz (256 g); global 2–3 day delivery costs from $15.50. Next-day delivery is also available from Federal Express and United Parcel Service. *Federal Express: 1 800 247 4747* *United Parcel Service: 1 800 742 5877*

10 Boston Newspapers

The *Boston Globe* is the dominant newspaper; the tabloid *Boston Herald* is widely available as well. Newsstands also carry *USA Today*, *The New York Times*, and *The Wall Street Journal*. For a good selection of non-Boston newspapers try Out of Town News or Borders. *Out of Town News: 0 Harvard Sq, Cambridge • 617 354 7777* *Borders: 10–24 School St • 617 557 7188*

Note: *The Yellow Pages telephone directory lists numbers organized by service. You can look them up online at www.superpages.com*

Left **Fire engine** Center **Local policeman** Right **Pedestrian crossing sign**

Top 10 Security & Health

1 Preventing Theft

Keep camera bags, backpacks, and purses on your person. Before you leave home, make photocopies of important documents, including your passport and visa, and keep them with you, separate from the originals. Also make a note of your credit card numbers (and the phone number to call if they are stolen).

2 Crossing the Street

Cross at marked crosswalks, obeying the "walk" signal lights. Intersections without "walk" signals indicate when pedestrians should cross the road with a combined red-and-amber signal.

3 Avoiding Muggers

Muggings are rare in Boston. Avoid poorly lit and deserted areas, like Boston Common, at night, especially if alone. Know where you are going and walk purposefully. Study your map before leaving, rather than on the street. Keep only small amounts of cash in your pockets and if confronted by a mugger, give up your money promptly.

4 Hotel Room Safety

When checking in, learn the fire escape route from your room. Keep valuables in your hotel safe, otherwise hotels will not guarantee their security. Use the peephole or chain to confirm the identity of anyone who knocks at your door before letting them in.

5 Telephone Hotlines

For police, fire, or ambulance, dial 911. Stay on the line even if you are unable to speak so the emergency locator system can track you. Emergency calls are free.

6 Hospitals

The Boston area has both city-run (public) hospitals and private hospitals. Public facilities, listed in the phone book Blue Pages, can be overcrowded but are often less expensive. Private hospitals, listed in the Yellow Pages, rank among some of the world's best and charge accordingly.

7 Dental Emergencies

The Massachusetts Dental Society can offer referrals to private dentists for emergency work. Tufts Dental School also runs an emergency dental clinic in Chinatown. *Massachusetts Dental Society • 1 800 342 8747 • www.massdental.org* *Tufts Dental School, 1 Kneeland St • 617 636 6828*

8 Medical Emergencies

Your medical insurer should cover all costs, but in order to avoid paying your medical bill and then have money reimbursed it is always best to contact your insurance company before seeking treatment. You will then be directed to a hospital that will deal directly with your insurer. If you need an ambulance, call 911. The Massachusetts General Hospital is centrally located for emergencies. For referrals, contact Massachusetts Medical Society. *Massachusetts General Hospital: 55 Fruit St • Map N2 • 617 726 2000* *Massachusetts Medical Society • 781 893 4610 or 1 800 322 2303*

9 Pharmacies

Bring copies of prescriptions for medications you are taking. Pharmacies abound; ask your hotel for the nearest one. *CVS Pharmacy: 35 White St, Cambridge • 617 876 5519 • Open 24 hrs* *CVS Pharmacy: 155 Charles St • 617 523 1028 • Open to midnight Mon–Fri & 9pm Sat–Sun*

10 Insect-borne Diseases

Three insect-borne infectious diseases (Lyme disease, eastern equine encephalitis, and West Nile virus) have been reported in rural areas of eastern Massachusetts. Exposure within metropolitan Boston is extremely unlikely. If worried, use mosquito repellent and keep arms, legs, and ankles covered.

***Note:** The Blue Pages telephone directory lists numbers for government agencies in alphabetical order by city, state, and federal*

Left **BosTix kiosk** Center **Discount tickets** Right **Free Hatch Shell concert, The Esplanade**

TOP 10 Boston on a Budget

1 Free Admission Times

Many Boston museums offer free admission at certain times. Harvard University art museums *(see p119)* are free on Saturday morning and all day Wednesday. There is no charge at the Institute of Contemporary Art *(see p82)* on Thursday from 5 to 9pm. Admission to the Museum of Fine Arts *(see pp22–5)* is by donation on Wednesday after 4pm.

2 Free Summer Venues

Hatch Shell *(see p52)* stages concerts during the summer as well as several of the Boston Pops concerts during the week around July 4 *(see p54)*. On Friday evenings, Hatch Shell shows big-screen family films. Check *Boston Globe* "Calendar" *(see p138)* for specifics, as well as for details on concerts on City Hall Plaza and Copley Square. The Commonwealth Shakespeare Company performs on Boston Common during July and August. *Concert hotline: 617 727 1300, ext. 555* *Commonwealth Shakespeare: 617 423 7600*

3 Gallery Hopping

College and university art galleries mount some of the city's most provocative exhibitions with free admission.

4 Bargain Tickets

BosTix kiosks sell half-price tickets to most non-commercial arts events and to some commercial productions from 11am on the day of performance. Purchases must be made in person and in cash. *Faneuil Hall Marketplace & Copley Sq • 617 482 2849 • www.bostix.com • Open 10am–6pm Mon–Sat, 11am–4pm Sun (Faneuil Hall closed Mon)*

5 Symphony Savings

Last-minute tickets for Boston Symphony Orchestra performances at the Symphony Hall *(see p52)* on Tuesday and Thursday evenings and Friday afternoons are 50–85 percent of the usual cost. General admission to open rehearsals is also available at a reduced price. *Symphony Hall, 301 Massachusetts Ave • 617 266 1492*

6 Theater Deals

Some of Boston's largest theaters offer ticket bargains: seats in the last row of the balcony at the Huntington Theatre cost $12; and on Mondays at 10am, you "pay what you can" for the American Repertory Theatre's upcoming Saturday matinee. *Huntington Theatre: 617 266 0800* *American Repertory Theatre: 617 547 8300*

7 Music Schools

Boston's music schools present ambitious performance seasons of students, faculty, and guest artists. Berklee Performance Center *(see p53)* at the Berklee School of Music has more than 100 shows per year (shows by students and faculty cost less than $10), as does The New England Conservatory *(see p52)*, which holds free performances at Jordan Hall. *Berklee Performance Center: 617 266 7455* *Jordan Hall: 617 585 1122*

8 Public Transit Passes

Cut transportation costs with a Visitor's Passport allowing unlimited travel on subways and buses for one, three, or five days *(see p136)*.

9 City Pass

A City Pass ($30.25) gives access to the John F. Kennedy Library and Museum, Prudential Skywalk, Museum of Fine Arts, Museum of Science, New England Aquarium, and Harvard's Natural History Museum. Valid for nine days, it's available at Visitor Information Centers and saves 50% on admission charges.

10 Special Discounts

Student and senior citizen discounts are often available with appropriate identification. Members of the American Automobile Association (AAA) or affiliated auto clubs of other countries should inquire about discounts at hotels, motels, and attractions.

Note: *For more information on Boston event listings, which include free/reduced price performances* **See p138**

Left **Line, USS *Constitution*** Center ***Cheers* sign** Right **Tow truck**

Top 10 Things to Avoid

1 Tourist Traps

Avoid any eating or drinking establishment that claims to have been around since colonial days. Also attractions that claim a close affiliation with TV series (such as *Cheers*!) have usually lost their original charm.

2 Lines & Crowds

A Visitor's Passport *(see p136)* lets you bypass the "T" token window. Avoid traveling from 8 to 9:30am and 4 to 6:30pm to beat the crowds. The biggest bottlenecks for entrance into most performance venues are at the "will-call" window, where you pick up pre-booked tickets, and the box office.

3 Taking the Wrong "T"

To avoid going the wrong direction on the subway, remember that all trains headed toward Downtown Crossing, Park Street, or State "T" stations are "inbound." All trains heading away are "outbound." Platforms for outbound and inbound trains often have different entrances. Be especially careful on the green line, which branches into four separate lines. The red line also branches into two south of the city. Check the final destination of the train you want against the MBTA map. Signs on the front and side of the train always list its final destination.

4 Parking Fines & Towing

You are likely to be towed if you park illegally in a tow zone, which will be signposted. In addition to towing fees, you'll also pay a large fine before your car is released. You will also get a ticket for parking at an expired meter or in a resident-only zone. It's impossible to escape payment. Rental companies will charge your credit card, and if it's your own car, your home state will not renew your license or registration until you pay.

5 Hotel Extras

Many hotels greatly inflate the cost of calls. Some may charge as much as $2 for a local call or a toll-free call. Save money by purchasing a prepaid phone card and using the lobby pay phone. Hotel breakfasts, unless explicitly included in the room rate, are also often outrageously priced. Most cafés will fill you to overflowing for $5 – the price of toast at some hotels.

6 Pickpockets

Boston has its share of pickpockets, who often work in pairs, with one creating a diversion while the other relieves you of your wallet. Be careful in crowds and when boarding or leaving buses and subway trains. Consider using a hidden travel wallet for the bulk of your funds.

7 Ticket Scalpers

Massachusetts law forbids anyone except a licensed ticket agent from selling tickets and only permits a reseller to add $2 over the face price. Scalpers nonetheless ply their trade openly outside sports venues and theaters.

8 Beggars

Boston has a large population of homeless people, many of whom beg on the street. One way to help the homeless is by purchasing a copy of *Spare Change*, the weekly newspaper produced and edited by the homeless.

9 Traffic Jams

Traffic jams are at their worst from 8 to 10am, and 4 to 6pm on weekdays. Highway traffic around Boston is very heavy on Fridays from noon to 7pm and on Sundays from 4 to 8pm. There are always jams around the Big Dig *(see p37)* area, which can have an impact on traffic up to 15 miles (24 km) away.

10 Jaywalking

The laws against jaywalking are rarely enforced by police, but crossing outside marked crosswalks is dangerous. Boston drivers have hair-trigger reflexes when they see an opening to accelerate, and much slower reflexes when it's time to stop.

Left **Prudential Center shopping mall** Center **Sign, Brattle Bookshop** Right **Fresh produce**

Top 10 Shopping Tips

1 Store Hours

Most stores open from 10am to 6pm Monday through Saturday (usually later on Thursday) and noon to 5 or 6pm on Sunday. Department stores often stay open a little later. Widely observed retail holidays are Christmas day, January 1, July 4, and Thanksgiving (4th Thursday in November).

2 Taxes

Five percent state sales tax is added to all purchases, except clothing and groceries. Clothing costing $175 or more, however, is subject to a 5 percent luxury tax.

3 Sales Periods

Look for end-of-season savings on merchandise. Expect sales during the Christmas shopping season, but greater discounts in January.

4 Department Stores

Boston's most traditional department stores, Macy's and Filene's *(see p56)*, are located at Downtown Crossing. In Back Bay, Lord and Taylor is known for classic clothing, Saks Fifth Avenue for following fashion trends, and Neiman Marcus for luxury items. ⊗ *Macy's: 450 Washington St • Map P4* ⊗ *Lord & Taylor: 760 Boylston St • Map L5* ⊗ *Saks Fifth Avenue: Prudential Center, 800 Boylston St • Map K6* ⊗ *Neiman Marcus: 5 Copley Pl • Map L5*

5 Shopping Malls

Boston's shopping malls are ideal for a rainy day. In Back Bay, a pedestrian walkway joins upscale Copley Place to the recently revitalized Prudential Center *(see p82)*. Cambridgeside Galleria has many mid-priced shops. ⊗ *Copley Place: 100 Huntington Ave • Map L5* ⊗ *Prudential Center: 800 Boylston St • Map K6* ⊗ *Cambridgeside Galleria: 100 Cambridgeside Pl • Map F2*

6 Discount Outlets

Wrentham Village Premium Outlets, a mall with 170 shops carrying low-priced top name brands in clothing and housewares, is a 45-minute drive southwest from Boston. Daily bus service ($33) includes hotel pick-up. ⊗ *Brush Hill Tours: 1 781 986 6100*

7 Food & Drink

For unusual gifts, and a taste of New England at home, James Hook & Co will airship live lobsters. For farmhouse cheeses, it's worth visiting Formaggio's Kitchen and South End Formaggio. ⊗ *Formaggio's Kitchen: 244 Huron Ave, Cambridge* ⊗ *James Hook & Co: 15 Northern Ave • Map R4* ⊗ *South End Formaggio: 268 Shawmut Ave • Map F6*

8 Music & Books

HMV and Tower Records have huge stocks at competitive prices. Try Skippy White's for R&B and gospel; Orpheus for classical and jazz; and Franklin's CD for Latin music. Harvard Square *(see p57)* has one of the largest bookstore concentrations in the country but collectors of rare books head to Brattle Book Shop in the square's center. ⊗ *Brattle Book Shop: 9 West St • Map C2* ⊗ *Franklin's CD: 314 Centre St, Jamaica Plain* ⊗ *HMV: 24 Winter St • Map P4* ⊗ *Orpheus: 362 Commonwealth Ave • Map J5* ⊗ *Skippy White's: 538 Massachusetts Ave, Cambridge • Map C3* ⊗ *Tower Records: 1249 Boylston St • Map D5*

9 Size Conversions

Size conversions between US, UK, and European countries are complicated, and differ for men's and women's clothing and shoes. The website www.onlineconversion.com/clothing.htm will help.

10 Fine Crafts

Boston is a prime market for artisan jewelry and other crafts. Mobilia is the leading gallery for an international selection. The venerable Society of Arts and Crafts *(see p21)* sells a range of work by local artists and emerging artists from around the US. ⊗ *Mobilia: 358 Huron Ave, Cambridge • Society of Arts & Crafts: 175 Newbury St • Map L5*

For antique shops on Charles Street **See p78**

Left **Bostonians dining out** Center **Seafood, Grill 23** Right **Apartment, B & B Agency of Boston**

TOP 10 Accommodation & Dining Tips

1 Location & Booking
Hotels and inns outside the city center charge the lowest prices. Those in central Boston close to principal tourist attractions, namely Back Bay, Beacon Hill, Downtown, and the Financial District, command higher prices. The Boston CVB offers a hotel booking service through its website but does not have a booking service for walk-ins. Otherwise contact the Boston and New England Reservation service and Citywide Reservations.
Boston CVB: www.bostonusa.com • *New England Reservation Service: 1 508 393 7470 • www.bostonhotelspecials.com* • *Citywide Reservations: 1 800 HOTEL 93 • www.cityres.com*

2 Room & Bed Sizes
Travelers accustomed to large motel rooms may be surprised by the small dimensions of some rooms in older Boston hotels. European-style twin-bedded rooms are uncommon; most have two double beds or one queen or king-size bed.

3 Efficiency Units
Significant savings on breakfasts, snacks, and light meals can be realized in "efficiency" (self catering) rooms or apartments. Booking agencies, such as the B&B Agency of Boston, can arrange for efficiencies in convenient locations.
B&B Agency of Boston: 617 720 3540 • www.boston-bnbagency.com

4 Taxes
Restaurant bills incur 5 percent sales tax. Hotel tax in the Boston area is 12.45 percent. Room rates are usually quoted without tax.

5 Meal Times
Restaurants start serving breakfast as early as 5:30am and usually continue until 10am. Lunch is usually available from 11:30am to 2pm. Tea falls between 4 and 6pm. Some restaurants begin serving dinner around 5:30pm and few restaurants serve meals after 10pm. Many restaurants, especially in the South End, have weekend brunch from late morning into early afternoon.

6 Reservations
Reservations are usually recommended. For Boston's Top 10 Restaurants *(see pp40–41)*, try to book two weeks ahead. Alternatively, call at dinner time to see if there are no-shows or cancelations. Some very popular restaurants do not accept reservations, assuming diners will simply stand and wait.

7 Etiquette
Be punctual for reservations. Many restaurants, both fancy and casual, now ban cellphones so it's best to switch yours off when dining.

8 Cuisine Styles
The best Boston chefs borrow liberally from cuisines all over the world, creating a complex style often called "New American". This new cuisine employs local produce and is lighter than traditional American cooking. The strongest influence on Boston cooking is Mediterranean fare of France and Italy, with a growing interest in Spanish, Portuguese, and North African traditions. Most fine-dining restaurants offer at least one vegetarian main dish.

9 Portions
Most Boston restaurants serve vast portions. One portion will often suffice for two people, and sharing can be a good way to save money. Immense portions also apply to sandwiches and most drinks.

10 Boston Seafood
Boston remains a major fishing port so fresh seafood is plentiful. Top choice is usually the sweet-tasting, large-clawed American lobster. In the Boston area, young haddock or cod is often called "scrod". Bluefish is a strong-flavored, oily fish in the mackerel/tuna family. A quahog is a large clam, and local oysters are known as American bluepoints.

Note: *Camping is available on Grape, Bumpkin, Lovell, & Peddock's islands* **See pp66–7**

Left **Dining room, Ritz-Carlton Boston** Right **Bar, XV Beacon**

TOP 10 Luxury Hotels

1 Ritz-Carlton Boston Common

Post-modernism triumphs in this classy hotel on the upper levels of the Common's tallest building. The rooms are the height of contemporary elegance. Another plus is that a fitness center and upscale cinema a few floors down are included in the price. *10 Avery St, 02111 • Map N4 • 617 574 7100 • www.ritz-carlton.com • $$$$$*

2 Four Seasons

Rock stars and visiting dignitaries often select the low-key luxury of this modern hotel situated on the edge of the Theater District. The lobby-level Bristol Lounge is a favorite spot for striking business deals, and the indoor pool is an added bonus. *200 Boylston St, 02116 • Map N4 • 617 338 4400 • www.fourseasons.com • $$$$$*

3 Le Méridien

The extremely posh Méridien occupies a jewel of an Art Nouveau building, the former Federal Reserve bank in the heart of the Financial District. Spacious rooms feature modernized Second Empire decor with rich brocades. *250 Franklin St, 02110 • Map Q3 • 617 451 1900 • www.lemeridien.com • $$$$–$$$$$*

4 Ritz-Carlton Boston

The 1927 "original" Boston Ritz on the edge of the Common had a thorough restoration in 2002 to revive its old-fashioned glory. This grand dame epitomizes opulence, decorum, and "old Boston" style. The lobby bar is a legendary venue for literary coteries. *15 Arlington St, 02116 • Map M4 • 617 536 5700 • www.ritz-carlton.com • $$$$–$$$$$*

5 XV Beacon

The design-conscious decor and extraordinary attention to detail makes this chic but cozy boutique hotel in Beacon Hill a favorite with business execs. With just 40 rooms, all with high-tech extras, it is the most masculine of Boston's new hotels. *15 Beacon St, 02108 • Map P3 • 617 670 1500 • www.xvbeacon.com • $$$$–$$$$$*

6 Nine Zero

Newcomer Nine Zero marries sleek and shiny steel, chrome, and glass with warm woods and designer furniture for a contemporary look with a soft edge. The Downtown Crossing location is ultra convenient. *90 Tremont St, 02108 • Map P3 • 617 772 5800 • www.ninezerohotel.com • $$$$–$$$$$*

7 Eliot

Back Bay grace characterizes this late 19th-century landmark hotel. Visiting musicians and baseball teams alike enjoy the spacious suites. Clio *(see p89)*, the ground-floor restaurant, is one of Boston's best and provides room service for guests. *370 Commonwealth Ave, 02215 • Map J5 • 617 267 1607 • www.eliot hotel.com • $$$–$$$$*

8 Lenox

Under family management for 35 years, this Edwardian landmark on Copley Square is intimate and European in style. The rooms are splendid (especially the corner suites), some with working fireplaces. *710 Boylston St, 02116 • Map L5 • 617 536 5300 • www.lenoxhotel.com • $$$–$$$$*

9 Boston Harbor

To enjoy one of the most beautiful locations in the city to the full, request a room with a harbor view and private balcony. There's no need to go anywhere else with restaurants, fitness center, and spa all on site. *70 Rowes Wharf, 02110 • Map R3 • 617 439 7000 • www.bhh.com • $$$$–$$$$$*

10 Millennium Boston

Rooms run the gamut from tiny to palatial in this elegant and swanky oasis close to bustling Faneuil Hall Marketplace *(see p12–13)*. Some suites even have their own jacuzzis. *Faneuil Hall Marketplace, 02109 • Map Q2 • 617 523 3600 • www.millennium-hotels.com • $$$–$$$$*

***Note:** Unless otherwise stated, all hotels accept credit cards and have en-suite bathrooms and air conditioning*

Price Categories

For a standard, double room per night (with breakfast if included), taxes, and extra charges.

$	under $150
$$	$150–250
$$$	$250–350
$$$$	$350–450
$$$$$	over $450

Left **Omni Parker House** Right **Seaport**

Top 10 Deluxe Hotels

1 Charles

Extra touches, such as handmade quilts hanging on the walls, personalize the surprisingly comfortable rooms at this modern hotel on the edge of Harvard Square. There's an indoor pool, an outstanding jazz club, Reggatabar *(see p47)*, and a leading Boston restaurant, Rialto *(see p40)*. *1 Bennett St, Cambridge, 02138 • Map B2 • 617 864 1200 • www.charleshotel.com • $$$*

2 Hyatt Harborside

When you're looking through the glass wall toward the harbor, the public areas here seem to resemble those of a deluxe cruise ship. But the rooms in this sleek hotel are far more spacious and comfortable than cabins. Alas, half of them overlook the airport. The Logan Airport water shuttle to downtown Rowes Wharf docks nearby. *101 Harborside Dr, 02128 • 617 568 1234 • www.harborside.hyatt.com • $–$$$*

3 Royal Sonesta

An outstanding art collection and a riverside location make the Sonesta a top choice for aesthetes. Bargain summer family packages include bicycles and other amenities. *5 Cambridge Pkwy, Cambridge, 02142 • Map F2 • 617 491 3600 • www.sonesta.com • $$–$$$$*

4 Seaport

Connected by a walkway to the World Trade Center, the Seaport was one of the first to pioneer the new waterfront district. The price is right for large and comfortable rooms and the pool is a bonus. Regular shuttles to downtown help ease the isolation. *1 Seaport Lane, 02210 • 617 385 4000 • www.seaport-hotel.com • $$–$$$*

5 Inn at Harvard

The clubby feel of this comfortable, modern, atrium-style hotel fits its Harvard association perfectly. The university often takes many of the 113 rooms for visiting academics, so the hotel can get very busy. *1201 Massachusetts Ave, Cambridge, 02138 • Map B1 • 617 491 2222 • www.theinnatharvard.com $$$$*

6 Swissôtel

This hotel at the edge of the Financial and Theater districts is true to its Swiss roots with low-key but impeccable hospitality. Upper-level corner suites have sweeping city views. Check on bargain last-minute deals. *1 Ave de Lafayette, 02111 • Map P4 • 617 451 2600 • www.swissotel.com • $$–$$$*

7 Colonnade

Frequently used by upscale bus groups, the Colonnade has some of the largest and most comfortable rooms in Back Bay, as well as the city's only outdoor rooftop pool. Very family-friendly. *120 Huntington Ave, 02116 • Map K6 • 617 424 7000 • www.colonnadehotel.com • $$–$$$*

8 Marriott Long Wharf

Recent renovations brought this hotel right up-to-date. The waterfront location means most of the bright, spacious rooms have superb harbor or city skyline views. *296 State St, 02109 • Map R2 • 617 227 0800 • www.marriotthotels.com • $$$–$$$$*

9 Wyndham Boston

Art Deco styling dresses up this mini-skyscraper hotel in the Financial District. Popular with business execs, the sedate library is a great spot to meet one-on-one with clients. *89 Broad St, 02110 • Map R3 • 617 556 0006 • www.wyndham.com • $$–$$$*

10 Omni Parker House

America's oldest hotel in continuous operation (1856), this opulent downtown hostelry gave the world Boston cream pie. Renovations costing $70 million brightened up all 551 rooms, although some remain compact. *60 School St, 02108 • Map P3 • 617 227 8600 • www.omniparkerhouse.com • $$–$$$*

Left **Charles Street Inn** Center **Fairmont Copley Plaza** Right **Gryphon House**

TOP 10 Hip/Historic Stays

1 Fairmont Copley Plaza

This sister hotel of New York's Plaza has been a Copley Square landmark since 1912. Public areas are opulent; rooms are small but comfy; and suites are truly grand. Richard Burton and Liz Taylor are among the star-studded guests who have stayed here. *138 St James Ave, 02116 • Map L5 • 617 267 5300 • www.fairmont.com • $$$–$$$$*

2 Hotel@MIT

Wired every which way, this adjunct to the Massachusetts Institute of Technology even incorporates circuit boards as a design motif. It's sleek and unfussy with ergonomic furniture and high-speed everything. There is a large garden terrace. *20 Sidney St, Cambridge, 02139 • Map D3 • 617 577 0200 • www.hotelatmit.com • $$$*

3 Charlesmark

Set in an 1892 Back Bay townhouse, the 33 rooms of this boutique hotel feature custom-made furniture, light-toned woodwork, and Italian tiles. Breakfast is included in the astonishingly low (for the area) rates. *655 Boylston St, 02216 • Map L5 • 617 247 1212 • www.charlesmarkhotel.com • $$*

4 Charles Street Inn

Carved marble fireplaces, Victorian furniture, and some of the finest linens in town give the nine rooms in this Beacon Hill hideaway a feeling of sumptuous luxury. High-speed Internet, mini-fridges, and stereos provide the finishing touches. *94 Charles St, 02114 • Map M3 • 617 314 8900 • www.charlesstreetinn.com • $$–$$$*

5 Beacon Hill Hotel & Bistro

This townhouse hotel is mere steps from Boston Common *(see p14–15)*. The rooms are mostly small but Euro-chic, and there's a first-floor bistro that serves breakfast (included in rates). There's even a private roofdeck for guests. *25 Charles St, 02114 • Map N3 • 617 723 7575 • www.beaconhillhotel.com • $$$*

6 Gryphon House

This brownstone townhouse, c.1895, boasts nine huge, elegant rooms – all with fireplaces, wet bars, CD-players, and high-speed Internet access. A quiet spot, it is equally convenient for Back Bay or the Fenway. *9 Bay State Rd, 02215 • Map D5 • 617 375 9003 • www.innboston.com • No DA • $$*

7 Commonwealth

This suave 150-room hotel (opened end of 2002) has all the high-tech essentials but the architecture and decor of France's Second Empire. *500 Commonwealth Ave, 02215 • Map D5 • 617 927 4445 • www.hotelcommonwealth.com • $$–$$$*

8 Clarendon Square Inn

A South End brick townhouse inn with magnificent 19th-century public areas, large suites with contemporary styling, wood-burning fireplaces, and decadent bathrooms. Excellent value for elegant lodgings. *198 West Brookline St, 02118 • Map F6 • 617 536 2229 • www.clarendonsquare.com • No DA • $–$$*

9 Boston Park Plaza

With 950 rooms on 15 floors, the 1927 Park Plaza is Boston's largest historic hotel. Recent restoration has thankfully put some glamour back. Popular with business travelers, convention goers, and tour packagers, it is convenient for Back Bay and the Theater District. *64 Arlington St, 02116 • Map M5 • 617 426 2000 • www.bostonparkplaza.com • $$–$$$*

10 Kendall

An artist-architect couple transformed this century-old Cambridge firehouse into a boutique hotel. The 65 spacious rooms are decorated with firehouse memorabilia and antiques. *350 Main St, Cambridge, 02142 • Map E3 • 617 577 1300 • www.kendallhotel.com • $$–$$$*

***Note:** Unless otherwise stated, all hotels accept credit cards and have en suite bathrooms and air conditioning*

Price Categories

For a standard, double room per night (with breakfast if included), taxes, and extra charges.

$	under $150
$$	$150–250
$$$	$250–350
$$$$	$350–450
$$$$$	over $450

Left **Encore B&B**

TOP 10 Mid-Range Hotels

1 Harborside Inn

This modest boutique hotel is in an old (1858) spice warehouse. Guest rooms have wood floors, exposed brick walls, oriental rugs, and traditional furnishings. ⓢ *185 State St, 02109 • Map Q3 • 617 723 7500 • www.hagopianhotels.com • $–$$*

2 Hyatt Regency Cambridge

With excellent parking, this large (415 rooms), pyramidal, riverfront hotel is ideal for travelers who have cars. Ask for one of the rooms facing the water for the great sunset views. The shuttle into Harvard Square compensates for those without cars. ⓢ *575 Memorial Dr, Cambridge, 02139 • Map C4 • 617 492 1234 • www.cambridge.hyatt.com • $$*

3 Best Western Roundhouse Suites

In a former railroad roundhouse, this hotel offers spacious suites with all modern conveniences. The service here is friendly and efficient. A frequent bus service makes up for the lack of subway. ⓢ *891 Massachusetts Ave, 02118 • 617 989 1000 • www.bestwestern.com • $–$$*

4 Days Inn

Barely within the city limits, the 117-room Days Inn offers clean and basic accommodation. Located on the Charles River, some rooms have water views, and it's only a 15-minute walk into Harvard Square. ⓢ *1234 Soldiers Field Rd, 02135 • Map B2 • 617 254 1234 • www.dayshotelboston.com • $–$$*

5 Radisson Cambridge

Large desks, good views, and an excellent on-site Greek restaurant are highlights of this older 200-room Cambridge riverfront hotel. For the best vistas climb up to the hotel's observation deck. The location isn't ideal unless you have a car. ⓢ *777 Memorial Dr, Cambridge, 02139 • Map B3 • 617 492 7777 • www.radisson.com • $$*

6 Sheraton Commander

Harvard Square's original (1927) hotel emerged more comfortable than ever following its latest facelift. Some rooms are small, but public areas are pleasant and clubby, and the Cambridge Common location is enchanting. ⓢ *16 Garden St, Cambridge, 02138 • Map B1 • 617 547 4800 • www.sheratoncommander.com • $$–$$$*

7 Harvard Square

This nicely renovated former motor inn is, indeed, right on Harvard Square. The rooms are tastefully decorated and the tiny lobby has one computer for those who need Internet access. ⓢ *110 Mt Auburn St, Cambridge, 02138 • Map B2 • 617 864 5200 • www.doubletree.com • $$*

8 Tremont Boston Wyndham

At the edge of the Theater District, this 1920s tower hotel underwent restoration that gave fresh glitter to its dramatic public spaces (think crystal chandeliers and marble columns). Rooms are small but modern with first rate amenities. There are conference rooms and executive floors for business travelers. ⓢ *275 Tremont St, 02116 • Map N5 • 617 426 1400 • www.wyndham.com • $$*

9 Encore B&B

This charming guest house in the heart of South End has just three rooms, all individually decorated. Continental breakfast is served in the sunny dining nook. ⓢ *116 West Newton St, 02118 • Map F6 • 617 247 3425 • www.encorebandb.com • No DA • $–$$*

10 Copley Square

This well-kept Back Bay hotel is frequented by conventioneers who balk at the rates of other nearby chains. Rooms are small, quirky, and old-fashioned in character. ⓢ *47 Huntington Ave, 02116 • Map L5 • 617 536 9000 • www.copleysquarehotel.com • $–$$*

Left **463 Beacon Guest House** Right **Bertram Inn**

TOP 10 Budget B&Bs

1 Isaac Harding House

Situated in a quiet Cambridge neighborhood, this 1860s Victorian home is now a popular B&B. The 14 guest rooms are spacious and bright. High-speed Internet connections are available in public rooms. *288 Harvard St, Cambridge 02139 • Map C2 • 617 876 2888 • www.irvinghouse.com • $–$$*

2 Beech Tree Inn

Most rooms in this friendly Victorian-style B&B have private baths, but four share. Guests also have use of a kitchen. *83 Longwood Ave, Brookline, 02446 • 617 277 1620 • No DA • $*

3 Mary Prentiss Inn

This fine Greek Revival house between Harvard and Porter squares has just 20 guest rooms, all delightfully decorated in traditional "historic B&B" style. Some rooms have wood-burning fireplaces and whirlpool tubs and there's a beautiful outdoor terrace. *6 Prentiss St, Cambridge, 02140 • 617 661 2929 • www.maryprentissinn.com • $–$$*

4 Bertram Inn

In a quiet residential neighborhood, this B&B began life as a private home built in the Tudor Revival style. It only has 10 rooms and four small suites, all tastefully decorated with styles varying between Arts & Crafts, late Victorian, and just downright eclectic. *92 Sewall Ave, Brookline, 02446 • 617 566 2234 • www.bertraminn.com • No DA • $–$$*

5 Irving House

An older rooming house turned B&B, Irving House is tucked away in a leafy neighborhood next to Harvard University. Rooms vary from tiny to spacious and some share bathrooms. *24 Irving St, Cambridge, 02138 • Map C1 • 617 547 4600 • www.irvinghouse.com • $–$$*

6 John Jeffries House

This former nurse's quarters now serves as a pleasant 46-room inn. Public areas sport the Neo-Federal look; guest rooms are bare but cheerful; and most have kitchenettes. *14 David G. Mugar Way, 02114 • Map M2 • 617 367 1866 • www.johnjeffrieshouse.com • $$*

7 Newbury Guest House

Several Back Bay residences have been linked inside to create this homey 32-room guest house. Rooms vary in size, but tend to be cozy with eclectic furnishings. Good value for the location. *261 Newbury St, 02116 • Map K5 • 617 437 7666 • www.hagopianhotels.com • $–$$*

8 463 Beacon Guest House

This late 19th-century brownstone building, on what was once Boston's most fashionable street, is a favorite stopover for European travelers on a budget. Most rooms have kitchenettes, private bath, phones with voice mail, and cable TV. Weekly apartment rentals are also available. *463 Beacon St, 02115 • Map J5 • 617 536 1302 • www.463beacon.com • No DA • $*

9 82 Chandler Bed & Breakfast

With just five spacious, Victorian-style rooms, this four-story brick townhouse in the South End feels like a private home. Each room is decorated differently but all have granite-tiled baths, a wet bar, and queen-size beds. A short walk from Copley and Back Bay "T" stops, it's pretty central, too. *82 Chandler St, 02116 • Map M6 • 617 482 0408 • www.channel1.com/82chandler • $–$$*

10 Constitution Inn

Officially listed as an "Armed Services YMCA," this 147-room facility in Charlestown Navy Yard welcomes all. Rooms are clean, bright, and modern – some have twin beds, others queen-size doubles. *150 2nd Ave, Charlestown Navy Yard, Charlestown, 02129 • Map G2 • 617 241 8400 • www.constitution inn.com• $*

***Note:** Unless otherwise stated, all hotels accept credit cards and have en suite bathrooms and air conditioning*

Price Categories

For a standard, [illegible] night (with breakfast if included), taxes, and extra charges.

$	under $150
[illegible]	[illegible]
$$$	$250–350
$$$$	$350–450
$$$$$	over $450

Left **Midtown**

TOP 10 Budget Hotels & Inns

1 Beacon Townhouse Inn

This four-story brownstone townhouse has been renovated to create quiet, elegant rooms that can, at a pinch, sleep four. Close to Fenway Park and Kenmore Square. *1023 Beacon St, Brookline, 02446 • Map C5 • 617 232 0292 • www.beacontownhouseinn.com • No DA • $*

2 Tage Inn

This new motor inn is a five-minute drive from downtown Boston (for non-drivers, there's a shuttle to the nearest "T"). Spacious rooms and suites have tasteful decor and include dual phone lines, 50-channel cable TV, and high-speed Internet connections. *23 Cummings St, Somerville, 02145 • 617 625 5300 • www.tageinn.com • $*

3 Chandler Inn

A popular choice for business travelers on a budget, this 56-room hotel in the South End is a short walk from Back Bay "T". Rooms are simple and comfy with TVs and phones with voice mail. *26 Chandler St, 02116 • Map M6 • 617 482 3450 • www.chandlerinn.com • No DA • $–$$*

4 Commonwealth Court Guest House

Handy for Back Bay, this former private residence usually rents room by the week or month. Each has kitchenette, cable TV, free local phone calls, and maid service twice weekly. *284 Commonwealth Ave, 02116 • Map K5 • 617 424 1230 • www.commonwealthcourt.com • No DA • $*

5 Inn at Longwood Medical Center

This Best Western affiliate is an attractive and comfortable 144-room hotel in the Longwood Medical Area. It caters principally to families of patients but is open to all travelers. *342 Longwood Ave, 02115 • 617 731 4700 • www.bestwestern.com • $–$$*

6 Midtown

This 159-room budget motor inn in Back Bay was built in the 1960s but has been renovated to bring it up-to-date. Kids appreciate the outdoor pool and drivers enjoy secure, inexpensive parking. *220 Huntington Ave, 02115 • Map E5 • 617 262 1000 • www.midtownhotel.com • $–$$*

7 Shawmut

Close to North Station, the 65 rooms and suites in this former office building all have well equipped kitchenettes for those on longer stays. Note, not all rooms have private bathrooms. Good value. *280 Friend St, 02114 • Map P1 • 617 720 5544 • www.shawmutinn.com • $–$$*

8 College Club

This private club devoted to promoting higher education also has 12 guest rooms available in its sophisticated Back Bay townhouse. Several smaller rooms share baths (only adequate for singles). *44 Commonwealth Ave, 02116 • Map L4 • 617 536 9510 • www.thecollegeclubofboston.com • No DA • $*

9 Hampton Inn

This new 114-room chain hotel features high speed Internet service in all rooms as well as underground parking for an additional fee. Rooms are modest but include a good desk area, making the hotel popular with business folk on a budget. *191 Monsignor O'Brien Hwy, Cambridge, 02141 • 617 661 5600 or 617 494 5300 • www.hamptoninn.com • $$*

10 Holiday Inn Express

Travelers hunting for a clean and dependable roadside lodging close to Boston need look no further. This eight-floor building has 112 rooms designed for short-term business stays – the rooms have good work areas. Limited free parking available. It's a short walk to Lechmere "T" stop. *250 Monsignor O'Brien Hwy, Cambridge, 02141 • Map F2 • 617 577 7600 • www.sixcontinentshotels.com • $–$$*

General Index

Acknowledgements

The Authors
Patricia Harris and David Lyon write about travel, food, fine arts, and popular culture for many publications including *Boston Magazine*, *Boston Globe*, *Yankee*, *Cooking Light*, and *Robb Report*. They also co-wrote the Dorling Kindersley *Eyewitness Travel Guide to Boston* and review restaurants online for Boston.citysearch.com

Jonathan Schultz is a travel writer based in Portland, Maine. He has contributed extensive local content to *Boston Magazine*, Boston.city-search.com; and LosAngeles.citysearch.com; as well as having compiled a guide to Boston for Z Publishing.

Produced by
Departure Lounge, London
Editorial Directors
Georgina Matthews, Ella Milroy
Art Director Lisa Kosky
Picture Researcher Naomi Peck
Editorial & Design Assistants
Alexandra Hajok, Sarah Billyard, Trond Wilhelmsen
Proofreader Stephanie Driver
Indexer Hilary Bird
Fact Checker Jillian Dudek

Photographer John Coletti

Additional Photography
Demetrio Carrasco, Ella Milroy, Linda Whitwam

Illustrators Lee Redmond

Maps Dominic Beddow, Simonetta Giori (Draughtsman Ltd, London)

AT DORLING KINDERSLEY
Senior Art Editor Marisa Renzullo
Publishing Manager
Helen Townsend
Publisher Douglas Amrine
Senior Cartographic Editor
Casper Morris
Senior DTP Designer Jason Little
Production Controller
Melanie Dowland
Additional editorial assistance
Karen Villabona

Picture Credits
t-top; tl-top left; tlc-top left center; tc-top center; tr-top right; cla-center left above; ca-center above; cra-center right above; cl-center left; c-center; cr-center right; clb-center left below; cb-center below; crb-center right below; bl-bottom left; b-bottom; bc-bottom center; bcl-bottom center left; br-bottom right; d-detail.

Every effort has been made to trace the copyright holders, and we apologize for any unintentional omissions. We would be pleased to insert the appropriate acknowledgements in any subsequent edition of this publication.

The publishers would like to thank the following individuals, companies, and picture libraries for their kind permission to reproduce their photographs.

BARBARA KRAKOW GALLERY: 84tr (*Wavy Horizontal Brush-strokes* by Sol Lewitt, 1995); BELL ATLANTIC BUILDING 98tl; BERKLEE PERFORMANCE CENTER: 33tr; 53tl (Bob Kramer)

CHILDREN'S MUSEUM: 60tc; 92cr

XV BEACON HOTEL: 79tl; 146tr (Richard Mandelkorn); FRANKLIN PARK ZOO: 60tr,126tl

GIBSON HOUSE: 21cr; 83c; GREATER BOSTON CONVENTION & VISITORS' BUREAU: 6t; 55tr; 80tr; 113b

HARRISON GRAY OTIS HOUSE: 76tl; HARVARD UNIVERSITY MUSEUMS: 17cl; 17bl; HULTON GETTY: 18tl; 18tr; 38tr; 38tl

ISABELLA STEWART GARDNER MUSEUM 2002: 7cr; 28tl; 28c; 28b; 28–29c; 29tl; 29tr; 29br

JAMES LEMASS: 4–5; 34–5; 54tl; 53tl, 55b, 60tl, 60tr; 68b; 70tl; 70tr; 93tl; 100–01; JOHN COLETTI: 118cl; JORDAN HALL: 112tr (Nick Wheeler)

MARY EVANS PICTURE LIBRARY: 36t; 37r; 38c; 39r; MASSACHUSETTS BAY TRANSPORTATION AUTHORITY: backflap; MASSACHUSETTS COLLEGE OF ART: 115tl; MASSACHUSETTS STATE HOUSE: 2c; 6tr; 8tr; 11cl; 11b; 75tr; MIT LIST VISUAL ARTS CENTER: 120b (*Amoreles vs Amorales* by Carlos Amorales, 2002); MUSEUM OF FINE ARTS: 3bl; 7tl; 22b; 22tl; 22–23c; 23tl; 23c; 23b; 24tl; 24tr; 24bl; 25t; 25c; MUSEUM OF SCIENCE: 60cb; 61tr; 118tr; 121tl

NICHOLS HOUSE MUSEUM: 75bl NIELSEN GALLERY: 84tl (*Summer Incoming Tide I* by John Walker, 2001 oil on linen); NEW ENGLAND AQUARIUM: 7br; 90tr; 32tl; 32b; 32–33c; 33tl; 33b

OLD NORTH CHURCH © Old North Church: 9cb; 10c; 90cr; 91c; 93tr; OLD STATE HOUSE frontflap; 97tr

PATRICIA HARRIS & DAVID LYONS: 108tl; 108tc; 108tr; 110tl; POWERSTOCK: 70b

RADIUS: 41tr (Keller & Keller); RITZ-CARLTON BOSTON: 146tl.

TRINITY CHURCH: frontflap; 7tr; 26bc, 26–7c,7tr (Jim Scherer); 27tr, 27cr (Peter Vanderwarker); 27bl (Trinity Church archives)

USS CONSTITUTION MUSEUM, BOSTON: 31t (Janet Stearns)

THE VAULT: 103 Matthew McKee

JACKET front: CORBIS tc (Dave Bartuff); DK PICTURE LIBRARY bl (Demetrio Carrasco); clb (Clive Streeter); cla (Linda Whitwam); back: DK PICTURE LIBRARY tl (Demetrio Carrasco); tc, tr (Linda Whitwam)

The publishers would like to thank all other churches, museums, hotels, restaurants, shops, galleries, clubs, and sights that have also supplied images but are too numerous to thank individually. All other images are © Dorling Kindersley. For further information see *www.dkimages.com*.

Special Editions

Top 10 Guides can be purchased in bulk quantities at discounted prices. Personalized jackets and excerpts can also be tailored to meet your needs.

Please contact (in the UK) – Sarah.Burgess@dk.com or Special Sales, Dorling Kindersley Ltd, 80 Strand, London WC2R 0RL; (in the US) – Special Markets Department, DK Publishing, Inc., 375 Hudson Street, New York, NY 10014.

Selected Street Index